By Lynn Fife

The Guaranteed Profit System

A quick and easy guide
to running a successful business

FOUR BOOKS IN ONE

Outskirts Press, Inc.
Denver, Colorado

The Guaranteed Profit System
A quick and easy guide to having a successful business
All Rights Reserved.
Copyright © 2008 Lynn Fife
V1.1

Outskirts Press, Inc.
http://www.outskirtspress.com

ISBN: 978-1-4327-1948-7

Outskirts Press and the "OP" logo are trademarks belonging to Outskirts Press, Inc.

PRINTED IN THE UNITED STATES OF AMERICA

Books by the Author

This Book

The Guaranteed Profit System, by Lynn H. Fife

Includes

Building A Strong Business Foundation, by Lynn H. Fife
The Stuff Called Money, by Lynn H Fife
Open The Door and Bring 'Em In, by Lynn H. Fife
Where The Good Employees Are, by Lynn H. Fife

Other Books By The Author

The Guaranteed Wealth System, By Lynn H. Fife
Sell, Sell, Sell, By Lynn H. Fife
Grow, Grow, Grow, by Lynn H. Fife
I Love My Employees, by Lynn H. Fife
Stop Making Money, Start Getting Rich, by Lynn H. Fife
Guaranteed Profit In The Painting Business, by Lynn H. Fife
Faux Estimating Made Easy, by Lynn H. Fife
Killer Contract Clauses, by Lynn H. Fife
Painter Meets Computer, by Lynn H. Fife

Other books by the author are available by calling (800) 697-5413

This book is available at quantity discounts for bulk purchases

First Part of this Book

As you can already see, I am a nonconformist. That's right! I don't like doing things the "typical" way. Wanna know why? In the "typical" business world, 80 percent of businesses fail in the first five years. Heck. That's nothin'. 95 percent go out of business by the 10 year mark. In short, that means only one out of 20 businesses makes it to the "success" level.

With that in mind, I ask you... Do *YOU* want to be "typical"? If you said "yes", then read that first paragraph again. I'll wait... OK? I think you get my drift by now.

The book in your hands will take you through the world of abnormality and show you what the successful people do *AND* show you what else you can do that even the successful businesses would envy. The main goal is to show you how you can take a "typical" business and turn it around into a highly profitable business.

So... With that in mind, get in, fasten your seat belt and hold on for the best ride down the road to business success you will ever have.

Table of Contents

Your Personal Security Code: **ET1207A1**

The Guaranteed Profit System
Book 1

Building a Strong Business Foundation

"A Quick and Easy Guide to
Understanding How to Have a Successful Business"

By: Lynn H. Fife

Building A Strong Foundation: Chapter One
Why Are You in Business Anyway?

I know. You've probably asked yourself that question a few times already, haven't you? But really, it's an important question. Just why ARE you in business?

When I put on a seminar or workshop, I ask that question, and almost every single time, I get the same answer. People respond with, "To make money." Honestly now, isn't that what you were thinking when you read the question?

But hey, here is where I want you to start thinking outside the box. Follow along with me.

Every single business out there is probably trying to make money. The term "making money" is tricky, though. Usually, it simply means bringing money in the front door. But let's think of the other side of the coin. Money comes in (called sales) and money goes…where? You guess the rest of that sentence. Right! Money goes out (called expenses). After the money comes in and the expenses go out, there is supposed to be something important left over, something called…? You can guess this one too. Right! Profit.

If your company does not make a profit, what will happen to your company? Oh, that was an easy one, wasn't it? No profit means you get to go right out of business.

That's "the bottom line" of good business. Even if you have other, more lofty goals than just making money, you won't be able to accomplish them if you don't make enough profit to stay in business. The sooner you get clear about this essential fact, the quicker you can be successful in all you want to do with your business.

What's so hard about making a profit? And why the heck am I starting this book with this stuff anyway? I'll tell you.

Business success does not begin with a great product, idea, service, business plan, instant customer base, or any of that stuff. Face it. Every business out there thinks they have (and actually may have) a great product or service, but the fact remains, 80% of all new businesses will be out of business in only five years. After ten years, only 5% will still be in business. All of them probably started out with a great product or service.

So what IS the key? The key actually is your particular attitude toward business. The whole idea of business is the business of business.

Let me explain that one.

The average person who goes into business is usually more or less good at making the product they want to sell, or they are good at performing the service they want to provide. If they weren't, they probably wouldn't start a business in the first place. What they lack is the knowledge of actually *how to go about* running a business profitably.

To drive this point home, here are a few things people typically say in my workshops:

"I'm great at making fudge, but what the heck is a balance sheet?"

"I give the best cleaning service around. Now, what was that budget thing about?"

"I'm a small hobby shop. Why do I need a business plan?"

This is where the number one reason for failure comes in.

People think success in business is only about having a product or service they can sell. But, let me repeat what has been said before, what they lack is the understanding that they are starting a *business*. In their product / service area, they may be on the top rung, they may be a graduate extraordinaire, but they are likely brand new apprentices at running a business. They may have spent years learning or perfecting their trade skills, but very little (if any) time learning about how actually to run a business or finding out about how the business world in general operates.

So. Where does a person learn this "business stuff" anyway?

Well, most people attend the School of Hard Knocks. The tuition is HUGE! The semesters seem endless, and you only get out by doing one of two things. One, you flunk out (this is called bankruptcy), or two, you graduate out (this is usually by learning from your mistakes). Maybe, by the grace of God, you keep your head above water and struggle your way out into the world as one of those 5% who succeed. Remember that statistic? Only 5% who start out in business actually succeed. Most of them attended the School of Hard Knocks. Not really a good choice of schools, is it?

Why the heck would you want to learn about business the hard way, in that familiar "school of hard knocks," where so few actually make it?

I say, "Bunk!" Let's find a better way. Let's find a way to learn, for example, from others' failures so we don't make them ourselves. And better yet, let's find a way to learn what successful people have done to succeed. If we can profit by others' experiences, we can perhaps avoid at least some of our time in the School of Hard Knocks. Maybe, just maybe, we can even guarantee our success.

If so, bingo! You graduate from the School of Hard Knocks without even having to attend. Man! I wish someone had told me how to do that years ago. It would have saved me SO many hours of frustration and bunches of bucks.

So, you ask, how do I start? Well, let's shift gears, going from talking about the big picture to talking about first things first.

Let's see what the successful people have to say about how they did it.

After watching literally hundreds of businesses struggle and only a few emerge on top, I got to wondering why some succeed while others fail.

I finally found a man who was willing to talk about it. He had started with his childhood work of mowing lawns, and by the time he was only twenty-six years old, his net worth was just over $6,000,000.00. BY CUTTING GRASS (the legal kind)!

Now think for a minute. If you were to meet this person and had a few hours of his time, what would you ask him?

I'm guessing you would ask the same thing I did. "How did you do it?"

I was very lucky and had that opportunity. I asked him how he did it. I was expecting stuff like, "You gotta have a good business plan, find great buys on stuff, treat your employees right," etc.

But, do you know what? He blew me completely out of my chair with the simplicity of what he told me. He said... (Are you ready for this?) "The most important thing about my success was and is getting my dreams out of my head into the world of _____".

Can you fill in the blank? Sure you can. We all have heard of getting things out of the dream world into the world of reality.

So I followed up with the important question, "How?"

(Now, this is the most important part of building a strong business foundation, so pay attention here.)

He said, "Almost every person alive will tell you they want to become a millionaire. Shoot, look at all the lambs flocking to the state lottery trying to win it. Almost every person alive will also tell you they are willing to do whatever it takes to get there (providing it's legal, that is). But the fact is, only one in a hundred people ever really get there."

He continued, "What it boils down to is that hardly anyone is actually shown how to get their dreams out of their heads and into practical reality."

Then, he said it again. "I repeat, it starts by getting it all out of the fuzzy place in your head and into the practical world of reality. It's got to be in a form you can see, touch, expand, change, modify, use, focus on. The best way to do that is start with something really so simple, anybody can do it. Start with a pencil and a piece of paper. Think about your dream, what you really want to do. Spell it out, write it down. Be specific, and then more specific. Say just what you want to do, and then what you need to do to get it done. Be specific. Then study it, expand it, change it, use it. Keep it in front of you so you look at it every day. It's that simple."

WOW! So simple. Or maybe not. Because it means we actually have to do it!

Let me help you do this first part an easy way.

Now, again, this is where your strong business foundation really begins. It starts with your getting your business dreams out of your head and down on paper so you have something real to work with.

To see how this works, let's first grasp the overall concept as it applies to life in general, and then we can focus on the business world. The concept of getting your dreams onto paper does NOT just relate to business. It can relate to ANYTHING in life, to include personal wealth, spiritual growth, family situations, social activities, you name it.

Let's start this section with a practice run on this concept as it applies to something you know well, your personal life. (Don't worry, it's just you out there, nobody's looking over your shoulder at what you write.)

Let me give you an illustration and make some suggestions from my own life so you get a feeling for what I mean. First, I thought a little. Then, I got out my paper and pencil, and I just sort of "blue skied it" for a while, and then I organized my first draft of my list, putting my dreams in order of priority for me. Here's what I wrote down:

"My Hopes and Dreams for My Life" by Lynn H. Fife

Spiritual Growth:
> Keeping my belief strong
> Appreciate how historical scriptures can apply to today
> Learn how to give to those in need without thought of personal benefit
> Etc.

Family Growth:
> Have quality time with family that involves interaction
> Build true friendship that will last into my children's adult life
> Become involved in activities enjoyed by all family members
> Etc.

Business Growth:
> Improve Sales
> Understand financial statements
> Adjust pricing based on facts to warrant a fair profit
> Gain respect and better production from my employees
> Etc.

Wealth Building:
> Become debt free
> Learn about different types of investments
> Learn about passive income options
> Develop multiple streams of income
> Etc.

Retirement Planning:
> What the heck do we want to do anyway?
> What will it cost at the point of retirement?
> How much income will I need to support my desired lifestyle?
> How soon can I have enough money to retire?
> Etc.

"Deep breath here," I said to myself… Lots of things in that list, aren't there? Maybe I'll keep them all, maybe not. But at least I have them down where I can look at them, work with them, scratch them off, or expand on them. They are right there in front of me, spelled out, and prioritized, waiting for me to take the next steps with them.

I feel that doing this is so very important that I want to stress it again. The fact of human nature is this. If you just dream about what you want to do in a vague way, keeping things in your head, you sort of believe it *might* automatically happen "someday." And we all know that "someday" usually never comes. So this is where you begin as far as becoming a success in business goes.

This book will show you over and over again exactly how to structure your own written objectives in a way that is not just an exercise, but is a tool, right there, down on paper in front of you, a tool you will use regularly to stay focused, in ways we will show you, ways that will guarantee your success.

This brings us to your first mantra / affirmation / goal / objective, or whatever you want to call it.

"WHEN I WRITE IT DOWN AND THEN ACTUALLY USE IT… SUCCESS WILL HAPPEN"

This, my friend, is the absolute starting point to success in any business.

OK. I'm going to get you started here. You'll find in a few pages from here a simple form you can use to start your own list. Now… Here's the WAY COOL thing about this book. You can go to our website www.evergreentech.net. On the home page, there is a picture of this book and below the picture, the link that says "FREE DOWNLOADABLE FORMS - Click Here". It will take you to a screen and ask you to enter your personal security code. This code is found at the bottom of the "Table of Contents" at the beginning of this book. When you enter the code on our website, you will be able to access all the forms mentioned in this book and download them. They will come to you in MS Word format so you can edit them, change them and make as many copies as you like. Now isn't that the coolest thing you have ever seen in a book. AND, MY! What value for your book dollar. WOW!

Go ahead. Print yourself a few copies of the form called "Needs Analysis". Remember the steps to all forms? Just as a bonus, I'll give it to you again in step by step format:

Step 1: Use your browser and enter the website: www.evergreentech.net
Step 2: Click on the button below the picture of this book that says: "Free Downloadable Forms"
Step 3: Enter your security code found on the bottom of the "Table of Contents" page.
Step 4: Click on the form you want to download.
Step 5: The form will be downloaded on your computer… Open it, Save it and Print it.

Easy squeezy. Now, here's how to use this form.

I like to use one sheet for each particular topic.

For example, if I were going to use this form with my previous list of dreams or goals, it would be like this. You will remember that under "Business Growth" I wrote "Improve Sales" as the first item. Using this form I'm giving you, I would therefore have a separate page for that item "Improving Sales, and so at the top of a copy of the form, I would write "Improving Sales."

My next step would be to write down everything I could think of that would help me improve sales. I would write down each one on a line on the form. Some ideas:

    Improve company image
    Modify business cards
    Print advertising brochures
    Etc.

If I transferred my list above to the form I'm giving you, it would look like this.

General Area of Improvement: __Improving Sales_____

What	Plan Needed	Plan Done	Immediate Needs
Improve company image	Yes No		
Modify business cards	Yes No		
Print advertising brochures	Yes No		
	Yes No		
	Yes No		

Pretty cool form, huh? The first three columns are self-explanatory. You just write in the item you want to accomplish as it relates to the subject matter. The second column asks if you need to put together a more detailed plan to break down the steps it takes to get it done. No need to break it down here, just circle "Yes" so you know that there is something that needs to be done later, and we'll get to the instructions for doing that shortly in this book. The third column allows you to check it off later when you have your breakdown complete. The last column is for those times when you find yourself saying, "Hey, self... I can't do this yet until I..." So you write down what you need to do first before you can do what you want to do.

What I have done, and what I want you to do, and what is so important here, is to categorize each general area into more specific areas. Then you'll be able to work with your initial ideas, figure out more and more what you must do specifically to make them work.

But, let's not get ahead of ourselves. That's often a mistake we make. Most people want to skip this initial "brainstorming." But it is the foundation. It has to be laid down first. The next steps are in the next chapters. So, let's do this one first.

The form you download will have a full page of lines for you to get as extensive in your planning as you desire. Now... take a look at the form and let's get started.

Wow! Lots to think of here. Lots of initial planning going on. Why don't we give you time to work on it for a while and when you get a few things written down, we can move on to the next chapter.

Oh... One more thing... You will notice some of the chapters have a blank area, just like the one below. I have left this "Notes" area so you can write down key things that will help you with your specific needs. You can use it to write down questions, and, at the end of this book, if you still have questions, you are welcome do call Evergreen Technology for any questions or help you may need. Our free help line is (800) 697-5413.

Now... Don't worry about writing in this book. You bought it. It's yours to use, so go ahead. No one is looking and no one really cares. Exception: Don't write in this book if you are borrowing it or checked it out from a library or something like that. But, you knew that anyway, didn't you.

Ok. Here's some space for notes:

Notes:

Building A Strong Foundation: Chapter Two
The Map

Let's imagine for a minute that you want to take a trip from your home to a vacation spot that is clear across the country. You have plenty of time, so you decide you want to drive and take in all the sights along the way. So. What's the first thing you do?

Unless you are one of the extreme venture types that just puts gas in the car, checks the wallet for credit cards, and heads that-a-way, it's my guess you start by making a travel plan. You look at where you want to stay when you get there. You grab a road map, decide which roads you want to take, and you map it out. You calculate distance. You decide where you would like to stop and eat, where you want to stay overnight at hotels, and which attractions you would like to see along the way. Am I right?

Now that you have this travel plan all written up and organized, what do you do with it? Just toss it in the trunk, forget about it, fill up the tank with gas, check your credit cards, and head that-a-way without ever looking at it again? NOT! Again, it's my guess you would keep that plan in your front seat right next to you so you can check it for reference and progress.

So what does this road trip have to do with business? I'll tell you.

Every single person alive who wants to start a business has probably been told, "You need to have a business plan." So, if you are that person who wants to start a business, you do a little research and find out you are supposed to write this whole long plan that has a mission statement, your resume, your cash flow projections, your competition, your advertising goals, sales goals, and a whole bunch of other stuff.

Enthusiastically, you get to work on it. Get a few pages written. Find out how much work it is. And many times, you end up making the excuse, "I'm a small company. I don't need to write this stuff down. I already have it in my head, so why waste the time…" End of story.

Other people who want to start a business may take a class, get a book, or get some help from a professional company. The business plan progresses as each person spends countless hours, until finally, after a few months, poof, it's done. So where does it go? Right! Not in the trunk of the car, maybe, but still, it sits on the shelf to collect dust, never to be seen again.

If this sounds familiar, you are part of the group I call the "typical" business owners.

The shocking part is that even though many business owners will spend months creating this thing called a Business Plan, they never look at it or use it from that point forward.

Now I don't know about you, but to me, that sounds like a lot of time spent for very little benefit. Let's compare it to your road trip.

A Business Plan is supposed to be …a PLAN, a plan you make for succeeding in business. Just like you plan your road trip, a smart business person (which you are), will plan their business success.

This is the point where I like to break the typical "rules" of business management that allows people to do all this work and then toss it aside without using it. Let's face it. If the Business Plan is not done in such a way that it *requires you* to use it for reference constantly (just as you would a road map on a trip) to be sure you are still on the right track, or to guarantee your success, I agree with the typical business owner who says, "Why do it?"

Thus, to me, a business plan should be *structured* in such a way that it *will* be used.

So, as I planned my business, I sat down with myself and said, "Self, what do I want my Business Plan to do for me (not just to satisfy the bank or to satisfy instructions in a book)." My mind took off and came up with the obvious answer. See if you agree…

A Business Plan should be a list of all the aspects of my business, including step by step instructions for getting each one operating successfully.

Ding, ding, ding. We have a winner here.

So let's get busy and do it, shall we?

The first thing you do is…well…if you followed Chapter One of this book, you have already done it. That is, you make a list of all the aspects of your business.
Things like:

> Office Organization
> Accounting
> Office Staff Job Descriptions
> Advertising
> Marketing
> Estimating
> Financial Statements
> Employee Relations
> Field Production
> Etc.

See… You have already started making your business road trip success plan. Good for you, because, let's face it here, folks. If you do not write it down, you're not apt to remember it all, and some things will not get done. You are a busy person, with a lot on your mind. It's easy to forget things, even something important. Agreed? So making a checklist, in writing, will ensure everything gets done.

So, the next step is obvious. This is where you think about everything that is involved in each category of your list. Example: For advertising, your company may need:
Advertising:
> Business Cards
> Vehicle Signs
> Information Brochure
> Direct Mailer
> Street Signs
> Photo Album
> Newspaper Ads
> Etc.

(I could go on here, but we have a whole book on advertising and how to make it effective so we won't go into all that now. And advertising is just one category.)

Now, to simplify all this thinking, you can use the next chart I have for you, the "Business Plan Overall View."

On it, the first thing you do is to place each category from your list in its own column at the top of the chart. Like this:

Business Plan Overall View

Office Organization	Accounting	Advertising	Marketing	Etc.	Etc.	Etc.

Guess what? You guessed it. This is also a form you can download from our website as explained in chapter one, page seven & eight. The form is called "Business Plan Overall View"

Go ahead. You can do it right now. Go make copies of that chart, and fill in your categories. After all, sooner is better than later (Mom told me that). I'll wait right here. When you get done, come back to this spot: ♦

Now that you have the categories in the columns across the top of the chart, why not continue to the next step? Put on your thinking cap now. (I like the beanie with the propeller on top, but whatever works for you is fine.)

Take them one category in one column at a time. Now think deeply about everything that you may need that is associated with that one category.

Need some help? OK. Let me offer a few suggestions. Keep in mind, though, that I don't know exactly what type of business you have, so I am just going to offer some generic things that most businesses need.

Let's start with the first column which I have labeled Off. Org. (Office Organization, remember?)

In the column labeled Office Organization, the list may look like this:

Business Plan Overall View

Off. Org.							
File system							
Message system							
Supplies							
Incoming Leads							
Etc.							

And on you go. Note. I am just listing the items right now. I am not listing all the steps I'll need to take for each one. For example, for "File System," I am not listing different file locations and their contents, details like that. I'm just listing the general item "File System." (We'll get to the steps you need to take for each item later, don't worry.)

This may take quite a while so you are free to take a break now, take a deep breath, clear your head, grab a brewsky (or soda, or hot cocoa). Once your mind is fresh, you are ready to go to work .

I think you have a good idea of how to proceed, so now is a good time for my nap. Go ahead and finish this sheet, then when you come back, we can talk about the next part of the Business Plan process.

Well… Go ahead…. What are you waiting for?

Yes, I know. It will take some time to get everything done, but think of it this way.

The poor stay poor because they don't plan on getting rich. Day by day, they keep doing the same ol' thing and, as a wise man once said… Wait! Let's make it your second mantra, affirmation, wise saying, or what ever you want to call it. Here it is:

If you keep doing what you are doing,
You'll keep getting what you are getting.

So, just buck up here and get busy. Let me know when you're done.

OK? Finished? Way cool!

On to the next step. Now that you have your master list of everything you need for your business, it's time to do the final planning.

This is where you get to put on that thinking cap again and make a list of everything needed to accomplish every item on your list. Ok…that was a weird sentence. Let's look at my chart again, and let me explain.

Business Plan Overall View

Off. Org.							
File system							
Desk top							
Messages							

Let's take my example of the Office Organization category. My first item was a file system. My list of steps to take care of this item may look like this:

File System:
      Draw a diagram of our office floor plan
      Mark locations of all file / paperwork locations.
      List what I want on my desktop
      List what paperwork I want at my fingertips on my desk top

11

Locate where I want to find blank forms
List what file folders I want in my blank forms drawer
Make file folder labels for the file folder tab for all files
Purchase file folders and label them… Etc.

And the beat goes on.

Yes. I know. You say, this is going to take a whole bunch of time. Most people take a couple of days just making the list (assuming they keep with it and turn off that dang Free Cell computer game; caught you, didn't I?)

Anyway. To give you even better value in this book, the following chart is yet another fantastic worksheet to help you get all that down in order and to keep your mind focused… BUT WAIT! Don't look at it yet.

I'll bet you did anyway just because I enticed you with waiting.

This form is the most powerful and important form in your business. It is the key to getting everything done. It allows you actually to assign who is going to do each task, when it is to be done, and when it is to be evaluated and finalized.

Note: Use one of these charts for each item on your previous chart. You can download and print this form from our website as explained in chapter one on pages seven and eight. Let's take a look at this make-believe one to give you a good idea of how it works:

BUSINESS PLAN

Category: <u>Office Organization</u>   Item: <u>File System</u>_____

	Design			Evaluate			
Task	Who	When	Done	Who	When	Done	Final
Draw a diagram of floor plan							
Mark paperwork locations							
List what files I want on my desktop							
List what I want at my fingertips, but not on desk							
Locate where I want blank forms							
Purchase file folders							

Don't worry about filling in the "Who, When, Done" columns yet. We'll do it later. For now, just make a list of everything you can think of that needs to be done to "get 'er done". Make a separate sheet for each item.

I'll bet there are some readers that have reached this point and have not yet started filling out the first form, let alone this one. Hey. Not a problem. That is normal. A lot of people like to read through to the end to get the entire concept so when they do go to work, it will be with full understanding. These are the "thinkers" of the world.

That's cool. I can get down with that. (Can you tell I have teenagers? I'm still learning the language, and they get a good chuckle out of me now and then).

It's actually a great idea, if you want to read ahead or even finish reading this book before you finalize (or in some cases, even work on) your Business Plan. As you read this book, you will learn about budgets, financial statement basics, pricing your goods or services, and a few other important items that make up a strong business foundation (sounds like a title to a book doesn't it). But if you want to take it one step at a time, just keep working with me here.

I also realize I am asking a lot. If you find yourself in a situation where you would like the "speed" method of getting this done, you have a couple of options. On our website, www.evergreentech.net, we have a completed Business Plan that is about 95 pages and we have done all this work for you. If you decide to purchase this option, it will come to you in MS Word format allowing you to simply edit what is there to fit your needs.

Another option is to give us a call and we can build a custom template for you. All we ask is you fill out a form that gives us basic information about your company and within a few days, we will have your customized business plan done, ready for you to spend a few hours to edit and perfect it to meet your needs. Both of these options are found on the website when you click on the "Free Downloaded Forms" button. The security screen shows all the optional items we have that can save you a bunch of time.

Anyway. I don't want to sound like a commercial, but on the other hand, I don't want you to lose a lot of time because the work may seems too time consuming. Most people can do all the work without spending additional money. They have the availability to spend about two hours a day on the "business" stuff needed for their company.

You decide for yourself. But in all cases… Git 'er done!
So, here's your next step.

Have a business meeting with…. Well, if you are a "one man" shop, have a meeting with yourself. For companies with key employees, have the meeting with them.

At this meeting, out comes your Business Plan. You flip to the first category, the first item. You look at what needs to be done. Now. Here's the fun part. Make assignments. In other words, you fill in the blanks on the rest of the form, the ones that say "Who" and "When."

See how easy this is? When you get to an item, stop and assign each task to someone, even if it is yourself, and write the name in the "Who" column.

Now, here comes the important thing. The box that says, "When." That's where you write in a specific date the person plans on doing the task.

Even more important, have the person (even if it is yourself) get their appointment book, turn to the date, and write in the exact time when they plan on doing the task.

Powerful stuff here. If a person does not assign it a time to get done, and write it down and schedule it, there is a very good chance they will come to the next meeting with an unfavorable report. We don't want that now, do we?

If the person has accomplished the task, they report it at the next meeting (yes, there is a next meeting, and a next meeting; in fact, you're going to have a meeting with this plan every week! You're not throwing *this* road map in the trunk of the car!). That way, when something gets done, it gets a check mark in the "Done" column.

When you are 100 percent happy with the task, then the "final" column gets checked off. Congratulations... The task is done, out of the way... on to the next item.

Now, I know there is someone out there reading this and thinking... "This all sounds like big business stuff. I work by myself or with a very small group of people. Is this all really necessary?"

You bet your sweet bippy it is. You will never make big profits, never be a bigger company, never see success if you don't start acting like a big, successful company.
Like I said earlier, this is the most important thing any person can do for their business. It is not just a stereotypical Business Plan. It is a success plan that will walk you step by step through getting everything done that is required to bring you the profit you need.

The importance is this. Remember our road trip? We had the travel plan right by our side the whole trip? Well, this new style of Business Plan will be by your side too.

Because every week, as I said, you will need to have a business meeting and go over your lists, over your assignments, check up on what needs to be done, what has been done, what is completed.

Do this, and... Congratulations! Your Business Plan is in action (instead of inaction by just sitting on the shelf).

What will absolutely blow you away is the amount of work you get done at record speed.

Think of it. Each week, you keep going back to the same page until it is complete and final. The person who was assigned the task gets to report on progress. The average person gets tired and sometimes embarrassed, to have to keep saying, "I forgot... I'll work on it this week." Excuses seem to diminish and work seems to get done.

Let me ask you now. Are you getting the vision of the power of this new type of Business Plan?

If not, then, remember the 80% percent of businesses that fail in the first five years? The reason they fail is they just let their businesses run by themselves. They only do "business stuff" when the urgent need arises. And lots of that stuff never seems to get done.

Here's what we hope to have happen with the information contained in this book. We want you to gain the full vision of a successful business. We want to lead you by the hand to show you how to apply these techniques to your business. Anyone can do it. It just takes your dedication to learn it and stick with it.

Any business is guaranteed to succeed when all the right principles are applied, so don't get overwhelmed. Just get in there and do it. The results will be greatly improved profits.

Wow! I just want to jump ahead here and give you the full picture, but I think it's best we take it one bite at a time. For now, let's just wrap up the Business Plan worksheets.

Remember to download this form from our website as explained in chapter one. Make a bunch of copies and three hole punch them so you can organize them in a binder. This particular form is called "Business Plan".

To organize them, I like to use the three-hole punched divider tabs you can get at the office supply store, and I use a tab for each category. Makes each category easy to find for my meetings.

That was a lot of work. So… go ahead and take another break. Let your brain re-charge and we can move on to the next subject. (I like lots of breaks. I think I learned that from my employees).

Here's a little bonus for you. Evergreen Technology has already done a business plan that will fit "most" business types. It is about 90 plus pages long and already filled out for you. Already in a three ring binder with tabs… etc. All you need to do is look at the items and edit a few to make it more specific to your trade. This could save you many hours of time doing something that is already done. The end of this book has a list of "Optional Items" that you can order to help you expedite this whole process. Take a look and see if it would be worth it to help you save time.

Any questions on the Business Plan building process? No? On we go.

Building A Strong Foundation: Chapter Three
The Concrete Foundation

Mind fresh? Alrighty then.

Welcome to the world of construction where you get to learn about the difference between a stick foundation and a concrete foundation.

Stick foundation is where builders use lumber to frame the exterior shape of the house and then put in more lumber to brace and build the ground floor. Even though they use pressure treated lumber, the life expectancy of the stick floor is only as good as the weather resistance of the treatment.

Concrete foundation, on the other hand, is man made rock. Solid. And it lasts far longer than wood products.

You can probably guess where I am going with this. OK. Let's just get it out. Your business foundation can be built on lumber or concrete. Your choice.

The words "Guess" compared to "Know" come into play in your choice.

Do you want to guess at your business management stuff or would you rather use the facts to help you build your business on knowledge?

I know. That was an obviously "dumb" question. But guess what?

Most people jump into business guessing at a whole bunch of stuff. Let's continue this chapter with some of the most common guessing games. See if you fall into any of these categories. And remember. If you do, that doesn't mean you are *not* broken, bad, evil, stupid or anything else. It just means you are normal (nothing wrong with that, except as far as business success is concerned). We just want to help you become abnormal so you can be among the few who succeed.

Here is a list of the typical guesswork stuff:

TOP THINGS PEOPLE GUESS:

1. I know what my competition charges. If they can sell it at that price, so can I.
2. If I charge more than my competition, I will go out of business.
3. I have a pretty good feel for what it costs me to be in business.
4. I'm pretty sure I can train my employees to work as well as I do.
5. I'm sure other people will agree that my stuff / services are better than others.
6. I think I will sell enough to keep me in business.

Let's look at these one at a time.

1. <u>I know what my competition charges. If they can sell it at that price, so should I.</u>

This is easy and should go fairly quickly.

Remember, 95% of your competition will be out of business in ten years or less. Why? They are not making enough money to show a profit. If they were, they would still be in business.

Summary: If you price your products or work to follow your competition, you will follow them right out of business.

The answer: Find out what you MUST charge (later in this book) and keep that figure in the back of your mind while always reminding yourself: "If I don't charge that much, I will go out of business, so I really have no choice."

I know what you're thinking, which is why item number two is next. You are thinking…

2. **If I charge more than my competition, I will go out of business.**

Think of it a different way and your logical mind will tell you, "If I must sell at higher prices (which I must), then I must make my product or service different / better / more attractive / more professional than my competition, AND I must get that message to my customers so they are willing to pay the higher price.

The answer: Focus on truly being the best there is. Honestly give your customers better value for their money spent. Do not be just another business, offering what everyone else offers. When you are not like your competition, you will not have any competition. Oooooo. I like that idea.

Again, it goes back to how you think about your business.

Let me give examples for two different categories of businesses. Almost all businesses fall into one category or the other: 1) the service industry, or 2) the retail industry.

The service industry is where you do some type of service for your customer. The retail industry is where a customer comes to you to buy an item.

Examples: A service industry would be anyone in the construction business where they provide the service of building a house, doing plumbing work, electrical work, painting work, etc. A retail industry might be a candy store, antique store, bakery, catering business. Can you see the difference? Sure you can.

The Service Industry:

Let's start here. Typically people don't just call you up and say, "Come do the work and send me the bill." (Wow! Wouldn't that be great?) Nope, they usually call and ask for an estimate.
Let's see what potential customers typically experience.

A. The potential customers call ten businesses and get three "I'm sorry, the number you have called is no longer in service." (these three businesses having gone the way of the 95% who go out of business). The potential customers then get six telephone message machines that say, "I'm sorry, we are not here to take your call…" of which only one may actually call them back. Finally, they get a real person. (Hopefully that is you!) So overall, if they want three estimates, they have to call 15 to 20 different companies. Very frustrating.

B. When potential customers do finally talk with someone live, they hear, "What is your name, address, phone…." Followed by, "We'll try to have someone there between the hours of 8:00 AM and Noon." A vague statement, so the customer has to take time off work, sit around and wait, only to hear (about half the time), "We're running late; they will be there between 1:00 PM and 3:00 PM." The potential customer then has to lose an entire day, just waiting. (I can hear you thinking to yourself… Exactly! Been there. Done that. Got the t-shirt.) Again, very frustrating.

C. The estimator finally comes, and shows up in blue jeans, t-shirt with a marijuana leaf embroidered on the pocket, smelling like stale cigars. (Been there, too, haven't you?) "Well," the potential customers reason, "it took so long to get them here, I've already lost half a day (or a full day) waiting for them, so I might as well get their estimate. Not my first choice, but, oh well."

D. The estimator listens to what the potential customers want, then starts to tell them what they should do (called up-selling). Here comes the pressure. The customers feel like they are sitting in front of a shady used car salesman who is trying to sell them something they don't really need. Yuck! More uncomfortable feelings.

(Side note: True story I'd like to share. I had an exterminator come and spray for typical household bugs. While there, he did a "free termite inspection." He came back and said that we definitely had termites, that he had seen them, and that for $1200 we could "save our house." I asked him to show me where he had found termites. He took me outside and showed me tiny holes in our deck wood against the house. I reminded him that he said he saw living termites, and I said I wanted to see them too. He showed me where he had dug into the lumber. He spent ten minutes digging into a lot of old soft lumber and failed to show me one termite. Needless to say, he walked away very embarrassed that he was caught in a lie. Do you think I still use that exterminator company? Not!)

OK. Back on track here.

E. estimator checks a few boxes on a form, writes a number showing the price, shows it to the customers, and pushes the customers for a signature on a contract. But the customers still want other prices to compare. Again, uncomfortable.

If we answer each of the above problems with things customers want, the list would include the following:

A. Make sure the phone is answered by a live person. Pay someone, if necessary, to do it. If you already have an office person who has other jobs but who can answer the phone, make sure they put priority on answering the phone. Or hire a receptionist. Put in a second line so you don't miss calls when you are on the phone. Transfer the phone to your cell phone. Get a live person answering service. Do everything to avoid the phone message experience for the customer. If, for any reason, customers do get bumped to the phone machine, check it regularly, call them back as soon as possible, and start the conversation with an apology for the phone machine.

B. Don't just take their name and address and schedule an appointment. Take time to talk with them about what they want to do. Ask questions that will help filter out the potential customers who are just looking for the lowest price rather than quality service. Don't waste your time doing an estimate where you know the end answer will be "I have a lower bid, sorry."

(We have a whole book about that one later in this volume, called *Open The Door & Bring 'Em In*.)

When you take time with customers, not only do you get a sense about them, they get a sense about you. They realize you are far more professional than is typical. They realize that you take time with them. You ask questions. Right here in your first conversation, you set the ground work for getting the job, even at higher prices, because you are demonstrating that you provide MORE than your competition. Make sense?

The second part of setting the appointment is to set an exact time. Be there about five minutes early, so you can ring their door bell just before or exactly at the time of your appointment. You now can easily say, "We have demonstrated our promptness by keeping this appointment, and you can expect the same when we do the work." Again, demonstrate that you ARE giving more value for their money.

C.   When you show up to meet the customer, be in a professional looking uniform. Slacks (not blue jeans), uniform shirt with a collar, pocket and hemmed sleeves. Company logo embroidered. Make sure your deodorant works and your breath mints are in use (better to impress them with your knowledge than with your breath). When you look ultra professional, you are saying strongly if silently into your customers' heads, "Wow! These guys ARE the best."

Side note here: I know body piercing and long hair is a "statement," but remember this: You are selling your goods. Your customers MUST feel comfortable. Some may be offended by long hair or body piercing, and you will immediately lose them. All customers can accept short hair. All customers can accept no body piercing. Moral of the story: being ultra-professional includes looking the part of a professional.

D.   Don't walk in like the "know it all" in your business, telling the customers what they need. Instead, listen to what they want, and then take the time to educate them on the choices they have. Let them build the scope of work. (This is also elaborated on in the section *Open The Door & Bring 'Em In*.) When you teach a customer in a professional manner and let them make the choices, you win. When you just try to push your services, you lose.

E.   Instead of giving a generic looking estimate, give them one sheet with the scope of work on it, and then put the price on a separate sheet. (If they take your estimate to another business for comparison, your price is not right there written on your page outlining the scope of work so the other guy can just easily match or lower his bid because he can see your price.) Make sure your bid is professional, personal, specific to the project. Your estimate demonstrates you are willing to take the time to prepare a far more professional and clear estimate than average, so it follows that the type of service they can expect from you will be above average.

Giving a good estimate and getting the contract involves a lot of things, like identifying a person's hot buttons, their learning profile, their ability to make a decision now or later, etc. (Want to guess where you can find out more about all that information? Right again. It's in the section *Open The Door & Bring 'Em In.* Can you tell I like that section? Good author, too.)

Overall summary for Service Industry:

Your main objective is to make your customers' frustration disappear and to demonstrate beyond all doubt that you ARE far better than your competition. You do that by always having a live person answering the phone, setting and keeping appointments, never being late, dressing and looking the part of a true professional, taking time to learn about customers' wants and needs, taking time to educate them, and giving them a professional and clear estimate.

FOR THE RETAIL INDUSTRY:

I know. We have spent a long time on the service industry, and you may have forgotten the original topic, which was, "If I charge more than my competition, I will go out of business." Here we go.

Again, look at it from the viewpoint of your customers. Hopefully, they have a hankering for your product. So they usually drive to your store (except, of course, for those businesses that deliver, like pizza places). The customers walk in, and the first thing they notice is the atmosphere of the place.

Ask yourself this. What does my customer "feel" when they walk in? Is this place a "plain Jane" typical place with nothing special for the floors? Does it have plain tables, plastic fixtures, typical acoustic ceiling tile, plain white (or solid color) walls, just like any other typical place? OR, do they walk in and see, for example, a design on the floor, unique countertops and table tops, linen, walls faux finished to fit the motif, and unique wall decorations? Overall, is this a place that "feels" elegant, or unique, or somehow distinctive, different?

If they feel that they are in a typical place, they will expect typical product and prices. If they feel that they are in a "special" place, they will expect "special" product and higher prices.

Next. Customers walk in and see you and your employees. Do they see blue jeans, t-shirts with that marijuana leaf imprint, or do they see professional looking uniforms that match the motif of your store? Again, many owners think a t-shirt with a pocket and screen printed logo is good enough. Really now, which would make you feel like you are in a "better" store: T-shirts or shirts with a collar, pocket, hemmed sleeves and embroidered logo? Obvious, isn't it?

Match the atmosphere with ultra-professional appearance. If you read the previous section for the service industry, we don't need to talk about long hair and body piercing.

Yeah, Yeah, I know. These "extra" things cost money which will drive the price up. That's exactly the point. When your place "feels" more elegant, special, the customers expect to pay more. You show that you are far better than your competition. You get to stay in business and become far more profitable. Good trade. (There's more on this later in this book, so hold on to that thought.)

Last, and most important for the retail industry, is your actual product better than the competition? Really? No, Really? If it isn't, then you need to do some thinking.

Let me give a few examples. If you are a bakery, what do you do different with your cinnamon rolls? Do you sprinkle the top lightly with cinnamon? Do you arrange the jalapenos on the jalapeno bread in a design? Do you give a baker's dozen? If you are selling computers, do you offer on-site installation? Do you offer hands-on software training? Do you offer free phone support for installation? Do your employees refuse to let any of your customers carry your products to their car? On and on.

Get the point? Your customers feel your professionalism, see they are getting more for their money. Special little "somethings" that bring them back to you.

SUMMARY FOR RETAIL INDUSTRY:

When you offer more in atmosphere, service and product quality, your customer expects to pay more, appreciates it, and spreads the word to bring you more customers.

(Again, there is much, much more in the section *Open The Door & Bring 'Em In.* later in this volume.)

OK. On to the next item. (Remember? Back at the beginning of this chapter, there were six items where unsuccessful business owners typically play guessing games?) Ok. Here we go, on to number three:

3. I have a pretty good feel for what it costs me to be in business.

Do you now? Every business owner alive can tell me "about" what it costs them to run a business. Most may even be pretty close. The answer they give is based on how much money they spend every month. People do have a feel for what they are spending day to day, even sometimes month to month. But what they miss is money they need to set aside for expenses they will have later but have to save for now (results of slow months or for taxes, etc.) and they forget to add that amount in when they set their prices to guarantee they end up profitable at the end of the year, after everything, even those "hidden" costs, is paid out. The first warning sign of a business being in trouble is when there is too much month at the end of the money because the owner forgot to account for things in setting the overall prices.

It doesn't matter if you are a service or retail business, it all boils down to having a business budget.

This is so important, I have dedicated the entire next chapter to it. The concept of budgets is broken into two different areas. Personal and Business. Both of these are fully explained, compete with worksheets to help you get through it all more efficiently and accurately. In the Budgeting chapter, we go into detail about several areas where business owners forget to budget for money that will be needed to be spent later (Income Taxes, Depreciation and a few others).

But for now, what you need to remember is that once you have an accurate picture of how much money you need for your personal income and for your business expenses, you can use that information to calculate exactly what you MUST charge your customers in order to hit your profit goals.

No guess work. You take comfort in knowing you are not charging your customer too much or too little. Your prices are the RIGHT prices to be fair to both you and your customers. Make sense?

Next item:

4. I'm pretty sure I can train my employees to work as well as I do.

Card on the table face up here. Honestly now, probably the only reason your employees are working for you is for that almighty paycheck. They come to work, put in time, get a paycheck. Do they *really* care about your profit, your professionalism, your image, giving better service, etc.? If you are completely honest with yourself you would answer, "They don't give a rat's back side about any of that stuff." All the typical employee does is exactly what you tell them and usually nothing more.

Owners keep saying, "I tell them over and over again what to do, but they just don't get it." I also hear, "I have the hardest time finding good employees." Sound familiar?

This is a normal situation. But, you do NOT want to be a normal business that follows the typical business pattern (remember… going out of business).

If you want to get good employees, you have to attract them with things your competition does not offer. Good employees are attracted by a better job, better working conditions, better benefits, etc. Yes, all those things cost money, but we can show you a way it will not affect your prices. The money it costs comes from their efforts and not your business budget. (this is discussed in detail in the book dedicated to employees, how to find the good ones and how to keep them. The book is called *Where The Good Employees Are* which is the last book in this volume).

If you want to get employees to match or surpass your abilities, look to that magic word "training." The average business owner thinks training is easy. Just tell the employees what you want them to do, and you have trained them. There is a huge difference between just telling an employee what to do as opposed to teaching them to think for themselves and remember on their own what to do.

Take an employee in the retail clothing business. You can tell the employee to keep the shelves stocked. Then you come out there, and the shelves are not stocked with the right sizes or items you want. You tell them again, and the same thing happens, again and again.

What if, instead, you teach them by telling them something like this: "If you were a customer and wanted a Hawaiian shirt, what would you like your shopping experience to include? Would you like all the Hawaiian shirts on the same rack? Would you like all the sizes to be in the same area? Would you like a wide variety of choices? When customers come to the counter and purchase Hawaiian shirts, that tells you those items have moved off the rack, so what do you think you should do? Right! Restock. How would you restock the rack?" Etc…..

Important note: In my example, did the owner "tell" the employee what to do? Hint. Look at the punctuation above. Wow. Lots of question marks. That's the point. When you ask questions, it forces a response. When you tell someone what to do, the communication goes in one direction. When you ask a question and get a response, the communication goes both directions, AND you are engaging their brains. They are learning to think for themselves and become responsible, because it all makes sense. If you jut tell them, they learn they can rely on you to think for them and direct them when needed.

On to the Next item.

5.   I'm sure other people will agree my stuff / services are better than others.

Cool. We've already addressed most of this item. Flip back to the second item where we discuss the difference in your product or service. Is it really better? I am very positive everyone feels their product or service is better than the competition, but the fact remains, if you operate, charge, conduct your business just like everyone else, you are very likely "almost" the same.

You don't want to be "almost" the same with a few differences. Your success demands that you do, in fact, become different. Far more professional looking. Far better ambiance. Far more respectful and compliant to your customer's needs.

And now… finally:

6.   I think I will sell enough to keep me in business.

I don't know about you, but to me the word "think" in this particular sentence is pretty much the same as "guess." Since I don't like the word "guess" (which usually means hope for and most likely fail), I would much rather see the word "know" in there.

We have all heard it many times before.

See if you can finish this sentence. History _____.

Not sure what to put in the blank? OK. History repeats itself. (You are probably saying, "Oh yeah. That saying.")

Well, it usually does. History does repeat itself. What smart business people (that's you) learn is to take a look at past history, watch volume trends, and use that information to project your needs for the future.

What it boils down to is this. For a service industry, you may be busy in the summer and extremely slow during the holiday season. When you are busier, you need more employees, more materials / goods. When you look back at past sales for a particular month, it will help you prepare for that month this year. Busier seasons mean there is a higher demand, and your prices can go over what they need to be so you can build up some surplus for the slow periods. In the slow periods, you may be able to use the busy season's surplus to bring down your price and still make your annual net profit.

Don't worry. That's a lot, I know. We will take all that one step at a time in future chapters. The main point for now is this: Do not worry about getting enough sales to keep you in business. Worry about setting your price so that no matter what your sales are, high or low, you are guaranteed enough to keep you in business and make your desired profit.

Please read that last paragraph again. It is so very important. Way too many people go out of business because they think they must compete with price. It is far more important to get what you must (price wise) from those who are willing to pay it than to chase those who only want the lowest price. Make sense? I sure hope so. Because that profit, that money left after all the expenses, is the foundation of a successful business.

Ladies and gentlemen, that brings us full circle back to that concrete foundation. You see, money is the foundation itself. It IS the main reason you are in business. The material used to build your foundation strong (the cement) is using facts. If you guess, you are using wood and can expect short term results. If you take the time to plan, based on the facts, you have a concrete foundation for success. Now let's talk budgets (yuck)!

Building A Strong Foundation: Chapter Four
Do I Really Need a Budget?

No. You do not have to do a budget. Not if you want to follow your competition right out of business, that is!

Do you really need a budget if you want to succeed? Absolutely. It is the starting point to knowing the right price for your product. Eliminate it and you are back to guessing and hoping. We all know the highly probable results of that "typical" world, don't we?

So, let's get started shall we?

Oh, come on now. It's not really that hard. Once you get started it will be over with in no time at all. The great thing is, you only have to set it up once (takes a few hours). The even better news is, you only have to adjust it once a month (takes a few minutes). The most important news is, this is where you start taking financial control over your business.

We'll start with a personal budget.

You are probably wondering why we don't start with the business budget and then see what's left over for the personal budget.

Actually, that is exactly the way "typical" business owners think. They bring in the money from sales, pay all the business bills, then take what's left, and that's what they get to live on. In their busy season, they get to go out to dinner and eat steaks and twice baked potatoes, buy the new Harley and a new big screen TV. When the slow season comes, there goes the Harley and the big screen TV, and they go back to eating macaroni and cheese with weenies (which, by the way, I developed a taste for when I was doing my own budget that way).

Well, since we don't want you to be the typical business owner who goes out of business, we are going to shift our thinking here a bit.

Your mission, Mr. Phelps (Mission Impossible theme song going on in the background here), is to determine how much money you need to make to pay yourself a decent salary to support your personal life style.

Some of you are thinking, "What? You mean I get a pay check just like my employees AND that paycheck is as much as I need to pay all my personal bills?

Yup-a-roo. You got it. Dead on. Right-o. Yes Sir-ee. Uh-huh. Exactly!

Think of it this way. If you don't *plan* to make the income you need, you will never get it.

Your objective is to have your company pay you what you need, so you can eliminate your own personal financial worries. After all, you have enough to worry about running that business, haven't you?

One word of warning here. Be careful not to fatten up your budgeted income with stuff you would "like" to have. I said to include stuff you "need." If you get too greedy, it will financially stress your business.

Remember, all that luxury stuff will come later, from cumulative business profits and wise investing. If you attempt to buy luxury items too early, you will enjoy it for a short time and end up being long term broke.

When you finish your budget, it will be used to calculate the price(s) you charge your customers for your product or service. Obviously, the higher your budget, the higher your prices or the higher your volume will need to be to cover your budget.

Warning. DO NOT cut back on necessary expenses just because you want to keep your prices low. The fact is, you WILL spend the money, and if you don't get it back from your customers, then you end up just digging deeper into your pocket, which is one of the biggest reasons people go out of business.

It is far more important to have your customer pay for your expenses and keep you in business than use your own money to go out of business. Really!

OK. On to the budgets. Personal first, so you can determine the salary your business needs to pay you on a regular basis (what a wonderful concept).

But wait! Before we start jotting numbers down on a piece of paper, we should talk about taxes and how they relate to your budgets.

Keep in mind, there is a distinct separation between personal finances and business finances. Uncle Sam agrees.

On the personal side, Uncle Sam starts with your total income to determine what tax bracket you fall into. The higher your income, the more you get to pay in taxes (like *that's* a real prize!). If you don't make a lot of money, you get to pay a lower amount of taxes, both dollar and percentage wise.

Most people in business (especially in the beginning years) take a low income and experience low taxes, but let's face it, you are not in business to make a low income. The more successful you become the more income you make, which will change your tax position.

Wouldn't it be simply lovely if we could take some of your personal expenses and transfer them over to your business budget and pay for them there, so you can still have the things you want, but show a lower income and thus lower your taxes?

Zingo! That's exactly what one of the best benefits of owning a business has in store for you.

Be careful now. We have to stay legal. We want to make sure you don't get in trouble with Uncle Sam by having your business pay for stuff that doesn't follow the tax rules. Here are some basic guidelines to help you keep your nose clean.

Imagine for a minute that you are a key employee for a major corporation like, oh, Microsoft for example. Now ask yourself, "Self. What could Microsoft give a key employee as a company benefit?"

Let's see now… What's behind curtain number one, Monte?

A NEW CAR!!! (Did you hear Monte Hall's voice there?)
Gas station credit card for all fuel for the car!
All maintenance expenses for your car!

25

All the insurance for the car!

And now… behind curtain number two?

Fully paid life insurance!
Fully paid health insurance!
All medical expenses!

Finally behind curtain number three?

Your house mortgage payment based on square foot used for business!
All telephone expenses (for all lines used for business)!
All of your cell phone bill!
All of your Pager / Nextel (or similar) bill!
Your electric / utilities bill based on square foot used for business!
Clothing considered uniform or required for business!

Well, hold on to your hat because today is your lucky day. You win the jackpot of…. ALL THREE CURTAINS!!! How can you stand the excitement?!?

One safeguard before we dive into your personal budget. Your safeguard is the person who does your taxes, or the person who should be doing your taxes.

Always check with them to make sure your state laws allow you to move these expenses from your personal to your business expenses.

Now I hesitate to mention this next thing because I really LOVE a good accountant who knows their stuff. But let's face it. Just like any profession, you can have good ones and bad ones.

Accountants are people and so there's competent ones and not so competent ones. Some accountants do not keep up with what a person can and cannot claim. Some accountants want to "play it safe," which means they don't want to use some of the things they *could* use on your behalf for fear it might flag an audit. (If you are doing everything legal, who cares about an audit?) Then there are the good ones who *know* what you can do and take advantage of all the tax laws to reduce your taxes substantially.

Simple procedure here. Ask your accountant about the above list. If they tell you, "You can't move that item," or "That usually flags an audit," it is a good time to find another opinion. It's OK to interview accountants. Go to several (at least three) and interview them asking them specifically about the above items that you want to move from personal to business expenses. When you find the one that knows how to take full advantage of the tax laws and are not afraid to do it, then you have found a good one.

Beware of "I've used this guy for years," or "They are my friend." Just remember, if a person is a true friend or if they truly care about you as a client, they will serve you best by letting you get your taxes done by someone who is comfortable taking advantage of tax laws and in turn saving you potentially thousands of dollars.

'Nuff said about that… let's get to work on your personal budget.

Here again... you can download the form "Personal Budget" from our website as described in Chapter 1. Go ahead and print out a copy right now so you can follow along and even start doing your personal budget.

Now remember, as you go over this list we have provided, *you* decide (with advice from a good accountant if needed) which items to shift over to your business. Either way, they will get paid for.

Remember. If you leave them on your personal expenses side, your income is higher, your tax bracket is higher, you pay more taxes.

If you move them to business expenses, they are 100 percent deductible (in most cases) from your gross sales. This means you only pay taxes on your net profit. I hope that makes sense. On the following page, you will see an example of what your personal budget may look like. Well, at least the first part anyway.

Now get settled in and get ready to start on your own Personal Budget worksheet that you downloaded from the website.

Here we go...

PERSONAL BUDGET WORKSHEET

ITEM	AMOUNT
Cable TV	$49.00
Child Support	$0.00
Clothing	$40.00 (take annual average, divide by 12)
Etc.	

Oh, yea. Here's a GREAT bonus for ya. We have an MS Excel worksheet that will automatically give you the total as you go along. Yup. It's on the website and it's called "Excel Personal Budget". Go ahead and bring it up and look at it now. This is where we have already put the personal budget form in Excel. It's really cool because you can enter the annual amount and it will automatically calculate the monthly amount (like the clothing item above). My! What value for your book dollar. Take a look.

While you're looking, you might as well go ahead and do your personal budgets right now. I'll wait.

Done? Great!

Now.... That wasn't so bad was it? Congratulations, you have just finished one of the most important business steps. The next step is almost like the previous step except there may be a little research and future forecasting.

I know you're curious, so why not just go ahead and download the "Business Budget" MS Word form, print it, then pop right back here for some instructions.
On to the instructions then...

The first item on the business budget is "Advertising." Well, remember back in chapter two where we talked about your pro-active business plan? Sure you do. There is an entire section of your business plan dedicated to advertising items and yet another for marketing (how you get your advertising pieces out).

Make a list of every single thing you would like to do for advertising and marketing. Then do a little research to determine the cost for each item. Just for grins, calculate the expense for each item based on a full year of expense. Total 'em up then divide by 12 to give you a monthly amount.

Note: The business budget is also one of the free MS Excel worksheet you get with this book. That's right. Just go to the website and download that one too. It will help with the automatic total calculation. My! What value!

Important note to remember when doing your budgets: There will be several accounts like advertising where you will not spend a set amount each month. It will be variable.

This type of variable budget item I like to call a "reserve" account. Meaning, there will be many months where nothing is spent for advertising, while there may be a few months where you spend a ton. For the months where you do not spend money for advertising, you should have excess income to set aside for the future months when you need it.

Since this is so important, I will give an example here: January (slow month), you don't spend anything for advertising, but your prices included an amount for advertising budget. Say, $500 per month. Since you didn't spend it, but your customers still paid that as part of the price, you should have an extra $500 bucks. You put this money in a reserve account (hide it from yourself) either by literally moving it to a savings account or hiding it from yourself in your accounting software by moving it into a "pretend" savings.

(I know there is someone out there asking how to hide it in your accounting software, but that is something we will have to let you discover based on what accounting software you are using. Our Extreme Business Makeover workshop shows hands on, how to do it in Quickbooks, but that's another day, another workshop.)

Now that you have a good idea about reserve accounting, as you do the business budget, take a look at each item in the overall budget and ask yourself, "Self, is this expense item something that is exactly the same or about the same each month?" If it is an expense that occurs only occasionally (like auto repairs), then it is a reserve account, and you do the same as you did with the advertising budget above. That is, you calculate the entire year's average expense, project anything additional you may want to include and add it to the yearly amount, then divide by twelve to give you a monthly amount.

Now. These next few paragraphs will really blow your mind. Get ready to find the most common things people do not budget for and therefore end up losing their Fruit of the Looms…

Money Leaking Accounts:

1. Bad Debt: Defined as any time you do work, or provide or give goods that are not donated to a non-profit organization, where you did not receive money. Mouthful, huh? Re-read it… Sample: You give free samples of your product (you paid for the labor and material but did not get money back). 'Nuther Sample: You did some free work that was not part of the scope of work. Same deal. Even 'nuther sample: You did a change order (construction) and did not get paid. Ouch.

What you have to do is document this (via a "change order" or "promotional expense" form) where you itemize what you gave away or did not get paid for. Stick it in a file folder, and then total up the amount of all these each month. You will come up with an average. Bingo. Your Bad Debt Budget.

Remember. When it is in your budget, you get money back from all customers to pay for the items other customers (or themselves) get for free. Way cool deal, and you don't end up taking the loss. WOW, is that worth the price of this book or what!

2. Depreciation: Not to be confused with depression, which is what you will feel if you don't account for it. This is where the accountant tells you "congratulations, you get to claim $6,000 (or whatever it is) for depreciation on taxes this year. Isn't that wonderful?" What they really mean is this: you just lost $6,000 in the real value of your depreciated items (car, equipment, computers etc.). Now, when the time comes when you need to replace these things, where does the money come from? Do *not* think you need to replace these items out of your own pocket. Your equipment, car, computers etc. do *not* appreciate. They depreciate which makes them an_____ (pause) can you guess? Right! An expense item in your budget.

So let's make a list of all of your items that depreciate and write down their current value. Now, divide each item by how many months that item usually lasts before it has to be replaced. Add up all the depreciated items monthly amount, and NOW, you have an accurate monthly depreciation amount to put in your budget. Not just what the tax prep person tells you.

Note: Here we go again with the "Optional Items" thing. We have an item there called "Excel Balance Sheet" which you enter all the depreciable assets you have related to your business. You can use it *both* for your depreciation calculation *and* your balance sheet which shows assets and liabilities described later in the book called *The Stuff Called Money* In this volume.

This fancy little worksheet will save you lots of hours each and every month.

3. Future (whatever). Could be you need more equipment that you do not have yet, or you need a new vehicle, or you need to add more computers, etc.

Here again, I ask, "Do you want to invest in your business forever out of your pocket or have your customers pay for it so you can keep your profits for retirement?"

I think you have a good handle on it. Just remember, an investment is supposed to grow money, not take it. Same concept with future whatevers.

Figure out how much they will cost, how long they will last, and come up with a monthly amount needed to buy them. Put it in the budget. As a few months go on, you should be accumulating money for the down payment. When the time comes to buy it, you already have the down payment and the monthly amount you have had in your budget all along becomes the monthly payment. As a bonus, you *know* you can afford it. Way cool.

4. Net Profit Estimate Tax: Just remember, net profit is money left over *after* taxes. Easy calculation here. Take your total annual estimated sales and multiply it by your target net profit. That is how much you should have in net profit for all year. Divide by 3 (Uncle Sam will take one third of it), then divide by 12 and ka-ching! You have your monthly net profit estimated tax budget. Now, when tax time comes, you go to reserves and get the tax money from there instead of out of your pocket!

Ok... You've waited long enough... here's the worksheet sample. You work on your own worksheet that you downloaded from our website.

BUSINESS BUDGET

ITEM	AMOUNT
Owner Salary	$4,500.00 (from personal budget)
Advertising	$850.00 (annual avg. divide by 12)
Auto Expense:	
Auto Payment	$425.00
Auto Fuel	$3600.00
Etc.	

Notice there are no expense items specific to your actual goods or service. Good observation there oh, smart one. Those types of things are called, "cost of goods sold" and are calculated into your price later. Hang in there.

Thanks a bunch for hangin' in there with me and getting the budgets over with. Now we can move on to the specifics of coming up with the "right" price to charge your customers.

Now don't forget to go to the website and download the free MS Excel Business Budget worksheet. It makes the chore a little more fun.

Since your brain is probably frying by now… go ahead and let it relax a bit, then you can dive into the next chapter for yet more exciting brain food.

Building A Strong Foundation: Chapter Five
What is the Right Price?

The "right" price. I'll be the first to say that I sure hate it when I pay too much, and my guess is that it's the same with your customers. When you charge too much, your customers get cheated, and when you don't charge enough, you end up out of business. Thus, the only price that is a win / win is the "right" price.

(Good preface, huh? I like it too.)

The only way you can know your price is the right price is when you have done your homework. You have already begun by gathering the facts of how much you need to pay the bills. There is only one more element involved in coming up with the right price.

That is the element we mentioned in the last chapter called "cost of sales." That's just a fancy accounting word that means what it costs to make your product or provide your services *above and beyond* those regularly budgeted overhead items we did in the last chapter.

What's the difference between overhead items and cost of sales? To put it simply, overhead involves *regular fixed* amounts you pay, while the amount paid for cost of sales items may vary.

Here's some examples:

Retail: Let's use a candy store for our example: The cost of sales in a candy store *begins with* the sugar, flavoring, butter… etc.

Service industry: If you are a plumber, your cost of sales items *begins with* the toilets, sinks, pipes, flux… etc.

But there is more to cost of sales than just the "goods" required to make your stuff or do your stuff. The tricky part is labor. Some labor items are "overhead," meaning they are fixed amounts you pay regularly. Some labor items are "cost of sales" because the amount you pay varies.

Let's look at the difference.

For the retail business, it does not matter if only one customer comes in all day to your store, or if 1,000 customers swarm your store, you have to have the same labor, day after day, making the candy before the store opens (or during operational hours). This labor that *does not change* is considered overhead because they have to make the goods whether or not you sell them. But if you get swamped and need more people behind the counter taking care of more customers, the *additional* counter labor will be considered in your "cost of goods."

Let me make that more clear. You service businesses, hang in there. We'll get to you in a minute.

Let's say I own a bakery. My volume is somewhat predictable. I need to make 200 loaves of bread and about 120 dozen donuts. Some days everyone seems to want a donut and get a loaf of bread, and you may run out by 4:00 PM, but the amount you spent on regular labor did not change. Thus the labor is "fixed." If it is fixed, then it goes in your overhead budget (use one of those blank lines at the bottom) and *don't forget to add the labor burden (meaning the taxes you take out and any workman's compensation insurance you may pay).*

Same bakery… A couple of people are considered the "regular" labor, meaning they work every day on a predictable shift, say 7:00 AM to 2:00 PM. Then there is "part time" labor, basically meaning they work as needed and could be required to go home if business is slow. The "part time" labor is *not* overhead because the amount you spend will be different from day to day based on sales. Ergo they become "cost of sales."

Do you understand how you split your labor between the two? Great. If not, go back and review the previous few sentences until you have it down 'cause it's another very important aspect of your guaranteed profit structure.

Now. Thanks to the service people for hanging in there. Here goes for you guys.

Service businesses have it easy. If the person *works in the field providing the actual service to your customers*, their wages and burden (taxes taken out plus workman's compensation insurance) *automatically* go in "cost of sales."

Simple rule. Receptionist, estimators, field managers, bookkeepers, secretaries, etc. that *do not actually do the service work* are all overhead. That leaves all field workers in "cost of sales." Easy squeezy.

Now, for the somewhat complex, but not to be afraid of "calculating the right price" part. Here's the meat and potatoes of this section and the most important part of building your guaranteed profit structure. Are you ready?

Here goes.

This first part is for service business, but retailers, go ahead and read it, because it will help you too, with only a few additional tricks to learn for the retail business.

For the service industry, typically (accountants, paralegal and similar businesses take the exception addressed just a little later) have two main parts to their price, most commonly known as T & M. The T stands for Time and the M stands for Material.

Let's start with the material since it is the easiest. If you are that plumber we were talking about earlier, you would take the cost of your toilets, sinks, PVC pipes, etc., as "cost of goods." So, if you are installing a toilet, you would list your materials (toilet, wax seal ,and a little extra for misc. sundries, plumbers putty if needed, etc.). Let's say the total cost of all goods was $100 to keep it easy. You go to the store, buy the goods, and pay sales tax, taking your expense up to $108.00 (so far).

Important. In order to hit your target *net* profit on the entire project AND to bring in a little to pay for those little incidentals you're likely to forget you need (duct tape, razor blades, etc.), we add to the base cost of goods so far ($108 in our example above) what is known as a *markup*. How do we get that figure?

Well, if your target net profit is 10% (sorry, you are on your own to find out what "typical industry standard" net profit is for your industry as it varies so much from trade to trade), then you need to mark up your cost so far ($108, remember) by the 10% for profit, plus I like about 5% more for those little incidentals, for a total of 15% markup. Let's see. To $108.00 add (your + key) 15 (then your % key) should give you around $124 to $125 bucks total for materials. Congrats... the M word (materials) is done.

Now the tricky part: calculating how much to charge for your labor. OK, it's not that tricky. Just focus and you'll get it right away.

Start with the *average wage* you pay your field labor (all those not part of your overhead as discussed above).

Then get your payroll person to let you know what your *labor burden* is "PER HOUR." (To do that, just get the federal tax percentages, state tax percentages, workman's comp. Rate, SSI rate, etc. and add them all up to give you a typical percentage.) Typical (non-union) will be between 25% and 40% depending on your trade and your safety rating for your workman's comp.

So, take your average wage and multiply it by the total percentage of your total labor burden to give you the tax burden you pay per hour. Sample: If your average wage is $15 per hour and your percentage is 33%, then you would have about 1/3 of $15 for a labor burden of $5 per hour. OK so far? Now you've got your labor rate, plus your tax burden.

Next is the magic part. How much do you need to add to that to cover your overhead expenses?

To calculate the amount you need to charge to cover overhead on an hourly basis is done by taking your *total monthly overhead Business Budget amount* and dividing it by the *total amount of FIELD hours your field labor (not overhead labor) works* in the field.

Total field hours? Easy. (Sample to get the total field hours: You have 4 employees that work 40 hours a week. 4 x 40 = 160 hours per week x 4 weeks per month = 640 hours worked per month.)

Yes, I realize there is more than 4 weeks in a month, but if you use only 4 weeks in a month, that will make your actual price just a tad higher which is OK because, it's OK to be a little fat. It's not OK to be short (talking about money here, you wise guys).

So, let's say your total overhead from your budget is $12,800 per month, and your total field labor hours is 640, you would divide the $12,800 by 640 to give you an answer of $20.00 per hour. What this means is that this company must charge $20 per hour just to cover the overhead (remember, overhead includes all business fixed expenses, including your salary, estimated taxes, etc.). But we're not done.

Last step is to add all the facts together. This is where you calculate as follows:

Average Wage you pay your field labor:	$15
Labor burden on the average wage:	$ 5
Overhead amount needed per hour:	$20

Total 'em up for your *"break even point"*: $40

We're not done yet. I know, I know. Some of you picked up on that term "break even point." In the "typical" business world, we have been taught this: Your break even point is based on sales. You must sell "X" amount of work to break even and when you sell more than needed to meet your expenses, then you get to start making a profit.

Sound familiar? Sure it does. This is where I like to think outside the box and *not* do what is "typical" (go out of business). I like to stay in business and *not* depend on sales volume to keep me alive. I like to take whatever sales volume I get and *adjust prices* accordingly to guarantee I stay in business. When you depend on sales volume alone without adjusting prices, you take a huge risk because if sales volume goes down or is not as good as you expect, you are guaranteed to lose! Boo! Hiss!

Back to finishing off the calculation process of your hourly rate.

There is only one thing missing. You are not in business to break even, meaning that in our example above, if your company charges only $40 per hour, you will pay your field labor, pay for labor tax burden, and pay for all business expenses, but have no profit.

Now. Get ready for the absolute biggest mistake made in the business world, bar none.

Let's look at the plumber: He calculates his cost for a pretty good size commercial project at $10,000. That is his cost for material and labor using the break even point price of $40 per hour.

So the plumber says, "My cost is $10,000. I need 10 percent net profit. So he adds how much (this is the proactive reader part where you answer) _____

Right. They put $1,000 net profit in there for a total price of $11,000 to the customer. Cool?

NOT! There is one little detail easily overlooked. Let's think backwards here. Start with the price he charged the customer. $11,000. Now, we are shooting for 10 percent net profit of our sales volume. What is 10 percent of $11,000?

Ooooooo. We have a problem here. You most likely said his net profit SHOULD be 10 percent of $11,000 (right you are) which calculates to $1,100. But wait! He only added $1,000 to his price for profit! Do you see the problem yet?

Bingo. He just lost $100 bucks because of a "typical" calculation error. Here's the right way to think about adding in profit.

Think of it from the world of percentage: (Now keep your powder dry, you'll get through this. I'm here to help, remember?)

You charge the customer:	100 Percent of the price
You want a net profit of:	10 Percent of the price
Leaving all your costs at:	90 Percent of the price

Simple math rule we learn from this little ditty is about a "factor" we can work with:

Let's make it simple. Take 100 (Percentage you charge the customer) and subtract 10 (the net percent profit you want), to give you a "factor" of 90 for calculating your amount.

Example: You want 10 percent net profit: 100 minus 10 = 90

The factor formula is used like this: Our plumber's break even amount is $40 so:
$40 DIVIDED BY FACTOR OF 90 = .4444
Move the decimal point so it makes sense = $44.44

Note the difference here. If you just added 10% in the example above, the resulting price would have been $44 bucks per hour. By doing the above calculation, you get $44.44, which rounds up to (always the nearest dollar and *never* round down) to $45 bucks per hour. You just hit your target profit by picking up the extra dollar per hour. *Or*, you could better say you just *stopped* losing $1 per hour. For the plumber in our example above $640 per month, or $640 x 12 months = $7,680 per year. Yes, indeedy, that's over $7 grand per year that could be lost by doing the wrong net profit calculation. MY! What value for your book dollar! How can you stand it?

Congratulations, all you service industry guys. You just learned how *you* can calculate an accurate labor rate.

Yes. The website has a manual calculation form called "Labor Rate Calculation Worksheet" which is laid out in a structured, easy to follow format.

Hey! Guess what? You guessed it. We even have a fancy little MS Excel item you can download for free from the website. It's called "Excel Labor Calc". All you do is plug in your employees, hours they work per week, and company budget. It will automatically calculate what you "should" be charging at the current time to hit your target profit. Go ahead and check it out. After all, it's free.

By the way. Make sure you use this program at least once a month to check your current labor rate AND you can forecast your up coming labor rate which changes when you hire or lay off employees or change your overhead.

One side note here. I know the construction industry has evolved around the "unit price," or how much money per square foot of floor space. Sorry to say, but this method of pricing is the main reason people in the construction industry go out of business. No two projects are the same. If you use the square foot price system, you play the game "Sometimes it's enough. Sometimes it ain't. Overall, I hope to win." Talk about huge risk. (More on this when we get to the "estimating" section of this book.)

Now. My sincere thanks to the retail business people who have so patiently been waiting in the background. Here's the pricing structure for you guys.

As mentioned earlier, labor for retail business is part of the overhead and *can* be controlled by reducing behind the counter or customer service type employees when volume drops.

So, let's take a look at...say, a deli business, for example. The deli *must* have people come in before the doors open to do food prep (slice onions, shred lettuce (if not pre-bagged), get sauces into bottles / bins, etc.). This labor is carved in stone, no matter how much volume you have, so we must dump the "prep" labor into your overhead budget.

In the food business, they have a real cool term called "Empty Plate Cost," which basically means what it costs you just to have an empty plate before you put food on it. This cost picks up food prep, as we mentioned above, plus other overhead, like dish washer, building rent, utilities, cost of dishes, forks, occasional replacement. etc. *This is where you retail people need to sit down and make a list of every single expense that is not already in that business budget you built and add to it these retail item specific things.*

So, the first thing you do is to use historical data (when available) to calculate how much it costs you just to keep your doors open, *based on a single customer's empty plate (before food cost).*

Example: Your total overhead and retail related product budgets come up to say $20,000 per month. You have kept track of how many customers you get on an average day and it comes out to 160. Let's see now. If you take:

160 customers per day average, multiplied by 30 days per month = 4,800 customers per month.
$20,000 overhead per month, divided by 4,800 customers per month= $4.17 Per Customer!

Remember... it is always better to be fat, not short, so we round that up to $4.50. That will allow for about a 10 percent variable in customers who actually come into your store. If you have 10% less, you are OK. If you have more, that's fantastic.

So. This $4.50 is where we *start* with your pricing. Now you breakdown the food cost. Let's see... we have meat ($x per lb divided by sandwiches per lb = $ per sandwich), lettuce (calculated same as the meat cost divided by number of sandwiches per head), bread, mayo, tomato... etc.) An easy thing to do is to set up an MS Excel spreadsheet which will allow you to easily calculate your food cost based on current price changes.

Let's say our food cost for the roast beef deli sandwich is $1.22. Add the $4.50 to it and you have $5.72. Congratulations. You have YOUR break even point for the price you charge, if you don't want to make a profit. (Remember, our calculation above for service industry.) What, you skipped over that part! Well, go back and review if you skipped over it. It's important.

Anyway, you take the $5.72 base price and divide it by your desired net profit factor (let's say you want a net profit of 20% this time). 100 minus 20 = 80 factor for calculating. The answer: $5.72 divided by 80 adjusts our price to $6.98 per sandwich. Don't forget to allow a little more for waste if needed.

Hurray! You have calculated exactly what you MUST charge if you want to make your target net profit. If you charge anything less than $6.98, then you will lose net profit. If you charge $5.72 then you will barely keep your doors open. If you charge less than $5.72, then you are digging into your pocket to pay for the privilege of feeding your customers.

Let's take it just one little concept further. There is the "magic" of numbers. Let's say your price calculated out to $6.74. The human mind sees six bucks and change. If you raise the price to $6.98, the human mind now sees... six bucks and change. Same thing. So , go for the gusto to allow for those slow periods.

Yes. You need to do this calculation for each food item you offer on your menu to make sure your price is the right price! We have just the thing for you. Another form that you can download from the internet called "Retail Price Calculation Worksheet".

But again., if you use an MS Excel spreadsheet, it can be an easy step which you can do once a month to check your prices based on food cost, price adjustments, or overhead budget adjustments. (In our Extreme Business Makeover workshops we show you how to use this Excel worksheet. 'Nuther plug there huh?)

And, yes. It wouldn't be fair to have a labor calculation Excel program for the service industry and not one for the retailers, so again, on the website, you can get your free download Excel worksheet called "Excel Retail Price Calc". This is really a handy little tool.

One final part. The retail business is different from the service industry in the fact that the service industry can adjust their labor rate, project by project, based on actual field hours being spent. For the retailers, your best bet is to keep track of number of customers (not sales volume) for each month. After the first two years of business, you will be able to assess accurately volume trends, focus on marketing your company during business hours, and adjust your menu prices monthly (if needed) to keep you in business based on *actual* volume instead of just "hoping" for business to be "good."

Make sense? Sure thing!

OK. I think we have touched enough on how to come up with the right price. On to the next exceedingly exciting chapter.

Building A Strong Foundation: Chapter Six
WAG, SWAG, T&M?

In the last chapter, I covered all of the aspects of pricing for the retail industry, but I need to hit just one more aspect of pricing for the service industry.

All of you retail business folks can skip over this entire chapter since absolutely nothing will apply to you. Go ahead… I'll catch up with you in the next chapter.

Ok. Now for you service businesses, let's talk estimating.

Estimating is where we use the facts you have gathered from previous chapters and come up with the final price you give to your customers.

We already have calculated materials (your cost, plus sales tax, plus markup) and your labor rate (average wage, labor burden, and overhead amount per hour). This is the chapter where we put them together and come up with a final price for your customers.

There are three basic methods of calculating the final price (also known as bid price, proposal, or estimate, or whatever you want to call it). The three methods are:

W.A.G. Method, which stands for wild ass guess method! This is where the estimator says to himself, "Self, you have been in business for over twenty years, and you know what this should go for, and you have a good feel for what customers are willing to pay, so…. OK!" If a WAG estimator extracts the price from a set of blueprints, for example, he weighs the plans and charges $2,000 per lb. (Just kidding… No, really, just kidding….) What? That's how you do it? You *wagger* you!

Obviously, this is not the best method, since it relies on pure 100% guesswork and a wild hope for a profit. This is "win some, lose some, hope to make it" type of bidding.

Needless to say, I do not support this type of bidding. I like my customers to know they are getting the absolute right price and not a price that is "average," when average means 1) they may be paying too much, or 2) they are getting cheated, or 3) when/if they find out, I lose a future customer, or 4) my business doesn't keep it's customers, or 5) customers spread the word and I lose my reputation, or 6) I slowly go out of business.

Next up is the *SWAG method* which literally stands for *scientific* wild ass guess method, but is more commonly recognized as "unit pricing." This is where the price is based on either 1) square footage of surface or 2) price per item. Example. I will install a door in your house for $150 per door. I will paint your walls for $.50 per square foot.

This is still mostly guessing because, for example, if the guy hanging a door only has one door to hang, he only gets $150, period, when various doors may take longer to hang and circumstances are almost always different. That $150, no matter what the variables, is supposed to cover all the estimating time, time to go get the door at the supplier location, drive time, set up time, installation time, cost of all the materials, clean up time, billing and collections time, and you have probably spent $100 in materials to make $50 gross profit to pay for a full day's labor. That really stinks!

So why do so many people still use this system? Easy. *They don't know how to take full advantage of current computer technology.*

You see, in the past, computing meant your brain and a pencil and paper. Massive calculations had to be done by hand for each project to calculate how much material is needed, how much time is needed for each step, etc. So, doing it once and calculating a unit price to use every time seemed much easier. The people who did this, though, played the game, "You lose some, you win some, and overall, hope to make a buck." Doesn't work 95% of the time (remember our "out of business" stats?).

As a smart business owner, you can use computers to help you come up with the right price. MS *Excel* is a good program since it is software specifically made to do all kinds of fancy calculations, *and* many computerized plan take off programs import to MS Excel.

But wait! First thing's first. We must first decide *how* we want the computer to do its thing. What are the steps? What information will it need? How does it get the final answer? We have these and many other related questions to answer.

Aren't you just one lucky person to have this book to give you some great ideas in that area? Here goes.

T & M Estimating...

Probably the best way to explain this is continue with my previously mentioned plumbing company (from the last chapter, remember?).

Let's live a typical experience with them, shall we? OK!

A general contractor calls and says they have a project for our plumber where they are taking over a house that already has the shell and core done, rough electrical and rough plumbing done, sheetrock in, etc. All they need is installation of three toilets, kitchen sink with disposal, and two bathroom sink vanities.

Questions need to be asked. First, will the house be empty of other trades so our plumber can focus on only his work? Where is the house located (hopefully close to the plumber's place of business)? What kind of toilets do they want? Have they already purchased the sinks and vanities? Etc. What the plumber is doing with these questions is getting information to use to develop what is called a "*scope of work.*"

Once the plumber has the scope of work defined, then he has basically three areas of estimating he needs to be concerned with. They are:

Inclusions: List of things included in the price
Exclusions: List of things not included in the price
Clarifications: Special conditions related to this particular project that need to be addressed.

Thus, a scope of work involves inclusions, exclusions and clarifications.

Let's start with the inclusions. This begins with a form I like to refer to as the "take off sheet." (Yes, another downloadable form from the website). In the service industry, the term "take off" means to count and measure the quantity of surface or the items related to the work. On the take off sheet, the plumber would start by itemizing everything he plans to do on this project. This inclusions list may look like:

Toilets	Qty 3
Kitchen Sink	Qty 1
Kitchen sink faucet set	Qty 1
1/3 hp disposal	Qty 1
Vanity w/ faucet	Qty 2

And so on….

Next step is to make a list of items not included. It may look like this:

Work specifically excluded:
> All rough plumbing work (scheduled to use existing)
> All exterior water fixtures, faucets, etc.
> All showers, tubs and related hardware
> All other surfaces not specifically mentioned above in the inclusions.

Cool! Did you catch that last "catch all" phrase. Basically what that says is, "If you don't see it on this scope of work, it is not included in my price, and it will be extra if you want it."

Now the plumber stops to think if there is anything else that may be an item that needs to be discussed before taking the contract to do the work.

Maybe it goes something like this. "Let's see now…. I could get on the job site and find that the existing rough-in plumbing is not correct for the sink and needs to be altered. Could happen." So, his clarification section may say:

> We understand all existing rough plumbing will be suitable for installation of all plumbing items selected. In the event rough plumbing is not suitable and requires adjustments, the customer/contractor will be notified of additions to the base price prior to proceeding with plumbing work.

Get the idea?

As the take off sheet is being filled in, questions arise. As the questions come up, write them down. When you have all your questions lined up (after making your inclusions, exclusions and clarifications list), then you get to call the contractor and ask your new questions and get a clearer picture of the scope of work and adjust accordingly.

Now is the time to start the calculation process.
For our example above, the plumber would look at materials first. What is the cost of the toilet, seal and related hardware (faucet, pipes, gaskets… etc.)? Let's say the total price for all the toilet and goodies is $100. Add the mark up as explained earlier. If your desired profit is 20%, you would add an additional 5% for any small items (flux, solder… etc) for a total of 25% mark up.

(Now, don't get confused again between mark up and profit calculation. For the profit calculation, remember, we took the 100 minus your desired net profit for a factor to divide by. Well, contractors don't do it that way. They do it the old way, so why not keep the math the same?)

The extra five percent will cover the math difference and pick up a little extra for those little sundry items. Thus, you would take the $100 material cost and multiply it by 25% (Calculator-- enter 100 then hit the plus key, then enter 25, then hit the percent key. This automatically gives you the final answer). This gives you an answer of $125 bucks just for the material side.

Now, on to the labor side. This is where you take into consideration your historical data to know how much time it takes to install the item, in this case toilets. Let's say our plumber knows that to unpack, get tools out, turn water off, open outlets, solder pipes, elbows, install faucet, place wax seal, position toilet bowl, install tank and innards, etc., until the thing is finished, including pack up time, takes a total of two hours per toilet. Well, we have three toilets for the above project, so we know it should take a total of six hours. Your labor amount is easy. Just take the 6 hours and multiply it by the labor rate. (Remember the labor rate? That was the $40 bucks based on average wage, burden, overhead and profit. Well, for a plumber it may be a bit more. OK. Quite a bit more. Say $75 bucks an hour.) Thus the labor portion of the price would be the 6 hours times $75 per hour for a total of $450. Add in the materials of $125, and you have the total price of $575.00

"But wait there, Fife" (you say). "You're forgetting the profit on the labor." Did we now?

Remember, the profit for the material side was put in by the mark up. The profit for the labor was already calculated in the labor rate.

Final concept here. Please remember, your labor rate will change often. Every time you hire an employee, every time you decide to make additional business purchases, every time you purchase a new piece of equipment, your labor rate will change.

Why? Remember, part of the labor rate is your *total overhead divided by field hours*. When your overhead changes, so will the labor rate. When you hire more employees, you have more field hours, which will change the labor rate.

I know this may be a bit confusing, but if you can just get that concept down, it will help you adjust your prices based on what is needed and not what is guessed.

I keep mentioning MS Excel as an Excellent calculation program and, you guessed it again. I have made a service industry MS Excel estimating program specially for youse guys. (Sorry, a touch of New Jersey hit me). It's on the website as a optional item you can purchase. Just click on the "Free Downloadable Books" link like you do for the free forms and the list of optional items will come up.

This is really a cool thing. It allows you to type in the item, number of steps, whether it is a sq. ft. item or a unit item and the quantity. From those items alone, it automatically gives you the total price following all the theories above AND gives you a field budget sheet, proposal for your customer (editable), and a financial evaluation showing your profit margin in advance. This way, you can play with it all you want to raise or lower your prices seeing the effect it has on your profit. Really a way cool program and recommended for easy calculations especially if you are not too comfortable with programming in MS Excel. Let us do that for you. We have even found a way to merge our program with an On Screen Take Off program. That's the cool software program that allows you to get plans from your contractors on CD or over the internet.

This software loads the plans and lets you do a *very* quick take off using your mouse and computer monitor. No expensive digitizer needed. Give us a call for more information on this plan reading take off software program thing I keep mentioning. As technology changes, so will we and this book may be outdated to the most current technology, so feel free to give us a call (800) 697-5413.

Now, shift gears into 5ᵗʰ gear and get ready for one more critical item that will keep your business running full speed ahead. (OK, not my best analogy).

Volume trends: This is where in the summer you seem to get lots of work and in the winter your customers are spending money on holiday stuff, so your work slows down. Rather than live on steaks in the summer and macaroni and cheese in the winter, you can actually take control and have a smooth business cash flow all year around.

Here's how.

The problem: In winter, volume is low. In summer, volume is high.

In winter, you have fewer employees. In summer you have more employees.

If you map it out…. It looks like this:

Calculated Labor rate:

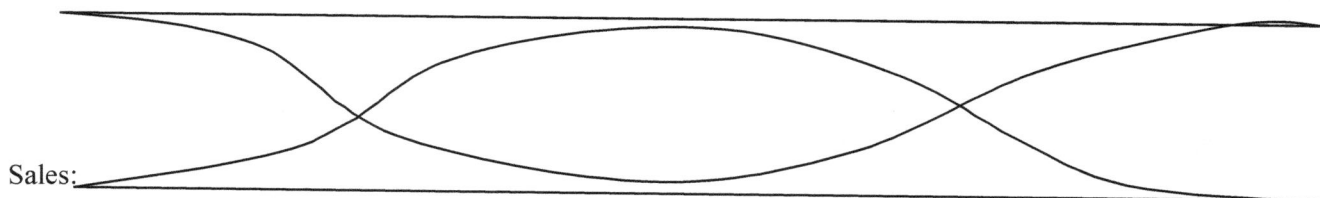

Sales:

Follow me closely here. When you have fewer employees during the slow periods, your *calculated labor rate* will go way up. Why? Because your overhead will stay the same (about) each month, but if you only have one employee to bring it all in, what you have to charge per hour will be huge. If you have more employees, giving you more field hours to spread your overhead, then your calculated labor rate goes down.

But wait. You need to lower your price in the winter to encourage work and raise it in the summer because your customers are willing to pay more.

Dilemma? Not really. Here's how you manage that situation.

In the summer, let's say your labor rate calculates all the way down to $35 per hour. BUT you can easily charge $45 per hour because it's your busy season. *Charge* the $45 per hour, call it "market value." (How much more can you *easily* charge in your business? We'll get to that later.)

My sample plumbing company had 640 hours per month. At $10 per hour *excess, or market value,* I should have *$6,400 per month to set aside for the winter months*. Make sense? Cool.

(The financial book we have will tell you how to use your accounting system to tell you exactly how much you need to set aside, and how much is left to be called true net profit. Later dude. See you in that book.)

The concept is this. When winter time comes and our plumbing company is only working 400 hours per month and that boosts the labor rate up to $80 per hour, our plumber has set aside $12,000 for the winter. This surplus has to last three months of slow time.

Math here. (Sorry, those who hate math, you gotta get over it). $12,000 split between three months gives you $4,000 per month to "buy down your labor rate." We are spending 400 hours per month, so that gives you a buy down of $10 per hour. Meaning…. Even though the labor rate will calculate out to $80 per hour, I can charge $70 per hour and still guarantee I hit my net profit goal.

This is what we call money management. Unlike the typical system of "when stuff happens, I just spend money, and when I run out of money, I get more from the bank. In the summer, I pay the bank back, and overall, I barely keep my head above water." Yuck!

I call that type of money management the "happen-ness" system. When stuff "happens," then react. I much prefer a guarantee profit system of knowledge. When stuff happens in that world, you have planned for it, know exactly how much you already have to cover it, financial worries are gone and you can have a much more happy life. Hey! Why not call it the "Happiness System" compared to the "Happen-ness" system. Way cool!

I think you have the critical elements of successful estimating for most of the service businesses.

Other service industries are somewhat different but still follow this same principal for estimating.

Let's take the paralegal service industry. You have your material expenses (paper, printer, filing fees, notary fees, etc.). Take what it cost you for a specific service and remember to *mark up by your desired net profit plus that "oops" factor of 5 percent.*

Now. For the labor part. Same thing. Use your historical data to determine how much time is needed to prepare your final product. Multiply the hours it takes by your needed labor rate and add that to the material costs. Vooalla. You have a price. Compare it to market value. If you are WAY too expensive, it's time to either figure out a way to do the work faster, or you flat-out have to charge a higher price to cover your inflated expenses.

The most important idea to gather from this entire chapter is this:

You have used your *actual expenses* based on your budget and your *actual field labor* hours to come up with the price you *must* charge per hour for your work. You have added *material.* The price you get is the RIGHT price because it's based on the facts.

Again, this will dictate to you what you MUST charge your customers to make a profit. If you charge less, you will not make a profit. If you charge way too little, you pay for the privilege of doing work for your customer. Exception to this rule is in summer time or busy time, you get to charge extra market value to cover your slow time volume by your good money management. Not by risk.

Can the computer do the estimating calculations you ask? Great question and thanks for asking.

You bet! There are many out there that are specific to your trade. I have made one for the service industry people, and yes, it does work very smoothly with a plan take off program. You guessed it. I have both our estimating software (can work stand alone) and the blueprint take off software which has templates for many different trades. They are listed on the website on the same page as the "free downloadable forms". You are more than welcome to call for information to see if these optional items would be a good fit for your company. By the way, I have researched many programs and found these to be the least expensive and best for most companies. May as well look into it. It will cut your estimating calculation time in half or more!

For those of you who don't mind doing it the calculator way, we have something special for you too. (Yea!!)

It's also on the website and is a free downloadable form called "Estimating Calculation Sheet". This will help keep your math structured and easy to follow and use for your business success. You will find later in this book that this form is used to help you monitor your field labor, so please don't feel that you can skip this part and just go back to the good ol' "I know what it should sell for so I'll just keep doing it the old way". Very dangerous!

There you have one of the two most important parts of your business identified. The other most important part is the field labor part, but (wouldn't you guess it), that's in another book.

Schewww! That got the ol' mind going. Break time here, then we can go on to the next chapter.

Building A Strong Foundation: Chapter Seven
Company Operations Manual

Company Operations Manual—that's just a fancy word for a book that has two main parts: 1) a section explaining the basic flow of the company's business, or "how the whole thing works," and 2) all of the employees' various job descriptions.

You are most likely thinking, "Oh, come on now! Do I really have to write all that down, especially job descriptions for my job and for all my employees' jobs?"

Well, let's look at it this way: if you are a one-person business that will never grow and you can carry all the details around in your head and never make a mistake, or if you never plan to hire employees, I'll admit the job descriptions may be a moot point. You are excused from this part of the book.

However, for the rest of us that have more to do than we can easily keep track of, or have even one employee, business partner, or, for the lucky ones, your spouse who works with you on the job, you need a Company Operations Manual.

Because let's face it, we all forget things, especially details, and there are lots of important details in business. And we don't learn new things or new routines easily either.

Let's take a tour of the average person's brain. The average person's brain shifts from one thought to another about 3000 times per day. (I love that statistic. It's my excuse for forgetting to do stuff my wife asks me to do. Think of it. What a perfect excuse. "Honey, there are 3000 things that hit my mind today, and your request was only one of them, so you should expect me to forget sometimes." OK. It doesn't work any more, but the fact is, it's still true. It is WAY easy to forget things.)

So, you cannot be expected to remember all the things you need to do each day for your company, and you cannot expect your employees to "get it" the first time they hear something from you, especially if your instruction is only verbal. (After all, the average person, even when paying full attention, will only remember 30% of what they hear the first time around.)

The answer to this dilemma is a Company Operations Manual. This manual gives you a chance to put, clearly and precisely, on paper, what you yourself need to remember, and also what you expect of each employee, and it also gives employees a chance to take the thing home, read it over and over again, and nail the training process in a couple of weeks instead of months (or years if you are trying to train a teenager).

Your Company Operations Manual we will develop together, here, step by easy step, starting with generalities and moving down to the particulars. And don't worry, we've got empty worksheets all ready for you to fill out, making it super easy for you.

Here's what will be involved, when we get around to doing it in a few minutes.

First, you will outline the general description of a typical day in your business by listing all the particular work items that usually need to be done in a day's time. Then you get to assign each of those same work items to its own "department" of the business. For the complicated departments (like accounting), you do a further breakdown of the work item into particular details showing how the task gets accomplished.

Then you write down an assignment of each item to a particular employee. When you get all this brainstorming and outlining done, you are ready to get to your computer and very easily type up your Company Manual.

Simple, really, and it helps you to be sure that nothing important, like, oh, let's say, recording the right information for taxes, gets done when it should. (And with your manual in hand, you'll be able easily to check with the right person in each department to be sure it's getting done!)

What? You don't have "departments." No prob. Just make 'em up as you go, thinking like the bigger company you may want to become someday. Remember. You are small now, but when the day comes when you grow big enough where you can delegate what you want to others, you'll be ready because, right now, you're making your overall plans for success.

So, what are your company's departments? Here's a couple of examples. Let's say one of your tasks in the service business may be to check for collections (people who owe you money). That would be the "Accounting" department. The task of checking for today's estimating appointments would be your "Estimating" department.

Retailers, same thing. Your departments may be "Management," "Front Counter," "Stock," "Custodial" etc.

Now, to begin. (Yes, we are still talking to both retail and service businesses on this one, so stay awake, both of you.)

Your first task will be to brainstorm before you actually start writing the manual itself.

First you will think about defining in a general way how you want your business to operate on a daily basis, to think for a minute about the typical *flow* of your business on an average day.

Here are some examples to make it easier to grasp. First let's look at a retail hobby shop, then we'll take a service business example.

The flow, or sequence of events that happens in this retail business, from the very first thing in the morning, may be:
- Arrive at the store location and check grounds to make sure it is clean.
- Open store, turn on lights, and check to make sure the store was left as is should be.
- Check stock and replenish items as needed.
- Go to office, get start up cash drawer, and count it for accuracy.
- Set up cash register and paper, check credit card machine and paper
- Check interior for overall cleanliness – sweep, dust… etc.
- Open the doors for business
- Ring up items for customers, bag and insert promotional items
- Spot check store for cleanliness every other hour
- Restock item if a large quantity of an item is purchased
- Shift change – cash machine reports (X tape)– cash drawer… etc.
- Upon closing, check to be sure restroom / other rooms are vacant.
- Close and lock doors
- Close out register (x and z tape), count morning start up, secure cash in safe.
- General clean up, sweep, dust… etc.

And there you have it, the basic daily flow of the business of that store.

And now an example for the service business people. Same thing, slightly different story, and yet, there's a kicker for you. You have two different business flows to consider. Both are similar to the one above, but separated into one for the *office* stuff and the other for *field* stuff.

Example. Typical service business flow for the office might look like this:

- Arrive at the office, check grounds, make sure it's clean and was left secure.
- Turn on lights and start coffee
- Check phone machine for messages
- Check schedule for appointments / to do list items (from your business plan)
- Take and screen phone calls as they come in
- Use phone message system to relay phone messages
- Schedule time slot for estimating activities
- Schedule time slot for billing / accounting activities
- Check in on all field projects (work in progress)
- Prepare reports as needed
- Handle customer new work, change orders, or general concerns.
- General maintenance of facilities (sweep, dust… etc).
- Assist others as needed
- Close the office, computer back up, general cleanliness, lights off… etc.

And for that other side, the field stuff, it may look like this:

- Arrive at job site 15 minutes early to orchestrate work
- Get tools organized and ready to move to job site in minimum moves
- Orchestrate labor with assigned tasks
- Observe all labor to check for efficiency and accuracy
- Evaluate material needs for the day and all day tomorrow
- Order material items as needed for delivery by supplier
- Lunch time activities-- check production and praise other workers
- Evaluate material needs again for the rest of today and all day tomorrow
- Order material items as needed for delivery by supplier
- Evaluate task progress, re-orchestrate for the afternoon
- Observe workers for efficiency and accuracy and correct as needed
- End of day, check time cards, paper work, schedule for tomorrow… etc.

I know. You are thinking, "Man! If I could get my foremen to do all that, we would be rich!" You can! ('Nuther book in this series. 'Nuther time.)

But for now, get ready for yet another great moment of "My, what value for my dollar I spent on *this* book!" Because now you get to do *easily* this very same brainstorming work for your company by outlining your company's daily work flow, assigning each task on the list to a "department" in your company, and then assigning each task also to a specific person. Don't panic, I said it's going to be easy, because you're going to use our easy worksheets as a sort of "first draft." Later you'll use the worksheets to help you actually write out your company manual.

Here it comes, your first worksheet, already prepared for you to fill out.

Just follow the same steps you did in chapter one and download the form from our web site called "Company Operations Sequence Worksheet". Go ahead. I'll wait…

Take a look at this form. It has only three easy columns:

Task   Department   Person

Pretty simple huh?

Now. Some of those departments were just darn easy, like, oh, janitorial duties, where you don't need to do a complete break-down of every little thing. But some departments, like Accounting, need a complete breakdown, since there are so many important detailed things to do, like accounts receivable, accounts payable, daily entry, weekly reports, monthly reports, and a bunch of other stuff that *has to precise and recorded*, so a detailed breakdown worksheet for each of those kinds of departments will be helpful.

Would you like to guess what the form is?

Right! A special worksheet we call the "Company Operations Task Breakdown Worksheet". Go ahead. Download that one and print out a few copies, then you can come back here and follow along.

As you can see, this worksheet has only three columns as well:

Item   Description   Person

Let me give you a little example that applies to both retail and service.

Here's what it may look like.

Item	Description	Person
Expenses	Check date for accuracy, check the check number, check who it's made out to, verify the amount, verify the expense account.	Pam
Deposits	Determine if the check is for an invoiced item or if it Is for a direct sale. Invoice item, enter under payment feature, check for Amount accuracy, date, check no, etc. Sale item, enter under sales feature, check for item Number, description, amount, check no… etc.	Pam

I know this seems like a bunch of work, but it really will go fast once you get to it. Now if you are just too busy and want the super fast way out, we have that previously mentioned "Extreme Business Makeover" workshop where we hand you the entire Company Operations template. Our template is customized for both the retail and service businesses *and* is available for purchase on the website "Free Downloadable Forms" page. It saves a ton of time and all you have to do is read it and edit it to match your desires. But for now, back to the task of doing this yourself.

I can feel the attitude of some of you out there. You want to skip this worksheet part and get on with it to actually writing the manual. Trust me. This is the easy way in the long run.

OK. Now's the time to get to work. I'll wait right here. Go ahead and put a post-it-note on this page so you can find it.

Homework done? Great job. Now comes the fun part. Aren't we having fun!?! OK. I know. It's not *really* fun, but it's just got to be done. That is, if you want everything in your company to go smoothly.

If you have done the homework by filling out a bunch of worksheets, this part will be easy.

Just take your worksheets and arrange them in the same sequence as things would usually happen in your company.

For retailers, it will be from the time you arrive at your store to the time you leave your store. Don't worry about the stuff that is done once in a while (printing profit and loss statements, etc.). You stick that in after the daily sequence stuff.

For servicers (my spell check loved that word) your flow is from the time the phone rings with a customer asking for an estimate all the way to the time you collect the final check.

Go ahead. I'll wait right here while you arrange them.

(Theme song from *Jeopardy* goes here.)

You are such a great worker! Way cool.

Now that you have all your worksheets lined up, you are going to make yourself an official Company Operations Manual!

We'll start with an *Opening Section*.

The Opening Section is written as if you have a new employee that knows absolutely nothing about your business. You give them a quick summary.

Here are a couple of suggestions to give you an idea. Feel free to use any part or modify to your heart's content.

For servicers it may look like this:

INTRODUCTION

Welcome to Veeblefesters Landscaping company where landscaping takes on a whole new meaning. Our company is unique because we don't just mow lawns and pull weeds, but rather we pride ourselves on providing elegant landscaping design that makes our customers' homes or businesses veritable show places.

This Company Operations Manual has been prepared to provide our employees with a complete description of how our company operates and to explain all the services we offer. We encourage our employees to read this manual several times to help them understand our business and how it relates to our expectations of our employees.

Retailers, same thing, just modified a bit. OK. I'll give you an example too:

INTRODUCTION

Welcome to Veeblefesters Music Store where music takes on a whole new meaning. Our company is unique because we don't just sell instruments, but pride ourselves in providing a wide range of sheet music, music books, all varieties of musical instruments, and quality instruction for beginners and professionals alike.

This Company Operations Manual has been prepared to provide our employees with a complete description of how our company operates and to explain all the services we offer. We encourage our employees to read this manual several times to help them understand our business and how it relates to our expectations of our employees.

So. Go write your own introduction.

Back now? Got-er-done? Fantastic.

Now to the meat and potatoes. Here's where we actually *write out* for the official manual the "flow" of your business that you spent all that time brainstorming and outlining. First you simply, in a bulleted list, name the tasks. Then each of your tasks or topics will be given a separate section in your manual and have it's own title at the top of the page. (This is where you use those worksheets where you broke down all the task descriptions and organized them in a somewhat logical fashion; just use those to get your sections and titles.)

If I know you, you may be thinking, "Where do I get all the possible breakdown items for each of these sections?" I'm down with that (my teenager says that's a cool expression). I wish I could give it all to you in this book, but understanding financial statements, advertising and marketing, or sales activities will require tons of explaining to learn how to do it very effectively. Here we're just trying to get you started. So I have saved that for the other templates we offer on the website. Yup. Same location as the others.

For now, you can put down what you are currently doing, then later add or edit in the great stuff you glean from the other books. Here's some examples for your company operations main points:

Example:

Retailers possible section titles:

- Operations
- Store Opening
- Store Operations
- Store Closing
- Cash Management
- Advertising & Marketing
- Accounting
- Price Evaluations & Adjustments
- Financial Statements

(Remember, you are *not* writing job descriptions at this point. You are just writing out the sequence of events.)

Now you take each one of those and write details for it.

Here at Hamhockers Specialty Jerky, it is our standard to give all of our customers a good and unique experience when visiting our store. We have maintained an Excellent reputation for our jerky products by following these general business guidelines:

STORE OPENING:

- *Arrive 15 minutes early.*
- *Check property for cleanliness*
- *Check inside store for cleanliness & security*
- *Note any item the closing crew may have missed*
- *Count start up cash*
- *Etc.*

Here are more examples:

STORE OPERATIONS:

- *Greet customers*
- *Assist customers in selection*
- *Give samples (discretionary)*
- *Take payment using cash register*
- *Etc.*

Service company examples:

Here at Klinkerdamps Karpet Kleaning, we pride ourselves on providing more than the average carpet cleaning business by giving our customers an experience that will bring them back for many years to come. Our unique service is demonstrated right from the first phone call down to the final exit. We have an Excellent reputation which is achieved by following these guidelines:

INITIAL CONTACT:

Telephone screening – set the stage
- *Promote the company*
- *Discuss options (color brighteners, de-odorizes, etc – discussed by estimator)*
- *Schedule an estimate (if needed)*
- *Etc.*

ESTIMATING:

- *Company uniform appearance*
- *Call to confirm appointment*
- *Arrive 5 minutes early*
- *Greet customer*

- *Etc.*

Other sections? OK. After all, I gave the retailers a breakdown of possible sections, so here's some for the servicers:

- Operations
- Initial Contact
- Estimating
- Sales techniques
- Advertising & Marketing
- Project Set Up
- Field Operations
- Services
- Project Completion
- Customer Follow Up & Promotions
- Billing & Collections Accounting
- Pricing Evaluation & Adjustments
- Financial Statements

Noticed it, didn't you. There are more sections for servicers than there are for retailers. Different ball game.

Ok. Everybody get to work on your own now. Then meet me back here.

Welcome back. Not too bad, now was it?

OK. On with the final part. The next part of your Operations Manual is writing the job descriptions part. This is where you write out all the tasks you have noted above, only this time around, your list relates to a job title. This way, your employees can find their job description and read all about work expectations for their positions.

We start again with the task description worksheets. (Aren't you glad you did them?) This time around, you arrange them according to an employee "title." For example, you may have one person doing the telephone greetings and the accounting, so you would give them the title of "Office Manager."

Remember. The critical part of this whole thing is to give your employees clear instructions of what you expect of them.

New employees must know about your product to better serve the customer, and new employees are not an expert at the point of hiring, so let's give them all the help we can.

Servicers, I know it will take much more training to get your employees up to all the aspects of their job whether it be office related (tons of stuff there) or field related (tons of stuff there too).

OK. How will the descriptions look?

Let's start out with the same type of opening section just to get into the flow of things. It may look like this:

JOB DESCRIPTIONS

It is very important that all employees of Pumpernicheski Premium Painting (take a shot at pronouncing that one!) understand all aspects of their employment. This will insure all of our customers experience the same level of professionalism from all people within this great organization. We encourage all employees to read and re-read as needed their respective job descriptions to assist in individual performance as proud employees of this company. Job descriptions are as follows:
RECEPTIONIST

The receptionist is the front person and usually the first person who makes contact with our new customers as well as the on-going contact for our existing customers. It is very important the receptionist maintain a polite, friendly and courteous attitude towards all people who call or visit our company. Items of responsibility for the receptionist are as follows:

INCOMING PHONE CALLS:

Estimate Request:

When a customer calls with a request for an estimate, it is important the receptionist gather information from our customer to make sure the customer meets our profile for potential business. Not all request for estimates fit our company standards. For example, if a person is selling their house and just want a "face lift" for a super discount (low) price, that type of painting does not fit our standards of quality and there are many painting contractors who operate in ways that we think cut corners and are basically just not the way we want to do business. These companies will charge substantially less. Thus, this type of customer will only use our time just to get a price, and almost always take the lowest price, thus a waste of our time.

To properly screen the customer on the telephone, one of the questions you will be required to ask is, "Are you in the process of selling your home?" If the answer is no, then proceed to the next question. If the answer is yes, then respond with the following concept using your own words: "We understand in selling your home you do not want to invest a lot of money for something you are selling. There are different types of painting companies. Some painting contractors operate in ways that we think cut corners and are basically just not the way we want to do business. These companies will charge substantially less. They pay cash under the table to their workers, don't pay workman's compensation insurance, don't have general liability insurance, and purchase lower quality materials to get the price down as low as possible. We are not that type of company. We do carry all insurances and operate 100 percent legally, thus our price will be higher than those other companies. You can decide, but if you are just looking for the cheapest price, you may want one of them instead of us. If you are moving to a new home in this area, we would love the opportunity to give you an estimate for that work because we realize you would want a higher quality, longer lasting painting job for that situation. For the house you are selling, may I suggest (another painting company who does that type of work where you can set up a commission structure for passing on the lead)."

Note here… you are breaking down the details of exactly what is expected and giving suggested "script" of what the employee is to say.

Here again, there is no one in the world who can read that only once and have it down. This is where it is very important the employee highlights that scripted section, and you (the ever so wise owner) test them with a couple of role playing times. Really! I did this for an actual painting company where out of the blue, I would call the receptionist and act as a new customer and tell them I was selling my house.

Interesting what happened. After about three times, the receptionist recognized my voice and still did the drill. It took about twenty times before she got smooth. Without the drilling, the employee would just do what is comfortable, which is get the name and address, schedule the appointment, only to have the estimator take the time to go out and then see the "for sale" sign in the front yard and waste the two hours with the appointment.

OK. Now for the retailers. Here's a sample.

JOB DESCRIPTIONS

It is very important that all employees of Beaulas Boutique understand all aspects of their employment. This will insure all of our customers experience the same level of professionalism from all people within this great organization. We encourage all employees to read and re-read as needed their respective job descriptions to assist in individual performance as proud employees of this company. Job descriptions are as follows:

OPENING SHIFT

The person opening the store is to arrive 15 minutes before the store opens to insure the store is ready to open in both appearance and to open early in the event a customer is outside waiting for the store to open. When our customers know we open early especially for them, it gives a feeling that our customers truly come first and will promote repeat business which is critical to our company.

Upon arrival at our store location, the opening person is to check all surrounding property to make sure it is free of all trash or anything that does not portray a clean and professional environment.

When entering the store, the opening person is to check. And on you go.

For content items you may want to have:

- Opening Shift
- Cash Register Procedures
- Customer Relations (how to greet customers… etc.)
- Stocking Products (food prep for restaurants)
- General Custodial
- Safety
- Manager Responsibilities
- Accounting and Security
- Closing Shift
- Etc.

OK, you got the idea. I realize your entire job descriptions will take a bunch of time to detail. The template we give at our workshops and available on line as an optional item is over 50 pages for the services industry people. Retailers can use much of the service industry template. However, we would prefer to work with you one on one if you feel the need to have additional help. Again, Phone calls are free. If you want us to actually do the work for you, we can help you out there too.

How to get-er-done yerself? You *must* schedule time in your appointment book. Just do one chunk at a time. If you set aside only two hours per week, and assuming you can type at, say, 40 words per minute, you should get one section done (four pages) per week. It may take you two to three months to get it done, but trust me. The time you take will save thousands of hours of frustration in training all of your employees in the future.

I have known one company that took eight months to write the job descriptions. Worth it? You bet. It was two years later that a franchise marketing company took interest in them, and their company operations manual became a critical part of franchising. The franchising company took interest because the company was "market ready." Was it worth it? Sure it was. By the way. This company only had three employees.

Some companies even give their employees the manual and have them highlight important parts of their job description directly in their copy of the manual. They sign a sheet stating they have read and understand it. The owners just look at their copy to see if they have highlighted it, proving they did in fact read it. Then, they take the first copy, give them a fresh new copy and have them repeat the process by highlighting their job description area again, noting important points. This proves they have re-read. Repeat a third time. Bingo. You are sure they probably have it down by now.

I know that sounds kind of "untrusting," but face it. The average person will read it once and say they "got it." They do not realize they really only got 30 percent of it *if* they had college level thinking turned on. That is just normal. They feel embarrassed if they are told "You really didn't get it the first time" indicating they are "stupid," so make sure you tell them the average genius only gets it 30 percent the first time and the re-read process only guarantees employee comfort with their job description.

Don't believe this? Just for grins and giggles, make up a test pinpointing the most important parts of your job descriptions. You can bet the average person gets less than 50 percent. It will amaze them too.

Anyway, I don't want to harp on this very much. You make the judgment call on how you feel your employees will grasp the job description.

So, take the time right now to schedule working on your Company Operations job descriptions. No need to post-it-note this page because that task may take a while and no need waiting to get the rest of the "great value" from this book.

Now. If you are one of these people who just hate the whole drudgery of making and writing your company operations manual or employee handbooks, feel free to give us a call. That's right, We offer the service of writing these company operations manuals. We have people that type up to 90 words per minute and we already have done this several times. This means we could "borrow" from what we have already done to save you time and money. Typically, we can get them done in as little as one week for an average size company (retail or service). Feel free to call to get a current quote.

And there you have it. Man! This was a long chapter, but none the less, a very important one.

Building A Strong Foundation: Chapter Eight
The Bible—According to Employees

So. You want to hire employees, huh? Great!

First, let me say this chapter is a preface to the forth book in this volume, _Where The Good Employees Are_. It's here because it will give you some important "foundation" things to think about before we get into the real meat and potatoes.

When it comes to employees, though, almost any business owner in the small business world will tell you the same thing. I hear it all the time. "I just can't seem to find good employees. If I do find one, I just can't seem to keep him."

No new news here. It's been that way for quite a while now. Different from the good ol' days in the 40's and 50's where it was easy to find good employees with good work ethics.

So what happened?

The employee mind shifted from "give the boss eight hours of work for eight hours of pay" to "I am blessing the boss by just showing up, and he owes me." From the time people start in the job market, they learn, "If your boss requires you to do anything (go to a meeting, work overtime, clean up your mistake, etc), they _must_ pay you for that time. If you work more than four hours, they _must_ give you a paid 10 minute break." It sometimes seems many employees are just there to do as little as possible.

Let's take a look at what we, the owners, are doing either to support or to combat any negative employee attitude. Let's begin with what I think an owner typically does. See if you agree.

(By the way, the last book in this volume goes into great detail on the subject of employees: where to find the good employees, how to pre-screen on the phone, how to conduct an effective interview, how to get applicants to compete for the job, how to hire them, orient them, train them, and offer them the type of working conditions and benefits that will keep them working for you. As far as this part of the book is concerned, though, we only need to suggest to you a basic mind set in establishing initial contact with employees, as well as some of the key elements in getting your employees to be the kind of employees you want them to be.)

Typically, the owner of a business puts an ad in the paper and waits for the phone to ring with the perfect employee on the other end of the line. Ten phone calls come in, three or four of the callers have a hard time understanding English, another three or four have a hard time comprehending English, and the remaining two seem to be ok, at least from phone impressions. The business owner sets two appointments for interviews, and, finally, only one person actually shows up.

The interview that takes place basically sounds like this, "Where have you worked before?" (Response from applicant). "Why do you want to work here?" (Response from applicant). "When can you start?"

This owner feels desperate to hire someone, and the person in front of him or her is breathing and seems to have a pleasant personality, so poof, a new employee is hired.

Once the employee is hired, the owner hands the new employee a "company policy" booklet (if they have one) which was written because... well... you choose:

1. You knew you needed something to help you with training.
2. Someone told you a company policy should be written.
3. You got really peeved at your employees, and you're "gunna fix 'em."

Most owners write it for the latter reason.

So. The employee gets this company policy thing and looks at it as "a bunch of rules the boss would like to see followed."

Do they read it? Typically, the owner sends the employee home with the booklet and tells the employee to read it. The employee starts, gets bored or doesn't understand it, so they put it--oh, anywhere, never to be seen again.

But we, of course, don't want to be typical. So let's take a different look at this thing called the Company Policy Statement.

First. The purpose of such a statement is to give your employees specific job-related rules *and* to let them know the consequences if they do or do not follow them.

Did you catch that word "consequences?" That's right. Most people just state the rules, but not the consequences.

Let's say the topic is the dress code. Your company policy may read:

DRESS CODE:

All employees are to wear the company uniform which will consist of black slacks, the company uniform, shirt or blouse and company hat.

That's it. Usually that's all she wrote.

Now, Michael Gerber, author of *The E-Myth,* spends a bunch of time on the importance of making all of your customers experience the same thing each time they walk in your store, including the appearance of your employees, the greeting customers get, etc. I agree. Customers *do* appreciate consistency, but does the Company Policy written above guarantee it?

Let's say that even after being given the Company Policy, an employee shows up in black Levis (not slacks). Their shirt was not washed from the precious day and has a few minor stains on it. They forgot their hat. So what do you do?

"Well," you may say to yourself, "I *need* them." So, you tell them, again, "I really would like you to wear slacks and the hat and have a clean shirt." That is, IF you tell them anything. Many owners are just glad an employee shows up for work at all, and so they just let such violations of company policy slide because, "Well, they really don't look *that* bad."

If you *do* actually follow up with anything more drastic, like, oh, implementing any type of punishment, then the employee often gets mad, leaves, quits, or worse, attempts to sue for harassment.

Why? Because there was no consequence defined in the company policy statement.

How to correct this?

Let's make another attempt at the same company's written policy.

DRESS CODE:

The dress code has been established to give all of our customers a feeling of entering a business that is clean and professional because this builds customer comfort and loyalty. For this reason, all employees are required to wear the company uniform, which will consist of black slacks, the company uniform shirt or blouse, company hat and black shoes with rubber sole. At no time will an employee be allowed to wear black Levis or similar denim material pants. Slacks are to have a crease in them. The company uniform shirt or blouse is to be clean with no visible stains. The hat is worn to provide hair protection (prevent hair from getting in our products) and must be worn at all times when on the job. If an employee comes to work with wrong style pants, uniform that is not clean, improper shoes, and / or they do not have their hat, they will be sent home, without pay, and be put on probation for one week.

See the difference? I don't just state the "rule," but I explain why it is important. Also, I let them know all the things I've already thought about, addressed, and am not about to let "slide by." They know exactly what the consequences are if they don't comply. No surprises and no exceptions.

By now, you are thinking, "Hey Lynn! What about the situation where I really need that employee to work? I can't just send him home and be short handed, now can I?"

Good point, oh worrisome one.

Here's the deal. If you don't enforce your consequences, you are proving to your employees that they can and will be allowed to break the rules. If you are not serious about the rule or the consequence, then, flat out, don't waste time with the rule in the first place. Moral: you just gotta send 'em home.

So, here's your solution. You have another person that is "on call." It's not too hard to find a person (either retired, in school, housewife with children, etc.) who doesn't really *need* to work, but who likes part time work just to break up the boredom. This is the person you call in at least twice a week to keep them happy and interested in staying employed part time with your company. When anyone breaks any rule in the company policy, you have a back up.

Yes. You may have to suffer for a half hour waiting for your on-call person to arrive, but the important thing is that employees breaking the rules *know* you are serious and that if they want to keep their jobs, they have to follow the rules. Period!

So, by now, we have looked at the company policy guidelines that will benefit you as the owner. But we have not addressed it from the viewpoint of your employee.

It is never a good thing to dictate to employees, "Here are the rules. Follow them, or you're fired!" Wowzer! Talk about negative! That sure doesn't get me excited about following the rules.

Ok then. What *would* make me excited? What makes *them* excited?

Ask yourself, "Self, what is the main reason people work for me?"

Obviously it is… Money!

People are not truly motivated by negative things (anger, yelling, hostility, threats, etc.) They are motivated by positive things (praise, thanks, acknowledgement, and, of course, money). Top of the list is money. Take money away, they will instantly quit. Take praise away, they can still "get down with that" and will keep working for the money.

So, if that's what motivates them, let's use *that* for a biggest motivating factor. How?

Here come a couple of retail terms: "average ticket" and "up-sell." Your customers come in to purchase something they have in mind. Many people, for example, go to the store simply to get milk. Where is the milk? Back-o-the-store. Right! You have to walk past the cookies, crackers, chips, soda pop display, etc. to get your milk. Impulse speaks up with, "Heck, why not?" And you end up with more than you came for. It doesn't stop there, either. There's one more shot at the cash register where they display candy, gum, tabloids, etc. *and* you have a check out person offering you even more temptations.

Every fast food employee (McDonalds, Taco Bell, etc.), always asks that oh-so-familiar question, "Would you like some desert with that? How about trying our new _____?" We all know this as an "up-sell" to increase the average ticket.

Well, rather than just tell your employees that doing this "up-sell" is part of their job and that you are counting on it for your pricing structure, you (the smart business owner) do your pricing based on typical average ticket *without* the up-sell. This guarantees you that hit your profit needs without the up-sell because the price you charge guarantees it. The up-sale is then extra frosting on the cake, gained by the employees' extra efforts in both super friendly service and up-selling.

Example. Ever go to a CiCi's Pizza (if you have them in your area)? Their advertisements are nuts. They show employees just bubbling and bouncing off the wall waiting to spring on customers with an over-abundance of joy and enthusiasm. When you go to the store, guess what? You get that bubbly enthusiasm with each employee. They are always asking what they can do to make your visit more enjoyable. "Get a napkin for you? Refill your drink? Get another chair for you?" And on and on.

When you have an employee that does these things, your sales go up, your profit margin goes up, and you have extra (not estimated or reflected in your pricing) profit. With this extra profit, you *give it back to the employee(s) who show the best effort* in promoting your company with perfect dress code, Excellent appearance, wonderful personality, up-selling, etc. Give them a cash bonus in front of other employees, along with praise and recognition.

What does it cost you? Nothing. It's free because the money comes from the extra profits they earn from their efforts.

What about service businesses? Same game, different day. Your price is based on estimates that are based on actual material and labor hours (see earlier chapters).

With you, it's even easier (lucky you!). We do not suggest you encourage any employee to cut corners with materials and so cheat your customer to bring in extra profit. That is a bad thing.

We do encourage employees to *save labor hours*. Example: You estimate twenty hours for a project. They get-er-done in only sixteen hours. You collected four hours of labor money that you didn't have to spend. Extra profit! Bingo! This too can come back to them in cash bonus and extra benefits.

I would love to take the time to explain all the details of a complete bonus program for both the retailers and servicers, but alas, the timing isn't quite right yet so we will save that for the last book in this volume. It goes into how to set up, prepare and implement good employee relations. It also talks about monthly meetings with employees that will cost you nothing. Providing all the benefits--vacation, holiday pay, sick leave, medical insurance--all of which will cost you nothing, due to this innovative program. We'll See you in that section later for all those details. Back on track with money motivation.

Now that your employees know there is money in it for them, you have their interest. If profits increase due to the quality work of all employees, then the employees benefit. And the company policy manual is the guide to showing the employees how this can be done.

The company policy then becomes a rule book that *benefits the employees,* not just the owner, and employees understand this. They realize showing up late is not good for the bonus program. They want a rule about getting to work early, getting ready so they can start the actual work at the designated start time. They understand the consequences and know they never have to worry about the consequences when they simply follow the rules. Employees can tell new employees, "Break the rules, and we are all serious about the consequences, because the person who breaks the rules takes money away from our bonus program, and we, the fellow employees, do not want to just let it slide and get smaller bonuses."

Is that powerful or what? Now, your company policy is not dictated to employees. It can be actually created by them and enforced by them because they want it. What a mind blower that is! Can you see how that is far more successful than the old way of, "Here it is. Follow it or get fired!?"

Your next thoughts are probably drifting to, "Hey Lynn, what is in this company policy anyway, besides the dress code you mentioned above?"

Man! You ask good questions.

Here are some general items you may want to address in your company policy:

Servicers:
- New hire qualifications
- Dress code
- Tools of the trade (what they are expected to have)
- Time card procedures (checked daily by foreman)
- Work Schedule (how they find out where/ when they work from day to day)
- Change Order / Additional work requested by the customer
- Material ordering and equipment request
- Personal conduct on the job site
- Project sequence (what to expect for production evaluation and goal setting)
- Company policy violation process (verbal, written warning, termination, etc.)
- Etc.

Retailers:
- New hire qualifications
- Dress code
- Time card procedures (checked daily by foreman)
- Work Schedule (how they find out where/ when they work from day to day)
- Personal conduct / customer relations (how to treat customers)

- Store cleanliness
- Company policy violation process (verbal, written warning, termination, etc.)
- Etc.

Hey, you can also use the previous "Company Operations Task Breakdown Worksheet" for this task. Just sit down at your computer and start typing the "basics" of what you would like to see in your company policy on this form. Then you can go to MS Word and just start expanding what you want into paragraphs as demonstrated above.

Remember, as you write this thing, write it as if you were training a new employee who is slow to "get it." Do not leave anything to common sense. Just like in our "Dress Code" examples earlier in this chapter, you have to take the time to address not only the rule, but the explanation of the rule, as well as the consequence for breaking the rule.

Also remember, you are only creating the template. After reading the last section about employees, you will understand how to gather the employees for a meeting to introduce your bonus / benefits program and get the employees proactive in creating your company policy. In this magic meeting, the employees will read your "suggestion," discuss it, offer suggestions for modifications, if any, vote on it, and you can then make your final copy.

This way when new employees are hired, you can honestly and literally say, "This is our company policy, written by your fellow employees, all for the benefit of having better working conditions and better opportunity for bonus and additional benefits. We have monthly meetings where you too will be invited to discuss any item in the company policy and make changes for the good of all."

Is that cool or what?

Takes time? Sure thing.

Worth it? Far more than you will ever imagine.

Remember. You, the owner, can only do so much to perfect the "business" side of your business. The employees really can make or break you.

Let's not be like most businesses and be frustrated with your employees. Work with them, so that you can *all* benefit by your business success. Makes it much easier and more enjoyable for all concerned. Don't you agree?

OK. Go ahead and get to work on your company policy template. You have the suggested categories above. Remember, you can also get a jump start with our optional Company Policy template offered on the website. Found the same place as the other options mentioned above.

Here's something else that will help. Give yourself the S.A.T. test. Oh, yeah, I haven't mentioned that yet.

S.A.T. test stands for Stop And Think.

Is there anything else in your business for which you need to have a policy?

In the "new hire requirements," for example, you may want to have a paragraph on general appearance including hair (no long hair permitted unless it is tucked under a hat and kept neat, or in a hair net. No scraggly beards. No body piercings. No smoking odor, body odor, or breath odor, etc.)

I know. Some may "think" they have rights to display their inner self.

Here's the thing they need to understand and something you may wish to add to the text of your company policy.

Everyone can accept a non smoker. Not everyone can accept the smell of cigarette smoke.

Everyone can accept someone with no body piercing. Not everyone thinks body piercing is cool.

Everyone can accept someone with no excessive tattoos. Not everyone thinks excessive tattoos are decorative.

On and on. Get the point? They (your employees) must too. You are dealing with All customers, which means ALL people, and you want ALL your customers to feel comfortable. We appeal to the masses, not to individuality. If employees are not comfortable with those types of concepts, they are telling you they have not matured enough to respect the rights of others. *They still put themselves first, and they will end up doing the same to your customers and business.* Statistics tell us that about 25% of the population flat out don't care, and if required to think of others where they work, they will flat out quit. They think their rights are more important than others' rights and will focus on themselves instead of your customers.

That's a good flag for you to let them go and find someone who does have respect and concern for others more than themselves.

Enough said on that.

So. Do you have enough to get started in your company policy?

Don't forget drug testing, negative attitudes, showing up for work early, etc.

OK, have fun then.

Oh, by the way, if you are planning to attend one of our Extreme Business Makeover workshops, don't worry about writing your company policy. That is part of the workshop where we give you an entire template. We have one for retailers and one for servicers, so most of that work is done for you (also available on our website as an option as mentioned earlier in this chapter).

And, remember we offer the service of writing your company policy for you for companies who really have a unique business and need that custom service. Just call for details and current rates.

On to the next chapter then…

Building A Strong Foundation: Chapter Nine
An Absolutely Essential Element of Success

Probably the most important aspect of being a truly successful business person is "Mind Set."

Here's the foundation to a proper mind set: "You get out of life exactly what you deserve, and you deserve what you get based on what you do."

We start with common sense. If you think you will never have a better life, you are absolutely right. If you think you "could" have a better life, then maybe you "might." If you think you "will" have a better life, you "_____" (yup. fill it in).

It goes way back to the time of Christ. "As a man thinketh, so is he." That is SO true. The first stage of "mind set" is to stop thinking negative things and start thinking resulting things. Note how the key words associate with each other in the following:

"Think"	=	It might or might not	=	Most likely will not = Fail
"Could"	=	Could or could not	=	Most likely will not = Fail
"If it works"	=	It might or might not	=	Most likely will not = Fail
"Maybe"	=	Maybe it will or won't	=	Most likely will not = Fail
"Try it"	=	A test to see if it works	=	Most likely will not = Fail

Get the idea?

Great substitution words for positive mind set that get you want you want:

"Will"	=	No room for failure	=	Success
"Do"	=	No room for escape	=	Success

So, when you catch yourself saying stuff like the following (and don't try to kid the teacher here, because I know what you have already said to yourself):

"This sounds like great stuff. I think I am going to give it a try. It might just work. If it works, my business could be great."

OK. Now go back to that last sentence and count how many "loser" words you can find.
Write your count here: _____

If you didn't get tempted to cheat by looking ahead ("Boy! How does this guy know about these things? He's just like my mom with her magic eyes in the back of her head."), you should have counted six. Go back and see if you can spot them.

I'll jam them together here: sounds like, think, try, might, if, and could.

If it "sounds like" then it could also possibly not be true. If you "think" (as in guessing), then you are not sure. If you "try," it, you could fail, but it's ok because you tried. If it "might" work, it might not... etc.

Now, *you* re-write that sentence replacing all the loser words with positive words and see how you do. Use this space:

Let's see how you did. Here's what I came up with:

"This IS great stuff. I AM going to DO IT. It WILL work. WHEN it works, my business WILL be great."

Can you see how that whole series just screams success, while the other way it was written just had all kinds of excuses for it not to work?

Positive Affirmations.

If you look in the mirror every day and say, "Man, you are U.G.L.Y." Guess what? You ARE ugly, and you become ugly.

Reverse it. When you say, "What a beautiful person you are," then guess what? You ARE beautiful (even though you still have that scar from the dog bite on your left cheek. No one cares because your smile and attitude cover it up).

Now. Let's turn to the business world. I can give you some very powerful business affirmations that will greatly assist in your success.

"I will re-read this book as many times as needed until I am clear on all aspects discussed."

"I will continue my business education with enthusiasm."

"I will start immediately on my personal and business budgets."

Now, you fill in the space below with a couple more affirmations that will get you going in the direction you want to go.

I will:

OK. I can see the fat lady out of the corner of my eye. She is warming up and getting ready to sing, so we'd better get with it because we have been given plenty of things to think about and have plenty of things to do.

One last word of caution, though. I was called to provide consulting services to a company whose manager had an entire wall of about 350 books, all on business management. This person had only been in business for four years and proudly said he had read all the books. I got to wondering, "Why the be-jeezees did this guy hire me?" If he read all those books, he should be expert enough to be a business consultant! The answer was that he spent all his time reading and not applying what he had read.

Moral: find only a couple of great books that are specific to the needs of your business and its growth. Read them. Re-read them. And then apply what you have learned. If you "over inform" yourself and do not follow up, you may overwhelm yourself with too much information, sometimes referred to as "paralysis by analysis".

So, team. Without further delay, now is the time to get out there and make it all happen.

This concludes this episode of the Guaranteed Profit System. Stay tuned for more exciting adventures with our other books in this volume.

- The End -

(Well… for this book anyway. On to the next)

What are you still doing here? Go on! Get to work!

The Guaranteed Profit System
Book 2

The Stuff Called Money

"A Quick and Easy Guide to
Understanding Financial Statements"

By: Lynn H. Fife

The Stuff Called Money: Chapter One
What is Money Now, Really?

Ah yes… The wonderful world of money.

First, let me give you a few things to think about that will help take you out of the world of "typical business" and into the world of "successful business."

Start with what your parents told you when you were just a wee tyke. As a matter of fact, I'll bet you tell (or told, or will tell) the same things to your kids (assuming you have or will have them.)

OK. What did your parents tell you about money?

Let me guess. If your folks were like mine, they told you…

"You can't buy happiness with money."

"Money is a tool of the Devil."

"Do not worship money."

"Don't beg for money."

"Don't steal money."

"Don't borrow money unless you absolutely must."

"Do not talk to anyone about how much money they make."

"Don't ask anyone how much money they paid for something."

And the list goes on.

It even branches into other areas concerning money. We also heard:

"Don't associate with rich people."
"Rich people are stuck up."

"Rich people don't care about the regular folk."

"Rich people think they are better than everyone else."

"Happiness has nothing to do with being rich."

On and on….

Well, I finally figured out why we heard all that stuff.

I don't know about you, but for my family, we heard it because we were broke.

That's right. Our folks taught us that it's OK to be broke, in debt, and struggling for a living all your life. That's what 99% of the world does.

Really? Really!

You take 100 people living in America and only one in one hundred gets to retire financially secure. In other word, rich.

Funny thing isn't it. You gather an audience of 1000 people and ask the magic question, "How many of youse guys wanna be rich?"

Watch almost every hand go up.

Next, you ask, "How many of you are willing to do whatever it takes to get rich, as long as it's legal?"

Watch almost every hand go up again.

The funny part is this: why is it that almost every person in America wants to be rich, are willing to do whatever it takes to get rich, but only one in 100 actually get rich?

The answer? We have been taught right from the git-go from our folks to fail in wealth building.

The only difference between a rich person and an average or poor person is that rich people understand that money is nothing more than a tool. That tool can give you an opportunity to have the things you want if you are in fact willing to do whatever it takes to have the life style you would like.

Break it down. Money is a tool. It is a tool of every society in the civilized world. It is nothing more than just a tool. It is *not* a tool of the Devil. It is *not* evil. Rich people are *not* bad because of money.

Opportunity is realized only when a person does in fact do what it takes to take their dreams out of their head and put them into the world of reality (discussed in Book One). Are you REALLY willing to do what it takes? If you are, then you do have every opportunity to make it happen.

Many people have heard this. They know it. They believe it. Why then do 99% of the people fail in accomplishing it?

Example: Take a candle maker. They think making candles and selling candles will make them rich.

Take a roofer. They think putting roofs on houses or buildings will make them rich.

But the fact is, nobody actually gets rich by simply doing their work or selling their services.

The work you do is nothing more than a way of making money. Heck. All of those 99% who fail in wealth building are *all* making some money. So is making the money the secret to getting rich?

No. Wealth is the aftermath of making money. Wealth is not how much money you make but instead how much money you (fill in the blank here): _____

Bingo! The PROFIT you make and keep.

Most business people think, "I sell my services or products. I spend money to pay the business' bills. What's left over is what I get to live on. In the busy times of my business, I get to eat steaks. In the slow periods, I get to eat Macaroni and Cheese."

Our Book One talked a little bit about this, but in this book we take it one step further.

When you let your sales happen, pay your bills based on who happens to be asking for it the most, and live on what you happen to have left over, well, this is the world I like to call "the world of happen-ness."

This is where 99 % of business people live. (Note the similarity between that and the people who fail to get rich?)

The successful business person has learned how to get out of the world of "Happen-ness" and into the world of "Happiness" by using one simple process.

It's called "Money Management."

That's right. Instead of letting money "happen" so that we adjust accordingly, we take control of our business by managing the money in a way that gives us control.

When you control your money, you get to pay your bills, plan on how much you want for your life style, and most importantly, plan how soon you get to retire a rich person.

Sounds wonderful, doesn't it? Well, is it a myth or a reality?

It can be a reality if you follow this simple process:

Step 1: Learn what money really is. WOW! You have this book to help you there.

Step 2: Learn what financial statements really are, from practical applications. Double WOW! Again, this book.

Step 3: Apply what you have learned. *This* is the main reason people fail. They learn it, think it's great, but don't take the time to do it. When they don't practice money management, are they *really* willing to do whatever it takes to become rich? I doubt it!

Congratulations. You have learned the first rule in becoming successful in business and even more important, how to become financially independent.

Success starts in your head. When you *think* like a successful business person, you will *be* a successful business person.

So.. Are you ready to get out of the world of happen-ness and into to the world of money management?

Great! Here we go.

The Stuff Called Money: Chapter Two
Your Monthly Report Card

School! Yuck! For those of us who didn't much care for school, that title may be off-putting, but don't be alarmed. This will be a piece of cake. The report card is just something that shows you regularly whether or not your business is making it or is about to fail. Important thing to know, right?

Sadly, the "normal" business only gets their report card once a year at tax time when our beloved Uncle Sam reminds us our report card is due by April 15th with penalties if it is not turned in on time.

Not being "normal" means you get a report card much more often. Why wait until the end of the year to find out if you are doing OK or not. If your business is failing, wouldn't you like to know it before it's too late, and you spend the entire year continuing to lose money to the point of bankruptcy?

I don't know about you, but for me, I like to have a good feel for my business success or failure at least once a month.

Suppose it took me less than a half an hour? I could know even more frequently. Even better, right?

Yes, the seemingly impossible is possible when you:

1) know what information you need to give you an accurate report card,
2) then take the time to set up a reporting system (only once, thank God),
3) use it to pinpoint how to correct things when things aren't going well.

So. What is this magic thing I have been referring to as the "report card?'

It is the business report affectionately known as the "Balance Sheet."

Once upon a time, you see, an owner of a company went to the accountant and said, "Take out a piece of paper and figure this up. Take all the money I have, and subtract all the money I owe, and tell me how much money would be left over? Or, let's put it this way: how much money am I worth right there on that paper?"

The Balance Sheet was born.

With only paper and pencil, accountants had to list all the money a company had and gave that a fancy name called "assets." Then, they listed all the money the company owed and came up with another fancy name called "liabilities." The accountant did the math and came up with the difference (what the company was actually worth) and gave it another business term called "equity." Some just made it simple and called it "Net Worth.

Well, here we are in the fast lane, new age, jet stream, etc. And since I like thinking a little outside the box, I got to asking myself, "Self, Why do I need this thing and IF I need it, what parts do I need that make sense to me?" So, I looked into it and found out a whole bunch of cool stuff.

I found out this report, this balance sheet, can give you a very accurate picture of your business success. It can let you know exactly if you are progressing, staying the same, or losing ground and if so, by exactly how much.

A quick summary: The balance sheet will give you a snap shot of where you stand money wise. It is NOT a historical report showing how much you spent. It just shows, "If you look at all the money you have, minus all the money you owe, you get your net worth as of RIGHT NOW, and how did it change compared to last month." If you did better than last month, your business success is positive. Congratulations, you got an A on your report card.

If the money is the same as it was last month, you get a C on your report card because nothing changed. You are just providing your service or product and not gaining any wealth.

If you have less money than the previous month, well, that stinks! You get a big fat F on your report card because you have now been paying for the privilege of selling your product or service.

We will make all this clear by the end of this chapter. All it takes is a little understanding, a little time setting it up, and only 15 to 30 minutes each month to do it.

Are you excited yet? How can you stand it?

So, let's get started in the wonderful world of the Balance Sheet report card.
First part: The money you have (the assets thing):

You can think of assets in two ways: 1) as money you have or can get your hands on that is in the form of cash, and 2) all the money you have spent on things that still have value (you can sell it if you had to).

The first one, in the business world, is called "Current Assets." That's the one where you list all the actual cash you have or could get your hands on. Let me be clear. It doesn't matter if you are a service business or a retail business, current assets are the same. Here are some examples of current assets:

1. Cash - That is the amount you have sitting in your checkbook available to use for your business. Now, don't get confused between your personal cash and your business cash. This is a *business* report card, so the cash listed in this item is *only* the cash you have in your business account(s).
2. Savings - Obviously, the amount of money you have in a business savings account. We talked a great deal about this in the first book when we talked about budgeting for your business. You know, when you budget ahead of time for depreciation and each month put your extra estimated expense money in reserves (savings) so you will have the money to purchase things when they need to be replaced and not effect your net profit.
3. A/R - Affectionately known as accounts receivable. This is the money that other people owe you for the work you have done. In the service industry, this amount will be much larger. Later in this book, we discuss how to keep this amount no more than 10% of your annual sales or how to warrant none of your accounts receivables go over 30 day net terms. For the retail business, accounts receivable may be where you have a favorite customer that you allow to carry a tab. They buy your goods, put it on a tab, and pay it off at the end of the month. This is a good idea of accounts receivable. Any accounting software package will tell you who owes you money. That is, if you have entered the invoice for them. Just click and look at the amount you are owed in your "customer reports" under "accounts receivable."

4. Work in Progress - For the servicers (service industry), this is the work you have done "so far" on a project that is not complete. Off hand, I can't think of a thing where the retailers would have this, since you are on a more cash basis at the counter. So, back to the servicers. You have done the work and the amount of work you have completed thus far has a value. Think of it this way: You paid for the materials, the labor, and your overhead bills for the period of time you have been on the project thus far. Right? Right! Thus, if push came to shove, you could go to the customer and say, "Hey, favorite customer. I have done (X percent) of the work and I could really use your help by asking you to pay for only the value of the work we have completed thus far. Whadda ya say?' Important note here: If you don't allow for the value of the work you have completed, your cash will go down (since you paid for labor, materials and overhead bills) but you will not have anything to show for it, thus your actual net worth will go down and give you a false picture of failure when in fact you may be actually doing quite well. To get this information, just make a list of all the jobs you have going. List what the value is of the work you have completed thus far (good and close estimate will do). Bingo, yer done with this info.

5. Inventory - What? How is that important? It's not cash. I have already spent the cash on it. How can it be an asset? Look at it this way. You DID spend the cash. Do you have anything to show for it? Yes! The stuff sitting on your shelf was purchased for stuff you will make or use in the future and get future money for it. AND, if push came to shove, you could return it and get your money back (or at least most of it). For servicers, you buy bulk supplies at trade show special deals (cases of masking tape, electrical tape, plumbing flux, cases of paper, etc.) For retailers, you purchase supplies in bulk quantities to get a great deal. Cash is gone, but is it really? If you do not allow for it in your accounting, it will show your cash has been spent but no value is there, when in fact the value is still sitting on your shelf. So, inventory is really not that hard to do. It only takes a little time to walk around your storage area, make a list of all the things that would be inventory items, then use your computer to make a form (I like Excel). List the things. Go count stuff. Write it on the paper form. Enter it on your computer as this month's inventory. Establish a cash value. Run the total and there you go. Your inventory form may look like this (Note: You only list things that are used up frequently in your business. Example: Do *not* list paper clips, scotch tape, etc. since they are rarely purchased and don't have a substantial value):

Item	Count	Total
Reams of Paper		
Ink Cartridges		
Etc.		
Masking Tape		
Sealant cases		
Etc.		

This sheet I visualize on a clipboard. It's purpose is to count stuff. The count column is used to write in your count. Take the total count and put it in the total area.

Once this sheet is done, you get to sit at the computer, load an Excel worksheet that may look like this:

	A	B	C	D
1	Item	Quantity	Price Ea.	Total Value

2	Reams of Paper		2.95	
3	Ink Cartridges		35.00	
4	Etc.		Etc.	
5				
6	Masking Tape sleeves		24.00	
7	Sealant cases		96.00	
8	Etc.		Etc.	
9				
1 0				
1 1	TOTALS:			

Easy squeezy! You just take the total quantities off the previous inventory form and transfer it to the quantity box in Excel. When you put in the quantity, the total value will automatically calculate.

By the way, Excel is not really that hard. Quick lesson: Each box is called a "Cell." Each cell is identified by the corresponding column letter and row number. Example, the word "Item" is found in cell A1.

All you do is type in the words you want in the first ROW (Row 1), which is called your header. Then type in the items you want in column A under your header. Next type in the price you want under row C / Price Each.

What? You want an Excel worksheet already made up for you so you can see it on screen and have this formula stuff already done? Ok, Ok. You got me. Go ahead and go the website as discussed in chapter one page 7 and download the free copy of "Excel Inventory". If you want, you can follow along on the computer screen except the cell numbers will be different on the computer. For those who would like to save a little time, you can follow the example right here in the book.

Let's continue with the cell formulas then…

For the automatic math part, using our example above, Click on Cell D2, then in cell D2, you would type exactly: =D2*D3

Let me break that down…

The "=" tells Excel you want an automatic calculation in that cell
The D2 is where you will type in your quantity.
The "*" is Excel's way of saying "multiply it by"…
Finally, the D3 is the number it will multiply it by.

A cool thing about Excel is once cell D4 has it's math formula, all you do is copy cell D4 all the way down to the bottom of your list.

Example:

Click on Cell D4.
Click on "Edit" at the top left of your screen, then click "Copy" from the list.
Click on Cell D5 and HOLD DOWN THE MOUSE BUTTON and move the pointer down to the bottom of your list, then release the mouse button. This will highlight all those cells.

Finally, click on "Edit" (top left again), then click on "Paste."

Bam! All cells have the correct cell formula and you don't have to type the math for each cell all the way down.

OK. The total box at the bottom of column D is where you want the total value of all your inventory stuff.

All you do is click on Cell D(whatever is at the bottom, i.e. if cell D56 is the last empty cell in the totals box, click on D56). In this cell, type exactly: =SUM(D2:D(last row of items (i.e. if cell D55 is the last row of items, then it would be D55). And follow it with an ")" on the end. If last row is Cell D55, then the finished formula would be : =SUM(D2:D55) then press "enter."

BAM AGAIN! Now you have the total inventory which can be used for your balance sheet.

Remember the balance sheet. The report card thing. I know. We've spent some time on this inventory thing so let's get back to the balance sheet shall we? The last item:
OK!

6. Misc. - Anything else that may have current cash value that you can get fast access to if needed. Example: If your buddy borrowed a cool C note ($100 for those not into hip slang), this could be listed as money you have coming soon. If it was borrowed by a family member, well, kiss that sucker goodbye. It doesn't count on the balance sheet.

Next section on the balance sheet: The long term assets.

This is the most misleading thing in business if it is not done properly.

Long term assets is simply the value of all the stuff you own (in the business now, not personal stuff).

Listing this is very similar to the inventory task. Just make a list of everything your business owns that is of "higher value."

Good stuff to have on your long term assets list:
        Company vehicle (if any)
        Company owned equipment
        Computer equipment
        Printers
        Digital cameras owned and used by the company
        Field equipment (servicers)
        Power tools or appliances
        Office Furniture
        Store fixtures (not part of rented building)
        Etc.

Not so good stuff to have on your long term assets list:
        Paper clips (come on now, they really don't have that much resale value)
        Cleaning supplies
        Seat cushions
        Etc.

I think you get the idea.

This is something that can also be done in MS Excel where you can modify it to show both what it is worth, *and* if you owe any money on it (making payments on anything). It may look like this:

	A	B	C
1	**ITEM**	**Value**	**Owe**
2	Delivery Van	12,000.00	4,000.00
3	Office Desk	1,100.00	0.00
4	File Cabinets	400.00	0.00
5	Computer Equipment	2,400.00	1,200.00
6	Etc		
7			
8			
9			

When you set up Excel like this, it can automatically calculate the totals for *both* your assets and liabilities (coming up later in this chapter).

The same math is used for getting the totals as described above for the other Excel sample. Again… Easy squeezy.

Now that you have all your long term assets listed, just get a grand total of *all* your assets (current and long term). It will look something like this (again, you could use MS Excel to build this balance sheet):

	A	B	C	D
1	**Item**	**Amount**	**Sub Total**	**Total Amount**
2	Current Assets:			
3	Cash	$ 8,200.00		
4	Savings	$4,000.00		
5	Etc	Etc		
6	Total Current Assets:		$32,600.00	
7				
8	Long Term Assets:			
9	Vehicles	$24,000.00		
10	Office Equipment & Furniture	$6,000.00		
11	Etc.			
12	Total Long Term Assets:		$68,200.00	
13				
14	Total Assets			$100,800.00
15				

Congratulations. You know more at this point than most people in business (believe it or not, and not a Ripley's thing).

On to the Liabilities: Liabilities is just another fancy word for "money you owe." Just like the assets, all you do is list the money you owe other people. Remember, this is only for business related debt.

It's pretty much the same for retailers as it is for servicers with only a few exceptions.

Ready? Ok, Here goes with the liabilities stuff.

Short term liabilities simply means "money you gotta pay off in full each month."

Retailers, this would be suppliers that you must pay off at the end of the month in full. Sample: If you are in any form of food business, you may have a food supplier that allows you to order on account as long as you pay it off in full at the end of each month. Or 30 day net terms.

Servicers are similar. Sample: If you are a painting contractor, your suppliers let you buy paint and put it on account on 30 day net terms (you gotta pay it off in full each month).

Other short term liabilities may include money you borrowed from your folks and you promised to pay it back (yea, right!). Ok. You really WILL pay it back at the end of the month, so list it here.

That's about all there is to short term liabilities. Just think about your company and list anyone that you are on 30 day net terms with. There ya go.
Next section is the long term liabilities.

Hey! Guess what! You have already done most of the long term liabilities if you have used the system we have shown you above. Sneak back a few pages and peek at the worksheet example where you listed your assets. There was a column for you to list their value *and* a column to list any money you owe. Bingo. Work done.

All you need to do now is add to it any other debts you may have. Those "other" debts may include stuff like:

- Credit card debts (list all those nasty little things and the amount you would have to pay if you paid them off in full).
- Money you borrowed from your mom (for those who *know* you have no intention of paying it back at the end of the month but fully intend to at some point).
- Small Business Administration loan (list the amount you still owe on it).
- Line of Credit at the bank (amount you owe on that sucker too).
- Factoring debt (where you can sell an invoice for a fee to a factoring company).
- Any other money you have borrowed from any other source.

Hey! This sounds like something you can also do in MS Excel to help you adjust that hummer every month for a more accurate picture.

OK. So much for liabilities. Now, your balance sheet should look something like this:

1	Item	Amount	Sub Total	Total Amount
2	Current Assets:			
3	Cash	$ 8,200.00		
4	Savings	$4,000.00		

5	Etc	Etc		
6	Total Current Assets:		$32,600.00	
7				
8	Long Term Assets:			
9	Vehicles	$24,000.00		
10	Office Equipment & Furniture	$6,000.00		
11	Etc.			
12	Total Long Term Assets:		$68,200.00	
13				
14	Total Assets			$100,800.00
15				
16	Short Term Liabilities			
17	Vendor 30 day net terms due:	$18,000.00		
18	Mom's bucks	$2,000.00		
19	Total Short Term Liabilities		$20,000.00	
20	Long Term Liabilities			
21	Vehicles	$16,000.00		
22	Office equipment and furniture	$1,200.00		
23	Etc.	Etc		
24	Total Long Term Liabilities		$33,200.00	
25				
26	Total Liabilities			$53,200.00
27				

And now ladies and gentlemen, the moment you have all been waiting for. The "Net Worth" (And the crowd goes wild with applause and deafening cheers).

All you gotta do is subtract the Total Liabilities from the Total Assets. Look at the previous page. When you do that with this example you come up with:

Write in your answer: _____

It's OK. You can write in this book. It's yours and your teacher doesn't care.

Your final Balance sheet should look like this:

1	Item	Amount	Sub Total	Total Amount
2	Current Assets:			
3	Cash	$ 8,200.00		
4	Savings	$4,000.00		
5	Etc	Etc		
6	Total Current Assets:		$32,600.00	
7				
8	Long Term Assets:			
9	Vehicles	$24,000.00		
10	Office Equipment & Furniture	$6,000.00		
11	Etc.			
12	Total Long Term Assets:		$68,200.00	
13				
14	Total Assets			$100,800.00
15				
16	Short Term Liabilities			
17	Vendor 30 day net terms due:	$18,000.00		
18	Mom's bucks	$2,000.00		
19	Total Short Term Liabities		$20,000.00	
20	Long Term Liabilities			
21	Vehicles	$16,000.00		
22	Office equipment and furniture	$1,200.00		
23	Etc.	Etc		
24	Total Long Term Liabilities		$33,200.00	
25				
26	Total Liabilities			$53,200.00
27				
28	Net Worth:			$47,600.00

Way cool dude! This guy here has a net worth of $47,600.00

So what? So what does it really mean anyway, and why have I done all this work just to get this number?

This is where it gets really cool. The whole thing here is to watch your net worth to let you know if you are successful in business (you get an A on your report card), if you are spinning your wheels (you got a C on your report card) or if you are losing your shirt at a rapid pace (definitely an F on your report card).

Where to make this determination? Great question.

This is where you look at your target net profit. In other words, how much net profit do you want to make in your business? This is typically identified by a percentage. Example: Industry average net profit for a subcontract business (construction related) is 10 percent. General contractors is between 3 to 5 percent. I don't really know exactly what net profit is standard for each and every type of business, so you will just have to decide that for yourself.

Anyway, if you have a desired net profit of 10 percent (keeps the math easy for this example), and you do an average of say $20,000.00 a month in total sales per month, then 10 percent of $20,000.00 is $2,000.00.

Thus, your Net Worth (bottom line of the balance sheet) should go up by $2,000.00 per month. Congratulations, you are a winner. You get an "A" on your report card. You get to stay up late and watch TV.

If your Net worth is staying about the same within a few bucks, you just got a "C." You didn't do your homework. You're just coasting, so you don't get to stay up and watch TV.

If your Net worth is going down, it's easy. You are losing money. You are paying for the privilege of staying in business. Keep it up, and you will end up a bum on the streets. Not only do you NOT get to stay up and watch TV. You are grounded for a month because you got an "F" on your report card.

Remember, your Net Worth should go UP (and only up) if you are running a successful business.

Next question. How often do you want to know if you're doing OK or not?

Most people wait till tax time and have their accountant tell them the bad news. Why wait? Wouldn't it be great to know each and every month so you can take immediate action to fix money leaks and save your business and guarantee you're getting rich sooner? You bet!

OK. So what IF you are staying the same or, worse, you're going backwards? What do you do about it? How do you find out where the money leaks are?

Here's another "great value for your book dollar" thing: It's a free downloadable form on our website called "Balance Sheet Worksheet". A great blank form you can fill out to get your balance sheet done a lot faster than most accounting programs. Oooo. I better explain that one. Ok.

Just a note about most accounting programs. Yes, they "can" to balance sheets for you *but* for most programs, it takes quite a while to set it up and then it will take about four to eight hours a month to make adjustments between your balance sheet and profit and loss features. I found this whole system takes about ½ hour a month do be dead on accurate and it requires *no* adjustments in your accounting program. Thus, I highly suggest you do *not* use the accounting feature for balance sheets (unless you are a huge company, that is). Use the Excel format.

What? I haven't mentioned the one we have? Sorry. We have a fully integrated balance sheet that helps you list your assets and liabilities. This is a double cool thing because you can also use it for insurance purposes in showing what you have and the related values and a couple of other cool things. It is an "optional item" you can purchase on our website and is found on the same page as the "free downloadable forms" page. Only a few bucks that will save you lots of hours.

On to the next chapter where we show you exactly where the money leaks are and how to stop those suckers.

The Stuff Called Money: Chapter Three
Money Leaks and the Cork

And now, just to get your heart started...

The shocking, amazing, astounding, resounding, and absolutely awesome news:

That famous *Profit and Loss* report you've heard of is not really a Profit and Loss report at all. As a matter of fact, it has almost nothing to do with your *actual* profit and loss! Now I ask you, is that astounding or what?

This is where the accountants are saying, "OK! Gloves off! This guy has gone too far!" But let me explain.

Most people think (remember that "most" will go out of business) that the *Profit and Loss* is there to show you the bottom line. As a matter of fact, the bottom line is all they look at, the bottom line that shows "Net Profit," and a dollar amount, and in some cases a percentage of sales. (Hopefully, they see it monthly instead of just at tax time when they get the shocking news of how much they owe in taxes.)

If most people look at the *Profit and Loss* report and see a positive number and a positive percent, they think, " Hummm, we must have done pretty good this time."

But we can do better than that.

Let's look at what the *Profit and Loss* report *really* is, if used properly.

The *Profit and Loss* report is a report that can show you where you have money leaks in your company. Doesn't that sound important?

And then there's that thing that goes with it, called a *Budget Comparison Report.* It helps you figure out how to *fix* those leaks. We'll get to both of them, one at a time.

Before we get to the "how to fix money leaks" part of this chapter, we'll have to start with understanding how to prepare and read a *Profit and Loss* report. Then we can move on to how you can make it one of the most important reports for your company's financial management.

So, here goes. Profit and Loss 101.

Basic overview and ground rules for this report (don't worry if you don't get this right off; I'll explain it all in detail below, since it sounds, well, arbitrary, at first.):

1. In your *Profit and Loss* report, you have three columns that must be headed: ITEM - DOLLARS - PERCENT

2. You must consider DOLLARS column and PERCENT column two completely separate things.

3. If one column (Dollars or Percent) changes a lot each month (is variable), the other column should be about the same (is fixed).

4. ***You manage your money by watching or managing the column that is fixed.*** You really don't care about the variable column.

Weird rules, I know. We will explain each one so you are very clear on how to make Excellent use of this report. Let's start over.

RULE 1:   Columns are ITEMS, DOLLARS, PERCENT

Regarding ITEMS column:

There are only three main "groups" of items in your column. These are:

1.   *Gross sales:* All the money you bring in, total sales.

2.   *Cost of sales:* What it cost you to make your product or provide your service
               Retailers: Cost of items you sell, or cost of ingredients that make up the   items   you   sell, etc.
               Servicers: Cost of materials used on a specific job AND labor on a job.

3.   *Overhead:* What it costs you whether you have any customers or not.
               Note: *Retail* labor is an *overhead* item since you must have someone
                  there all the time to greet customers even if no one comes in.

Here's a sample:

ITEMS	DOLLARS	PERCENT
Start with Gross Sales:	$ 20,000	100% of sales
Subtract Cost of sales:	- $ 6,000	30% of sales
Equals Gross Profit:	$ 14,000	70% of Sales
Subtract Overhead:	- $ 12,000	60% of Sales
Equals Net Profit:	$ 2,000	10% of Sales

Let's look at this again now to make sure we all understand how the *Profit and Loss* Report *really* works to help us find money leaks.

Remember RULE 2. *Dollars and Percent are two completely different things.*

And remember RULE 3. *If one is variable, the other is fixed.*

So how do we find our leaks?

Not sure? Well, here we go:

Gross sales. Is your gross sales amount exactly the same each month?   Yes   No (circle one)

Almost all businesses have different sales totals each month. That makes the *Dollar* column *variable* and thus the percent column should be fixed. Really? Let's see…

The *total sales* you get will always be "total" or "all" or "100%." Right? Right! The percent for this item will always be 100%, meaning it is a "fixed" number. Tricky, right?

Let's check out *cost of sales* stuff now.

Retailers: Is the amount you spend on your re-saleable items or ingredients exactly the same each month? Yes No

Servicers: Is the amount you spend on material the same each month?   Yes   No

Answers for both Retailers and Servicers is No. Even if you sell more stuff, you then have to purchase more stuff to replace what you have sold. Make sense? Sure thing.

Thus, our *cost of sales* items will vary up or down *based on our sales*. In other words, the dollar column will be variable, which makes the percentage column fixed (or very close).

Let's check that out too. If you sell, say, $1,000 worth of your stuff or service, you need to have, say, $200 to purchase goods or materials. Right? So 20% of your money collected is spent on goods.

Now, if you sell $2,000 worth of stuff or services (twice as much), you will need twice as much materials or goods, making your dollars go up to $400 (variable dollars) but it is still 20%. Thus, your percent column is fixed.

Bingo… Rule two and three have proven true.

So, what does all this matter to you, anyway?

Cool question. You are such a great thinker.

Let's apply RULE 4. *"You manage your money by the column that is FIXED."*

Let's check THAT out. (Loads of checking out here.)

In our *cost of sales* column, the *dollar* amount will go up or down, and who cares. The *percent* is fixed in our example above at, say, 20%.

But, month to month, we watch the percent column. Let's say next month, our materials percent goes up to 26%. The previous two months is was at 19% and 21 percent. So you just had a 5 percent jump in materials. *THAT creates a FLAG.*

A flag is just a term that means "this is something that needs your attention." So you go back over your material expenses and see what happened.

Most accounting packages like Peachtree or Quickbooks allow you to double-click on the *materials total* amount and it will pop into a *material expense report,* giving a full list of materials. You scan the expenses and look for possible problems. Examples would be:

I just bought a bunch of surplus stuff at a great price. I have much more than I would usually have. For a retail donut shop, it may be I purchased 1000 lbs of flour that will last three months. Or, a servicer may have purchased several cases of masking tape, or PVC pipe, or whatever.

This is where I get to back up my statement at the beginning of this chapter. The *Profit and Loss* really does not show Profit and Loss.

In the above example, the *Profit and Loss* would show you that your profit was negative, that you had a loss! *but*, we know that the goods the money was spent on will last for months to come. You will have *less expense* over the next few months. Thus, you really didn't lose money this month, even though it looks that way on the *Profit and Loss Report*.

Starting to get the picture?

Anyway, back to the breakdown of the typical *Profit and Loss* report....

Thus far, we have discovered that the columns look like this:

ITEM	DOLLARS	PERCENT
Gross Sales	Variable	Fixed (100%)
Cost of sales:		
Materials	Variable	Fixed
Service field labor	Variable	Fixed
Etc…	Variable	Fixed
Gross Profit:	Variable	Fixed

Cool…. Now let's stop and look closer at *Overhead* expenses:

These are the expenses you will have already listed in your budget (That's for those of you who have read the first book. For those who haven't, what are you waiting for? Go get it, and get caught up.)

Overhead items are basically items that eat your bank account each month whether or not you do any business.

Let's take a look at some of the things that would be in there, just so we can have an example for this part of this chapter.

Your Salary! Should the amount you get for a salary be the same each month or different? Is this item fixed or variable?

If you have done a personal budget as explained in the first book, you will know your salary should be a fixed dollar amount. The company in trouble will hear themselves saying, "My business just can't afford to pay me that much this month, so I will just take what I have available." This is a sure sign you are on your way out of business.

"OK, OK", you say, "We get the picture. The amount our company pays us in salary is *fixed*". Well, I say, "that makes the *percent* column variable". And you say, "What the…."? Example:

If you have sales of $10,000 and you take a $4,000 per month salary that is 40%. If your volume goes up to $20,000, you still take a $4,000 per month salary which now calculates out to 20%. See. Told you. The percent goes all over the place. Variable.

Applying RULE 4 here, we don't care about the variable column, and we *do* care about the fixed column. After all, you do care that you always get your guaranteed salary don't you?

Now, if you have followed that last part about overhead, your *Profit and Loss* will now look something like this…

Blah, blah, blah, blah..

Blah, blah, blah, blah,

OK… The above two lines are there just as a filler so the next page break will start the report fresh. You got me.

ITEM	Dollars	Percent
Gross Sales	Variable	Fixed (100%)
Cost of sales:		
Materials	Variable	Fixed
Service field labor	Variable	Fixed
Etc…	Variable	Fixed
Gross Profit:	Variable	Fixed
Overhead:		
Owner Salary	Fixed	Variable
Building Rent	Fixed	Variable
General Liab. Ins.	Fixed	Variable
Telephone	Fixed	Variable
Etc.	Fixed	Variable
Net Profit:	???	???

Note the test at the bottom. We'll get there in a minute.

First, let's notice something way cool. Note that the FIXED and VARIABLE columns switched sides. The Cost of Sales variable items related to the dollars while the variable items related to the overhead is under the dollars column. Interesting, huh?

Back to RULE 4. We manage our money by the FIXED column, not the variable.

Now, here's where it gets fun.

Remember the budget thing in the first book. This is where you made a list of every single dime your company spends for overhead items. This budget now becomes critically important.

Your *budget,* remember, is a list of the amount(s) you PLAN TO spend. The *Profit and Loss* report will show you the amount(s) you ARE spending.

Wouldn't it be wonderful if we could have one report that would show these side by side: my list of what I AM spending compared to what I *planned* to spend? And even better yet, show the difference?

Just imagine the power there. If this report showed me that I am spending more on an item (say, cell phone) than I planned to spend, then I could adjust my budget somewhere else to allow for the difference. How?

Well, remember, that budget thing is tied to how you come up with your prices. Thus, when you need more money to spend on your business, your prices will go up just a little bit so that you have enough money to pay for the things you need and do not have to use up all your profits to pay for them.

That really is powerful. That takes me to the next shocking bit of news about the *Profit and Loss* report. It isn't enough.

What you need is called a ***BUDGET COMPARISON REPORT.*** IMPORTANT: IF you have done your business budgets in an accounting software and IF you have entered all your expenses in your accounting software, then this report (or one very similar) is free and instant.

Example: In *Quickbooks,* click on *"Reports,"* then click on *"Budget Reports,"* or *"Planning and Budgets"* depending on the version you have, then click on *"Budget vs Actual"* and poof, you have it.

This is a cool report that looks like this:

Budget Comparison Report

Item	Actual	Budget	Budget Over/Short
Gross Sales	20,000.00	0.00	20,000.00
Cost of Sales			
Materials	5,000.00	0.00	5,000.00
Etc.	3,000.00	0.00	3,000.00
Gross Profit	11,000.00	0.00	13,000.00
Overhead Expenses			
Owner Salary	4,000.00	4,000.00	0.00
Building Rent	1,000.00	1,000.00	0.00
Gen. Liab. Insurance	0.00	200.00	<- 200.00
Telephone	170.00	160.00	10.00
Etc.	4,230.00	5,630.00	<- 1,600.00>
Total Expenses (overhead)	9,400.00	11,000.00	<- 1,800.00>
Net Profit:	1,600.00	0.00	1,600.00

ANOTHER IMPORTANT NOTE: You may have noticed in this example there are no budget numbers for the Gross sales, Cost of Sales, Gross Profit or Net profit. That's because those are VARIABLE DOLLAR items and according to RULE 4, we only care about that which is FIXED.

The important parts of this report are:

When you spend more than you had budgeted (*Actual* column is LARGER than the *budget* column), the *Budget Over / Short* shows a POSITIVE number, meaning YOU ARE OVER BUDGET. NOT good. Thus, in this report POSITIVE NUMBERS ARE FLAGS (bad things to look at and correct).

Reverse of that, when you spend less than you think (*Actual* Column is SMALLER than the *budget* column), the *Budget Over / Short* shows a NEGATIVE number, meaning YOU ARE UNDER BUDGET, which is typical, and not necessarily a red flag None the less, it is STILL a flag to let you know not to put it in savings or give yourself a raise, maybe, because "At some point in time, your budget reminds you that you WILL need that money to pay for the item when the time comes. Why?

Example above shows General Liability Insurance. You may pay it yearly. Your yearly budget shows you need an average of $200 per month (discussed in detail in the first book) to pay for your general liability insurance. This means you will need to collect and save $200 per month to give you the $2,400.00 per year you need for insurance. When the time comes for you to pay the insurance, you will have the money in savings.

Again, this is discussed in detail in the first book on how to budget and reserve money for future expenses.

This is where the *Budget Comparison Report* is so very important. It shows you exactly where your overhead money is going and where you need to make adjustments each month.

If your phone bill goes up by 40 bucks a month, you need to adjust the budget, ***which will adjust your price to the customer***. Failure to do this means that as things go up in price and you don't make immediate adjustments, you are just setting yourself up for using net profit to pay for those things that come up, which lowers your net profit and eventually puts you right out of business. Boo.

So. Let's summarize the *Profit and Loss* and *Balance Sheet Comparison Reports* before we move on to the next chapter. The *Profit and Loss* report will show you PERCENTAGES to help you see those big 'ol red flags for your *Cost of Sales* items ONLY. (Remember RULE 4 - Watch that which is fixed).

THEN, you also need to print that *Budget Comparison Report* so you can again apply RULE 4 by watching that which is fixed (*Overhead* this time, those dollar amounts being about the same each month whether you have any sales or not). The *Budget Comparison Report* will show you the difference between what you THINK you are spending (*Budget*) to what you ARE spending (*Actual*). This will help you easily see the "Red Flags" for your overhead expenses so you can make adjustments each month and adjust your prices accordingly.

One more thing to help you get a real clear picture of the *Profit and Loss* (yes... back to that thing).

The bottom of the report... the "*Net Profit*" line. Is the *Dollars* variable or fixed?

Good question. In business, our goal is to pay all our expenses, pay ourselves a salary AND have money left over for profit. The *target amount of profit* we use is expressed in PERCENTAGE. Example: Your business may merit a 10% net profit, thus the *Percent column is fixed and the dollar is variable.* More about that later.

I Know, I Know. You have a huge number of questions. Just hang in there for a few more chapters and we will tie in a whole bunch more money management stuff to show you how to take total control of your money management on a monthly basis and guarantee your success.

This chapter was on the subject of how to find money leaks (look at **percentages** on *Profit and Loss* report and **Dollars** on the *Budget Comparison Report*). This chapter was also on how to fix money leaks: 1) evaluate cost of sales to find where money was spent, and 2) adjust budgets to take care of increased overhead expenses. *Both of these will fix money problems only when you have accurate information and facts to help you make those all so important decisions about how much to charge your customers.*

So much for this chapter. Next up is the exciting world of knowing exactly WHAT to do with your money to plan for those up-coming expenses, how to allow for slow periods vs. busy periods, and how to plan for your actual, real, true, pure money-in-the-bank profit!

So, without further ado, on to the next chapter…

The Stuff Called Money: Chapter Four
Moving Money

WOW! In those last few chapters, we learned about how to look at money in a different way. We learned how to use financial reports to have an accurate picture of our business as it is right now, and we learned how to watch our money by using the budget comparison report.

Now we get to talk about what to do with the money you have left in your bank account at the end of each month.

First (you knew it was coming, didn't you), the mental part.

Remember, the first book in this series talked about the typical business person who lives off the money they have left over each month after paying their bills? And remember how we, instead, were told to set up a personal budget and a business budget so that we can plan our cash flow better? Sure you do. So, let's take it to the next level.

Most people (I mean 99% of people out there, including me) have this huge habit of spending money if we "know" that we have it. That's right. We look in the checkbook, see some extra money hanging around, and we get this inner feeling: "Cool. I'm not broke anymore. I have money now. I can go to any restaurant I want and look at the menu from left to right. I can go to the grocery store to get anything I want. I can go to Costco and get all that cool stuff I have always been tempted to get."

Next thing you know, the money is gone. Some surprising bills pop up that weren't expected and poof, we are back to living month-to-month again, eating macaroni and cheese with wieners.

Come on now. Admit it. It happens to you too.

Guess what. That's fine, to an extent, but only if you are managing ALL your money correctly. Let me show you how.

I'll start with a cool picture that should stick in your head. Here it comes:

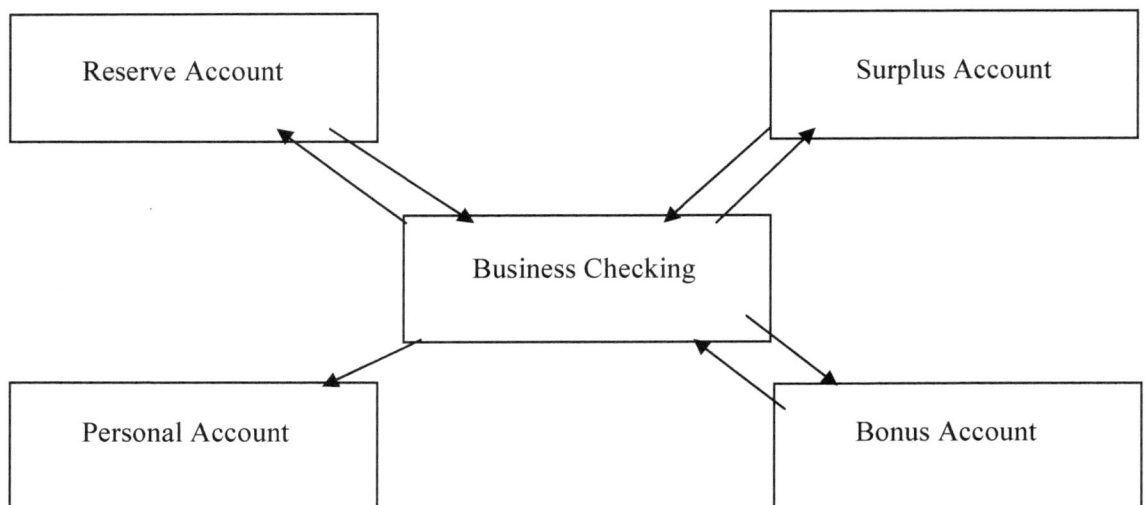

OK. I didn't say it was an "artistic" rendering, but these "stick" figures will get the point across.

Each box is supposed to represent a checkbook (use your imagination).

The center box is your business checking account which is the hub of all your money since it is the source of income and expenses. Yes, even your personal expenses come from a paycheck from your business, so it really is the center of all your money.

Those fancy arrows will be discussed in detail in just a bit (for you "ahead thinkers", you).

First, let me introduce you to the other bank accounts you will need for control of your cash flow.

Reader, I would like you to meet the "Reserve Account" in the upper left corner.

This, believe it or not, is literally a separate savings or checking account where you hide money from yourself! The money you put in here is used to pay for things you know are coming, but that just haven't gotten here yet. So you hide the money from yourself so you don't spend it.

Example: You set up an account for purchasing a new computer for your company. You add to the reserve account an amount of say $100 per month for this item. And, you *adjust your pricing* so this item is now included in your price structure (See first book for details).

At the end of each month, you should have an extra $100 left over in your business account because you have put it in your price and collected the money, but have not purchased the computer yet. So, the Reserve Account is where you put this extra hundred bucks so that it is out of your sight and will still be available for you in a few months when the time comes to actually purchase the electronic wonder box.

Next account is the "Surplus Account." This is a little more tricky.

We all know there are slow periods and fast periods. Retailers, let's say, during the Christmas season, are swamped from November through mid-January. Then, things slow down in the summer time. Or, let's say, servicers who work on exterior stuff (landscaping, painting, concrete, etc.) will be eating Cheetos and watching football in the winter months and swamped with work during the summer months.

This seasonal trend does not need to be emotionally draining. We all *know* the slow months are coming, but seem to just not have enough money to maintain the same life style during the slow months. Thus, ta da!! The surplus account is born.

In the busy months, a business can charge more due to demand, and when the demand lessens, the price follows suit. Right?

Since we all know this, now is the time to start money management that will greatly help us in this area. So set up this surplus account where you stuff your "surplus" money from the busy season to help you later to get through the slow periods.

One more little note on this. "Surplus money" is defined as money you have left over *after* you have paid your bills, *after* you have paid yourself, *after* you have put money aside for reserves and *after* you have allowed for your "target" net profit (which we will explain more in just a bit).

Basically, after all is said and done (accounted for), what is left is *still* not yours! You will need it later for slow periods, so stick it where you can't see it—in the Surplus Account.

Remember, now, the surplus account is a separate bank account so you don't get it mixed up with money that is spoken for (your reserve account).

Next account is your "Personal Account." Do I really need to explain this? Just kidding.

Easy enough. You cut a check to yourself and put it into your own personal account. This is your personal income which is used to pay your personal bills as you have so cleverly itemized in your personal budget.

That leaves us with only one more account. The "Bonus Account." This is money that you set aside to pay for employee incentives. What's that, you ask? Well, I would love to tell you all about it here, but that takes another hundred plus pages, so I've made a special book just for that reason. Book number four in this volume is all about employees and incentives. I know you'll just love that book too.

OK, now to the actual, amazing, fun, thrilling and exhilarating part of knowing exactly how to manage your money so you never have to worry about financial stress again. Look at all the psychiatrist bills you can save.

For this we must recall a report from Chapter three of this book called the "Budget Comparison Report." This is the most important report of your company money management, bar none.

Remember, this report shows what you are *actually* spending compared to what you *think* you might be spending and it shows you the over or short column to let you know if you need to adjust budget or flag stuff that may be a money leak.

Without further ado, let's have a look:

Budget Comparison Report

Item	Actual	Budget	Budget Over/Short
Gross Sales	20,000.00	0.00	20,000.00
Cost of Sales			
Materials	5,000.00	0.00	5,000.00
Etc.	3,000.00	0.00	3,000.00
Gross Profit	11,000.00	0.00	13,000.00
Overhead Expenses			
Owner Salary	4,000.00	4,000.00	0.00
Building Rent	1,000.00	1,000.00	0.00
Gen. Liab. Insurance	0.00	200.00	<- 200.00
Telephone	170.00	160.00	10.00
Etc.	4,230.00	5,630.00	<- 1,600.00>
Total Expenses (overhead)	9,400.00	11,000.00	<- 1,800.00>
Net Profit:	1,600.00	0.00	1,600.00

Let's quickly evaluate this company.

The first column of ACTUAL is basically the Profit and Loss report. According to the Profit and Loss, this company made a net profit of $1,600 bucks. Not Bad.

Oh reeeeeeeely now? According to our Budget Over – Short column, in the Total Expense (overhead) box, it says we were $1,800 UNDER budget.

This reeeeeeeely means, this company has $1,800 still in the business account right now, but it is earmarked to pay for stuff that is coming (taxes, insurance, that new computer, etc.). So, that $1,800 bucks should be put in reserves so the money will be there when the time comes to purchase the items this money is reserved for.

VERY IMPORTANT: Please re-read that last part to make sure you are 100 percent in sync with this concept as it is critical to the next step in money management.

If you understood that last section correctly, when you look at this company's budget comparison, you would come to this conclusion:

The company above did not do "OK." They did not make enough to pay for the current bills and the ones that are coming. They only show an extra $1,600 available, while $1,800 is needed for reserves, which mean they are $200 bucks short just to make the reserves! That leaves *nothing* for profit. They actually *lost* $200 bucks that month.

This once again confirms our previous statement that the Profit and Loss really does not accurately reflect profit or loss. It is misleading. So, here's what this company needs to do.

This company will take all the $1,600 available and put that into reserves because it is needed. The $200 bucks they are short will come out of the Surplus Account (if there is any money in there).

WAIT! This company had NO profit. OR did they??? Hummmmmm…

If there is money in the surplus account, they could also take their own 'Target Profit" out of the Surplus Account, because, under this system, their monthly profit is guaranteed--even in a slow month.

I know. I know. You want to know how the money gets in the Surplus Account in the first place so that this incredible luxury can be realized.

Good thinking. Great question.

Here goes.

Let's look at the next Budget Comparison Report for a busy month.

Item	Actual	Budget	Budget Over/Short
Gross Sales	30,000.00	0.00	30,000.00
Cost of Sales			
Materials	7,000.00	0.00	7,000.00
Etc.	5,000.00	0.00	5,000.00
Gross Profit:	18,000.00	0.00	18,000.00
Overhead:			
Owner Salary	4,000.00	4,000.00	0.00
Building Rent:	1,000.00	1,000.00	0.00
Gen. Liab. Ins.	0.00	200.00	<- 200.00>
Telephone	170.00	170.00	10.00
Etc.	4,640.00	5,640.00	<-1,000.00>
Total Expense (Overhead)	9,800.00	11,000.00	<- 1,200.00>
Net Profit:	8,200.00	0.00	8,200.00

This time around, the money seems to be GREAT! The company president can go out to dinner and buy extravagant things, right? Reeeeeeeeely now?

Profit SHOWS $8,200, but:

> $1,200 Goes into the reserve account for future expenses (spoken for)
> $3,000 Goes to the owners for their normal "target" profit assuming 10% target (10% of gross

sales
> $30,000 = $3,000)
> $4,000 Goes to SURPLUS Account for slow months.

That's it. $8,200 taken care of.

The most important thing to remember:

GET IT OUT OF YOUR SIGHT.
IT ISN'T YOURS.
YOU WILL NEED IT LATER.

Here's a map of what the cash flow we just talked about would look like:

I'll have to put in another blank space so the cash flow chart is all on the same page.

Hey, I know, you can use this space for…

Notes:

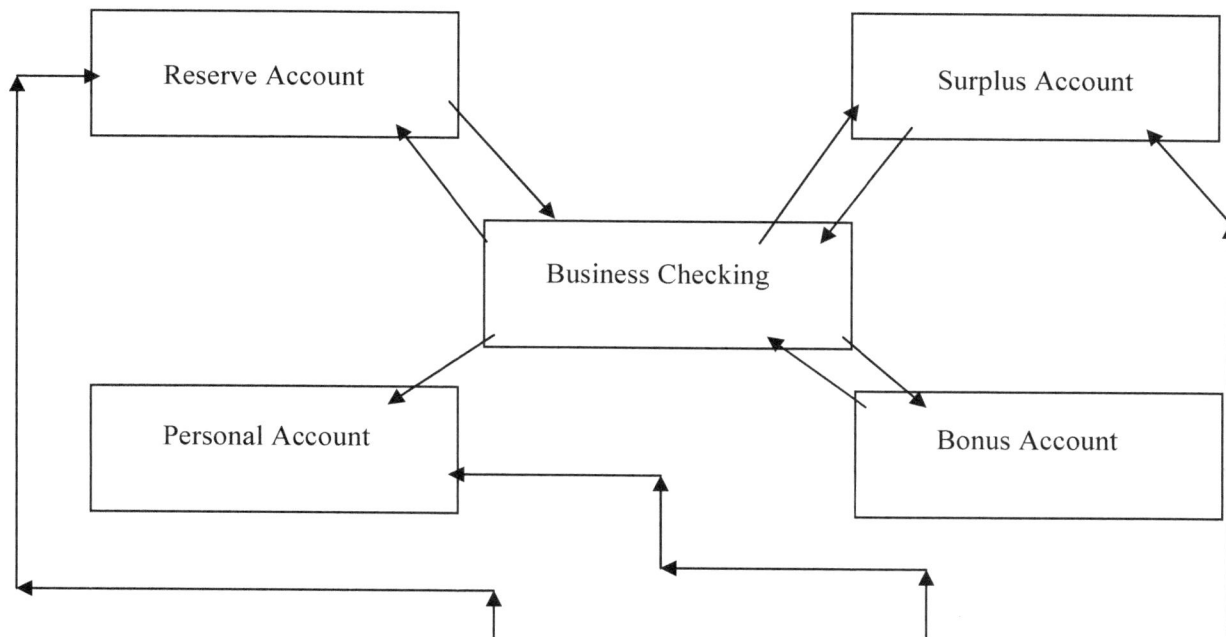

P & L Gross Sales	P & L Net Profit	Budget Over or Short	Calculated Actual Profit	Business Net Profit	Surplus Over or Short
30,000.00	8,200.00	- <1,200.00>	7,000.00	- <3,000.00>	4,000.00

Write this in   Write this in   Subtract this   equals this   Subtract this   Equals this.

Budget Over or Short: This money goes into or out of reserves. Minus goes in. Plus comes out.

Business Net Profit: *This money stays with your business account until you have two Months Overhead.*

Then, you get to keep it for your personal investments.

Surplus Over or Short: This is money you put in during busy months and take out during slow months. Your

"nest eggs."

Hey, this sounds like a great thing to program into MS Excel. Easy spread sheet.

On the website, download the form called "Money Manager Worksheet". That is a blank form you can use to track your money management. We will use this form for reference, so go ahead and print out a copy or two. After you use this form a couple of times, you will have it down pat.

As an extra option, we have on the same downloadable forms page on our website, an MS Excel version where you enter only the first three column items right off of your Quickbooks budget comparison report. The rest is automatically calculated for you and it will show you how much money you should have in reserve account and surplus account. This again will save a lot of time, but is your choice if you want it or not. Check it out.

We call this whole process Money Management. *this*, my friends, is called money "happiness" instead of money "happen-ness." It only takes about one year to get the flow going to the point where you should have no financial worries. Really? Really!

Before we move to the next chapter, let's just re-cap this one to make absolutely sure we understand the total control money management system.

Summary: (You'll need a copy of the Money Manager Worksheet from the free downloadable forms area from our website. Remember how to get it? It's explained in book one, page seven if you need reference).

Print your Budget Comparison Report from your accounting program. Note: It is only accurate if you have done your business budgets as instructed in the first book.

Look at the Profit and Loss Actual Column and see what it says for the Gross Sales. Write this number in the first column of the worksheet on the previous page.

Look at the Profit and Loss Actual Column and see what it says for the Net Profit. Write this number in the second column of the worksheet on the previous page.

Look at the Budget Over / Short column in the row that says "Total Overhead Expenses: If it is a negative, leave it negative and write a negative number in the third column in the form on the previous page. This is also the amount you take out of your Business Account and put into your Reserve Account

If the number for the Total Overhead Expenses in the Budget Over / Short column is Positive (you spent more than your budget), you write in a positive number, take money OUT of your Reserve Account, put it back into the Business Account. You also add the P & L net profit to the positive Budget Over /Short column and write the answer in the 4th column showing company Actual Net Profit.

The 5th column is your company "Target" net profit amount. Write in the amount that represents your target net profit percentage of the gross sales. Sample: If gross sales is $10,000 and your target net profit is 15 percent, you take 15 percent of $10,000 to give you a target net profit amount of $1,500.00. Easy?

If the Calculated actual profit (4th column) is LESS than your target Business Net Profit (5th column), you take money OUT of Surplus Account (if available). If it is MORE, then you put the extra cash over your target net profit INTO the Surplus Account,

I know, I know. Each time I have a live workshop it takes us about eight to ten times to go over this before it becomes clear. Just re-read this. Make a copy of the form and practice a few times. I know you can figure it out since you have been an Excellent student thus far.

Most important, stay with it. This whole process of printing the report, evaluating what to do, filling out your monthly management form and moving your money accordingly will take no more than 15 minutes per month once you get it down.

So much for this chapter.

I know it seems like a mind full, but you will get it with just a little practice.

Next up, the ominous "Bell Curve Monster."

The Stuff Called Money: Chapter Five
Taming the Bell Curve Monster

We all have heard about the "bell curve" and how it affects your business. What? Not everyone knows this? Really?

Ok. Here's the story. When business is slow, money seems to get tight. When you are selling lots of work or doing lots of work, your money situation seems to be better. This up and down swing can be both financially and emotionally draining.

I don't like to ride that "roller coaster" bell curve, so I have found a way to tame it.

It's really not that hard. Common sense tells you: "Hey you! When you are busy and are making lots of money, that's when you need to sock it away for when it's slow."

The concept is sound and easy to understand, but many of us have a hard time doing it.

"Why," you ask? Great question.

Most people in business don't have a specific system to follow. We just live in the "by guess and by golly" mode. Or, as another friend of mine put it, the world of "happen-ness." Basically, we let things happen and deal with them. So, it's easy to understand why that roller coaster monster bell curve can be so stressful.

Well, then, how *do* we get control?

In the last chapter, we talked a whole bunch about how to put money in reserves (money you *will* spend on stuff later), and how to calculate your "target" net profit and take that for yourself. What is left over *after* your reserve items and *after* your target net profit amount is taken out leaves what we will now called "Surplus" money. But it isn't really surplus to spend, because this, my friend, is the money you sock away for the slow periods.

There is just one little problem that seems to keep popping up. It happens when the first slow month uses up all or most of our surplus, and so for the rest of the slow period, we still end up sucking in the gut and tightening up the belt.

The key word in the solution here is *control* and *management*. This requires that you keep historical data so you can take a look at historical volume trends, or when you typically do the most business and when things get slow.

To best explain this, let me talk with the Servicers out there first.

Let's use a painting contractor for our example. In warm, sunny weather, you are swamped with jobs for exterior painting. When the sun tends to go away during the winter months, your business slows down. This we call volume fluctuation.

Let's look at this volume fluctuation more closely. In the summer, the customers create a higher demand, you are busy, and customers are willing to pay more to get their jobs done. So market value (the price customers are willing to pay) automatically goes up.

So, for the year, the bell curve of sales, combined with the bell curve of what can be charged, may look like this:

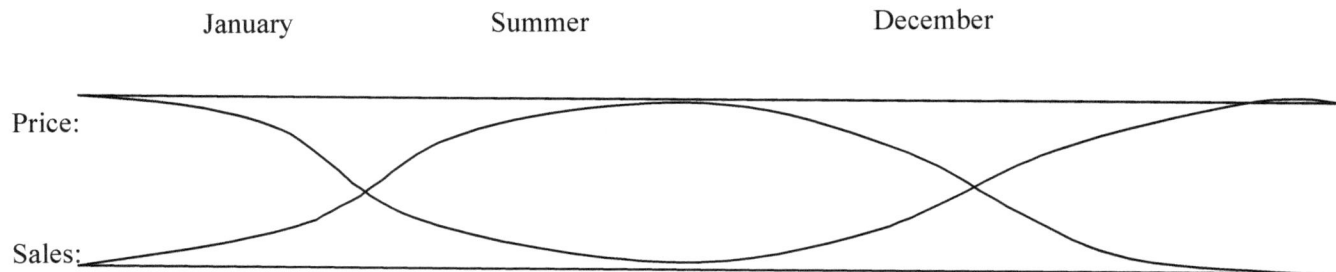

	January	Summer	December

Price:

Sales:

(The PRICE line in this chart is what the painting contractor has projected that he MUST charge to be profitable. Yes, the price line does go down in summer. Why, you ask, since what his budgeted amount needed to be profitable is the same? Because the painting contractor has *more business and more hours in the field*, and this distributes his overhead expense over more hours which lowers the amount he *needs* to charge to meet his projected price. Get that?)

But remember, the customer is *willing* to pay *more* due to demand in summer months, so the painting contractor *should* still charge "Market Value," or what the customer is willing to pay even though that is higher than his projected amount needed to cover his expenses.

Why? Here is where understanding the entire last chapter becomes so important.

He needs this extra summer money to carry him through the winter slow months.

In the winter months there is less business volume, but overhead remains the same, so some businesses tend to have to raise prices in the winter just to cover their overhead. But in winter, when demand is low, average market prices generally go down, so these people tend to lose business due to their high prices. Double bind.

Let's look more closely at the situation to see if we can work all this out.

Example: Let's say that in the summer, our painting contractor only needs to charge about $35 per hour to make his profit, but he knows he can get $45 per hour. He charges the $45 per hour, and then, when he does the reports at the end of the month, there is an extra $10 bucks per hour for every hour worked.

Now, this is where he does the magic trick to beat the bell curve! He maps out how much of the extra money actually goes into *reserves* for those things he knows he will need to spend money on, how much of the extra money he can keep for his deserved *target net profit*, and *then* all the rest is an amount that goes into his *surplus account to set aside for those slow months in winter.*

Let's say that this painting contractor has earned an extra $20,000 over the summer. He needs to ask himself how many months does this extra money have to last to cover the slow months? Let's say the answer is only four months, December through March. He has $20,000 to divide into four months, or $5,000 per month to use for the slow period.

Let's see how that affects what he charges his customers in *winter*. Remember, in winter volume goes down, but overhead and targeted net profit remain the same. That drives the required price up, let's say, to $40.00 per hour.

Let's say he dropped down to five painters with total hours worked in the field at 1000 (makes the math easy). He worked 1000 hours at $40 an hour.

But the company has $5,000 per month already sitting there in the surplus earned the previous summer. Do the math. In winter, they can *lower the labor rate* by $5.00 per hour down to $35, sell more work, and still hit target profit, still have money left over for other slow months, still get to keep a stable income, and totally release all financial stress. How cool is *that*!

Now, I realize that reading that for the first time may have swizzled your gray matter a bit, so you may want to go back and re-read that until you've got it down pat.

Now, let's focus on the retailers who are reading this book.

For the retail market, it is a similar situation, with only a few slight variations. Your "bell curve" may not always be driven by the time of year.

Then again, it might. If, for example, you sell Christmas goods, then you definitely are driven by a calendar period which is pretty consistent.

Or, if you sell cotton candy, your busy season would be during street fairs, state fairs, and summer party months, with a few spikes for off season events that may happen.

You caterers will be swamped during the wedding months and during the holiday season, with surges and spikes for convention and workshop activities, etc.

Your tire business is just plain based on when peoples' tires start wearing out. People drive more in summer for vacation, and that may affect you. Car dealers selling out last years models and moving more cars may affect you, etc.

But notice. This is where your own historical data is important, so you can take a look at volume trends and plan accordingly.

Retailers have a tighter market when it comes to price. If I own a candy store, I can't raise the price of my chocolate bars from a buck a bar to a buck fifty a bar just because it's slow or I think the market will pay it. People purchasing consumables like to feel they are getting a fair deal or they won't give you repeat business.

Retailers *do*, however, have a means of control. That is with their day-to-day labor expense.

Retailers, let's say the candy store manager, *must* have a person standing behind the counter whether or not there are customers. If you have ten customers all day or if you have 500 customers all day, the same labor dude or dudette *must* be there. This makes your labor expense more of a "fixed" item.

This is where part time people on a "flexible" schedule come in handy. If you "think" you need five people to run your candy store on what "should" be a busy day, but the day progresses and your first two hours of business have been substantially less than anticipated, you can have one or two of your part time employees clock out. (Remember, a two hour minimum is all that is required by law in most states.) Just because they are scheduled for a six hour shift does not mean they must work it.

Danger Zone item here: An owner of a business will say, "I don't want to lose these people," or "They are my cousins," or "They will suffer financially if I cut their hours", and the beat goes on.

Just remember this. Count up the total number of people affected by their employment with your company and by its staying in business. Your six employees may each be married with a child or two or three. Plus, there is you and your own family. That means that up to thirty people (or more) depend on your company success.

So, the danger is this. If your company does not make a profit, and you go out of business, then all thirty people are out of work, suffering the loss of *all* their pay. In other words, thirty people lose. Not just one.

On the other hand, if you send one or two people home for the rest of the day, only one or two (maybe up to five including their family members) suffer only part of one day's pay. They still have a job. *and* the other twenty-five people are not affected at all. You get to stay in business and keep all thirty people employed.

Moral of the story: it is far better to have one person sacrifice a few hours pay than to have everybody lose all their pay because you can't meet your overhead.

Be aware of what is *needed* to keep things going. You may even have to get in there and sweep some floors yourself. Yes, I know you hired people to do that, but when things get slow, it's time to get more involved, doing more of the tasks yourself. That will help you keep your prices more stable.

For the truth is, with a retail business, the overhead must be paid (rent, utilities, etc.) So, you must project how many slow months you will have and how many busy months you will have. Then you must record what actually happens, and adjust accordingly.

Let's give our candy store example some numbers to work with to get a better idea of exactly what I mean.

Candy store had four great months, putting aside $8,000.00. They looked at last year's sales and saw four slow months coming up. (Oh, this is way too easy for the math.) Each of the four slow months gets how much out of the surplus account??? Right! Two grand each slow month.

Now. IF the two grand is *not quite enough* to cover the expenses *and* leave you a nice salary *and* leave money for profit, what do you do?

You adjust your *price*. (We will talk a whole bunch in one of our other books, on the subject of sales and marketing, about setting prices and adjusting for benefit and repeat business. But for now, let me give you a quick "sum up.")

Let's say you are the owner of a sandwich shop. Typically you sell your "monster hoagie" for, say, $8.59. People love this thing. They buy it the most. You raise your price for only one week to, say, and $9.15, and see what happens. Guess what? Those customers still love the sandwich, and they are still ordering it. Sales go up. Money in hand goes up. You have more money to pay bills and to use for the little extras. Next week, bump the price to $9.39, and you see what happens. Still, they are ordering the thing, and no one has even mentioned or noticed your price going up. Keep 'er a goin' 'till the crowd starts to squeal. When you start to hear that high pitched whine, then it's time to go back down, bit by bit.

Ever notice how gasoline companies do it to us. They bump the price from $2.89 all the way up to $3.50 and hold for a month. When it comes down to $3.19 we all feel like we are getting a great deal on gasoline. Go figure. Note: These prices based on 2008 time era. Actual may vary in your actual time but you get the idea.

I think you're getting the idea by now. Your bell curve is controlled by using surplus dollars you have managed (as shown in the previous chapter), by controlling your employee work force (and doing more yourself if you need to), and by adjusting prices based on tolerances of your customers.

I think that's enough on the bell curve monster.

Just remember this:

You can *not* control the financial stress of a slow period if you do not have a budget.

You can not control reserves without a budget

You can not control your actual profit without a budget

You can not control actual surplus and have that slow period money relief if you don't have a budget.

So. What is the first and foremost important thing you must do to get started?

Right! The "B" word. Once you have that as the hub, and you follow the financial controls used in the previous chapter and this one, you can now enjoy much more relaxing and stress-free slow periods simply by managing your money based on the facts. No more guessing. No more "happen-ness." Instead, happiness!

Ready for the next chapter?

Me too.

The Stuff Called Money: Chapter Six
The Money vs. Inventory Battle

Let's get started with a brief description of that word "inventory," shall we?

"Sellable" inventory is basically the stuff you need either to make your product(s) or to provide your service. For restaurants, it's the food you must buy in order to make your delicious stuff. For a carpenter, it may be lumber and nails, screws and glue—the things that directly go into what you build. This inventory goes out and money comes in for them.

There is also "non-direct" or "secondary" inventory items. You don't sell these items, but you have to have them in order to make the things you do sell. For a restaurant, it would be dish washing liquid, napkins, plates, silverware, etc.—things that don't directly go into the food you sell, but you must have to do the job. For the carpenter it would be the saws, hammers, drills, etc.—things you must use to build with.

The battle between Money and Inventory usually starts right from the very first day you open your business. Didn't know there was a battle? Well, there is. And it starts with the secondary inventory—the stuff you have to have to make the stuff you actually sell.

Retailers first this time. You start your business by buying all the "secondary stuff" you need. Guess what? It doesn't last forever, does it? Nope! You gotta keep replacing the stuff . And that starts the first battle between inventory and money.

Many retailers soon find themselves asking themselves, "Hey, self! How long do I have to keep buying this secondary stuff anyway? It seems to nickel and dime me right out of any extra money that happens to come in once in a while." We all say it.

So, to win this little battle is really easy. It just takes planning and financial control, as explained in our first book. You know--the one about the strong financial foundation?

Let me sum up the victory dance here. When you make that first list of all the stuff you need (secondary items that get used up, and any equipment or tools you need to work with), then, on your list, right by each item, you put it right away as an item in that oh-so-important business budget. When you plan for having to buy it or replace it, your price will reflect it, and so you will have money when the time comes to buy it. How sweet that is!

Servicers now. You have exactly the same thing. You buy tools, machines, computers, hardware, software, field equipment, etc. Right? Right! So the same concept applies to you. Make your list of every item you need for your company, showing how much it costs, etc. Put that into your budget, adjust your price structure, and you have the money to pay for the new stuff when you need it.

The battle is finally won over secondary inventory by adding one last concept about money management. Sure! It's easy to calculate how much soap you will use, or nails you will pound, because you work with those types of items almost daily. The tricky part is the equipment side of things.

For equipment (retailers or servicers), your list will have a couple of extra columns in it. Once you make your list of each and every piece of equipment in your company, you add columns that say: "Cost to replace," "Months of Use," "Cost per Month."

Did you catch the key column there? Right! The last one, where you can accurately calculate (well, OK. Maybe very close estimate), how much you need to put in your monthly budget to allow for equipment replacement.

The basic concept is this. You want to know how much money you will need to replace things when they wear out. You want to have the money available to pay for it, so you DON'T have to dig into your net profit or personal pocket to pay for it (constant re-investing in your company is a bad thing). By putting your equipment usage in your company budget, you gather money a little at a time so that when the time comes to purchase the item—poof!—you have the bucks to do it.

We have already gone over "reserves" in this book and the previous one, so there's no need to drill it into you again.

Now. For the "typical" inventory stuff—stuff you actually sell or that actually moves out of the shop and brings in the bucks. (Food, for example, for restaurants, nails for carpenters, paper stock for paralegal firms, etc.).

This type of "sellable inventory items," can be somewhat dangerous, because you may be in for a huge shock when tax time comes around.

The tax game (retailers and servicers alike) goes something like this:

The end of the year draws near (or the end of your tax year). You think, "You know, I have a couple of thousand bucks sitting there for my profit picture. I know my favorite Uncle (Sam that is) will be there to take about a third of my profit. My tax dude / dudette says if I don't spend it, the IRS will get it, so I may as well get stuff I need and get my profit down as low as possible so I don't get killed in taxes."

Very, very dangerous game. Here's why.

You go out and buy a bunch of these "sellable inventory items" *thinking* you just spent money and lowered your profit which will lower your taxes. Buzzzzzz! Wrongo!

The IRS knows this type of thinking oh-so-well since they have seen it hundreds of thousands of times. They just quietly sit back and break the news to you, knowing full well your attempts to pay less taxes will only come back and bite you in the back side.

The IRS says, "Nice try there. But how it works actually is this. Your inventory is considered "liquid assets," and that counts the same as profit. In other words, we know you spent the money to lower your profits, but guess what? We know you have "cash value" in inventory sitting on your shelf that represents the extra cash you had to purchase this stuff and for which you could have otherwise paid taxes. The extra cash you had came from (here it comes), your extra profit, which (slam the door shut on my foot) is taxable the same as profit."

In short, they tell you your net profit may show as $3,000, but you have another $12,000 in inventory that is taxable. Last year, you ended the year with only $3,000 in inventory so we know your cash value in inventory grew by $9,000. Add that to your showing profit of $3,000, and you're taxed on $12,0000 profit. "One third, please." Which, in this case is about $4,000, but wait! You already spent the money on inventory. You are now short on cash and have to borrow money to pay taxes!

A better picture: Take very close inventory at the end of your tax year. One month before the end of the tax year, manage your inventory so that its value is about the same as last years. In the case above, the $12,000 actual profit is kept by the company and NOT spent on inventory to reduce your profit. In this case, you still pay taxes on the $12,000, but guess what? You have $12,000 in the bank and only $4,000 goes to taxes leaving you with $8,000 cash in hand.

Summary of the above picture: Which would you rather have (Circle one):

1. A shelf full of too much inventory and $1,000 short to pay taxes

2. Inventory of only what you need and $8,000 in the bank free and clear

GOOD CHOICE (assuming you picked choice 2).

That my friends is another Money vs. Inventory battle won.

But, the war is not over yet.

Winning the *war* boils down to the main focus of this book. Money management. The war is won when you KNOW how much inventory you "use up" of the "Sellable Inventory Items" and KNOWING how long a piece of equipment lasts related to how much it costs per month to build money to replace it.

So, the final battle is in knowing how to handle inventory based on volume trends.

When business gets busier, the more stuff you need. When it slows down, the less stuff you need. Watching this, planning for this, and managing this will help reduce a ton of wasted money.

Have historical data. Restaurants know they will get busy during the holiday season from all the shoppers wanting to eat on the run. During the same time period, painting contractors sit at home wishing for any kind of work because people are spending all their money on gifts and Christmas parties and the like, festive stuff and all that. Work slows down for many other servicers for the same reason.

Well, smart business person that you are, you know these trends from past history. You know a time of less work is coming, so you can start to use up your "Sellable Inventory Items" and NOT replace them up to higher volume levels.

Now remember, for the "Sellable Inventory Items," it is important to watch inventory levels for tax time, but not so important for the "equipment" type of inventory items.

Why? Good question!

The "equipment" inventory items are considered an "Expense" which is 100% tax write off.

Another good thing. For taxes, you get to put many equipment items on a depreciation schedule and get further tax benefit from that.

As a kicker bonus, you have your equipment listed and have come up with your own depreciation schedule as explained above where you calculate how much your equipment costs you per month (build reserves to pay for it when the time comes to purchase it).

Making sense? Hope so.

I would much rather you learn about it from this book instead of learning about it from the IRS.

This also is a good place to mention the importance of a good accountant. Make sure your tax preparation accountant type person really knows her stuff. I see too many times where an accountant wants to take the quick and easy way by not taking advantage of all the tax breaks we business people can take advantage of.

A good test is to ask them how inventory (both types) affects your taxes. If they suggest that you just don't mention it or that it has no effect, that would be a good time to look for another accountant. After all, the IRS doesn't give it "no effect," and when they catch up to you (which they eventually will), it will come back with some financially distressing outcomes.

Aren't you glad you bought this book?

Cool. On to the next exciting subject…

Notes:

The Stuff Called Money: Chapter Seven
Money and Growth

Time goes on and your business is doing just fine (because you're actually doing all the stuff suggested in this book). Also, as time goes on, your customers spread the word because of the high quality and value you give your customers.

Although that may sound like a nice thing to happen (which it really is), often times it becomes a hidden monster that ends up eating you and your business alive!

Here's the deal. Like it or not, when business grows, so does your overhead, your need for more people, your need for more management, your need for you to get out of the active day to day customer dealings and spend time on your business management stuff so you have to have more trust in your employees to run things efficiently.

Many companies have actually increased in sales and ended up losing more money that when they had fewer sales.

WOW! Look at all the hands!

You are absolutely right! Many times a company will actually lose money with growth. They think more sales means more profit. Not necessarily.

More sales always means you need more product (Retailers) or more people to manage your service technicians (Servicers). There is a point in time where your need to hire more people or buy more product *now*, which will increase your overhead *now*, which will throw your pricing structure off.

To cover these costs, prices will go up, many times to a price that is not easy or feasible to sell. At the same time, your employee production (when left in the hands of others who are new and / or in training) will decrease.

OK. So you decide not to raise your prices in order to sell, and at the same time your production goes down. What do you think will happen to your company? Duh!

This is where the previous book and previous chapters in this book are very important. First. as a refresher, the objective is to gather the facts and come up with the right price for your product, and use the financial reports to tell you where there are potential money leaks and lets you know how to fix them.

Second, be careful *not* to overextend yourself. To accomplish that, you must learn about something called "projections." Planning ahead with accuracy can make your growth stable for your company.

We all have heard that the ideal tool for projections is a good working crystal ball that can do a little fortune telling. I actually have one, but I have yet to get it to work correctly. It just stares back at me as if to say, "What? You want *me* to take a shot at it? I'm only a piece of glass."

So, you have to do it yourself without the crystal ball. Projections are really not all that hard to do, and you will find with a little practice, you can become quite accurate at it.

Basic rule for projections is to use the facts to the best of your ability, and project in a way that will be conservative. Too many times people get hooked on the "potential" and not the "reality". They say, "Gee, if I just purchase this new type oven, I can sell twice the product." That is what the oven people want you to think, so they can sell their oven. Fact is, though, if the business buys the oven but it just sits there, and sales increase only 10%, let's say, which doesn't even cover the payment of the new oven, then it was counter-productive to buy the oven right now. And maybe now, they've got to sell the dern oven and hope they can get out with only a few thousand dollars loss instead of a gain.

The main point here is this. It is always *far* better to get the demand in place before you expand. Get a feel from your customers or competition. *When* your customers give you the indication they will actually buy, then and only then get only what you need plus a little more to allow for growth. Be careful *not* to overextend yourself.

Hey! Remember the budget trick? You know, the one where you put any item in your budget for a future purchase. You leave it in there in the budget for six months, setting aside money to purchase it. And then, you analyze your market to see if it makes financial sense to buy it, if the prices you are charging can support paying for it, and then you can use your six months of reserve budget money to pay for the down payment, and you get the dern thing *knowing* you can afford it and it won't put you out of business.

So much for equipment, though. Let's get back to that man-power thing.

When your sales grow to the point where you need more management people, this is where you need to keep in mind one very important thing. The new person you are hiring does *not* think like you do, nor do they know your business like you do.

Check out this question. How many of you have told an employee to do something, even reviewed it with them only to have them do something totally different?

A business I know about told their meeting secretary to take more accurate minutes for their weekly meetings. At the next meeting, the secretary produced and presented the minutes from the previous meeting that looked like this:

> John: OK…. Let's get started. Everyone please take a seat.
> Kathy: Just a minute… I have to get the financial reports off my desk.
> John: Is everyone ready?
> Robert: Yup. I'm ready
> Etc.

The boss asked the secretary why she scripted every single word that was said and how did she do it. She said she recorded the meeting and then went back and played the tape so she could type up the meeting minutes. The boss asked how long it took her. She said. "Oh, not more than six or eight hours over three days!!!"

What a waste, but this sort of thing happens. The employee did exactly as she was told. Who is at fault? Actually the employer is the one at fault here.

It is our job as owners to make tasks clear to employees, even new management people.

Human nature tells any new employee "make the boss happy and don't look like an idiot, so pretend you understand and try to figure it out later."

A simple trick is to have the employee repeat what they heard so you can verify they got it right the first time. When you listen to their response, think of things they might mean other than what you intended, and verify what you heard using different words.

I would love to spend a ton of time on this topic, but that will be covered in full in the book called _Where The Good Employees Are_ which just happens to be the last book in this volume. Hard to wait isn't it?

I just touched on it here because it does have a lot to do with growth in this way. When you hire a new people for management positions, just remember, they typically will not be generating their full value for as much as three months (providing you stick with them to train them properly).

Example. You hire someone to do the books that you were doing yourself. In the past, it took you fifteen minutes a day to enter the expenses. It took you one hour a day to track the sales. I could go on but I think you get my drift.

But now that you have someone standing next to you getting trained, it took you a half hour to explain it, 30 minutes to do it while explaining, and another 30 minutes watching them do it. Where it was 15 minutes for you, it is now 2 hours.

We're not done yet. Remember, telling them once does not mean that they got it, so you will have to review it with them and correct them as needed taking maybe another 30 minutes a day. You are still spending 30 minutes a day instead of 15 minutes a day.

Ever caught yourself saying about new employees, "I can do it much faster myself. Why have these guys"?

You are right. You can do it faster because you are the "master" at it. They have not mastered it yet and need time to do so.

So what does this mean for your profitability. It just goes to figure. You now have two people doing the job of one and it takes more time, not less, to get the job done.

This is normal _and needs to be in your budget_. The budget hint is put the management person's salary and burden in your budget at least three to six months before you hire them. This will help you build up financial reserves so when you do hire them, you can expect to lose time / money during the training process and it will not surprise you and put you out of business.

You see, the management people will be introduced into your company similar to the way equipment is: with budgeting and planning.

Planning for management people may mean you make a list of what you expect them to do. Write a job description using the forms introduced in the first book so you can give them a great tool to know what is expected of them. This will help greatly as a training guide and a reference for your new management person. It will also allow you to get far better performance from them at a much sooner time.

Bad thing to do: You know what you want. It is all in your head. Just hire them and tell them what you want. Correct and fix as you go and try not to get peeved!

Remember, successful growth comes from planning, preparing, and budgeting for it. This will greatly reduce the risk of losing money while growing. Also remember, it should be growth with financial gain, not growth with financial pain.

Speed of growth is very important.

Let's say you literally double your sales on one week. BAM! A good thing for cooking, but not for business.

Now you have to produce twice as much service / product with new employees who are not properly trained or skilled. Supervision time is doubled which is often not possible so quality starts to go out the window, and your free time (what's that?) is now down to nothing with way too much work left undone at the end of the day.

Thus, a slower growth pattern allows you to take what you *know* you can handle without sacrificing quality, service, profitability and a happy life balance (first book). If you have more than you can handle, it is far better to explain the situation to your customers and have them return later with a good experience compared to taking them on only to give them a bad experience and damage your company reputation (no repeat business... Boooooo).

For restaurant owners or retailers, way too much volume (sales) may mean your prices are too low. This is where you can do a profit structure evaluation and bump up prices to increase your profit margin. More money for the same work. Customers will not go away if they are already banging down your door.

Servicers, we addressed this in the first book under the estimating / pricing chapter where you adjust for market value (seasonal high periods to compensate for seasonal low periods). Thus, we don't need to be a broken record on this one.

In either case, just remember. Never sacrifice quality, service, or profitability for the sake of more sales. You are far better off in the long run to handle what you know you can handle for now and make plans for a smooth, financially risk-free growth in the future.

That should give you some great stuff to think about for growth.

On to some more hot topics.

The Stuff Called Money: Chapter Eight
Wealth! More Than a Concept!

For the finale of this book, I thought we could take a really long view, toward your retirement. Like everything else, this requires planning.

So, first you take care of your business' needs, and with what profit you have, you plan for your retirement.

As for your business, it is always a good idea to have anywhere between two and three months of your total overhead amount in the bank for that thing called "operating capitol." Basically, operating capitol is the money you have in reserve that will sustain your business in the event of an extended slow period. You will have to determine how much is enough to have in the bank so you will never have to worry about paying bills or using a line of credit again.

Once you have your nest egg for your business operating capital, you can use the profit from your business to reach your financial goals for retirement.

Wealth is really nothing more than being able to afford the life style you would like to have, even in retirement.

Plan your retirement the same way you did your business.

That means you start out by writing down exactly what you want to do when you retire.

Once you have the general concept of what you want in retirement, then identify everything that will cost money at the point of retirement and then a list of what it will cost in monthly expenses to maintain the life style you have chosen.

You can even use the same business forms in the first book and modify them to mean retirement instead of business.

Think of it this way. Some people may want to retire owning a small cabin in the Kentucky mountains and just live off the land. Someone else may want to visit all the countries of the world and go on a cruise at least once a month.

The first person will only need perhaps $250,000 at the point of retirement and an income of only $4,000 per month while the second person could need $5,000,000 at the point of retirement with an income of $20,000 per month.

It really doesn't matter. What *does* matter is how *you* want to retire and how much you will need in the bank at the point of retirement *and* how much income you will need to sustain your life style.

Whatever the numbers are, your goal is to get there as fast as possible so you can enjoy a long and fulfilling retirement.

What happens with most of us is that we wait until we hit 65 years old and then take a look at how much money we have and at our income. Sad to say, but 88% of Americans are working to afford their current life style, with no hope of retiring the way they really wanted. Only one in 100 Americans *can* retire the way they want. Only *you* can make it happen for you, if, and only if, you plan for it and work that plan.

So, let's talk about how your business money effects your retirement and wealth picture.

1.   PROFIT:

Yes, your company profit is obviously one of the first things that will help you build your wealth at the pace you desire.

We have a another book called "The Guaranteed Wealth System" which will give you all the methods, forms, calculation sheets and even software that will help you in your planning and actual wealth picture. So, we don't need to repeat the whole book here. It is available as an "optional" item on the website. Same page where you get the free downloaded forms. We decided to make that it's own separate book since it has absolutely nothing to do with business. It's entire focus is on your personal wealth. No forms to download. It has all the forms with it and a CD with all the Excel worksheets for your current and future planning. Really cool because it shows how long it should take you to hit the financial wealth point of retirement. Note: The concept is, Retirement happens when you have enough money. Not when you reach 65. Well, for those who win the wealth game that is.

OK. Back to *this* book.

If you remember, all company expenses are taken into account in your overhead budget, and when you reserve ahead of time for all the items that do not occur monthly (taxes, membership dues, equipment purchases, etc.) the money is there to pay for them when they are due. Then you set aside operating capitol for emergencies. After that, profit is then 100 percent retirement money.

Your company volume will only allow so much profit for your retirement account and it may or may not be enough to meet your retirement goals. Example: If you are already 58 years old and figure only 5 years of business life left in you, and your company can only net say $10,000 per year, you will be stuck with $50,000 (plus interest, of course).

If you are young and have all the time in the world, why use it up working. Get to the point of retirement as soon as you can, so you can enjoy retirement with some youth in your body. I don't know many 70 year old people who want to go bungee jumping.

Anyway, here's where having a business gets really cool.

Profit is not the only retirement venue. You have your business value, a fact that can also add greatly to your retirement picture.

WARNING! Your business can only help your retirement picture when you run your business correctly with intent of using it for retirement.

Here's how it can work for you:

When you run a profitable business, you can have options for exiting your business without going out of business.

The obvious first choice is to sell your business.

Really now. Who wants to buy a business that does not have a balance sheet for the past few years showing steady growth in assets and wealth?

Who wants to buy a business that cannot show a profit and loss statement for each month for the past few years, all showing a healthy profit?

Who wants to buy a business that cannot show the owners taking a healthy salary out of the business?

Who wants to buy a business that does not have any instructions on how to run it profitably (no Company Operations Manual).

NOT ME!

No one else will either. Can you see how important *everything* is in these series of books? When you have it all together as a fine-tuned, well-oiled machine showing increase in assets, profit and guaranteed owner salary, *now* you have something to sell.

There are many different ideas of what your business is worth. All the theories are useless if you can't sell your business.

We had one business owner (Construction industry Service Company) who had about $250,000 in company assets (field equipment, lift equipment, company vans, etc). Showed a net profit of $25,000 per year and took a salary of $60,000 per year.

One business consultant told him to sell his company for the value of all the assets, five year net profit and a five year salary. For this company it came to $675,000.

It never sold. Why? No one was willing to spend *that* much for equipment that was "used and depreciating" and only $25,000 per year gain. It would have taken them 25 years to break even on the investment. Not a good deal.

On the other hand, we had a Retailer who had about $80,000 in product inventory with a profit of $30,000 per year and an owner salary of $50,000 per year. They were advised to show a two year salary and profit plus inventory for a sale price of $240,000.

Here, they owned $80,000 in retail products which can sell for 40% higher, giving the new owner about $50,000 in product profit, plus $30,000 per year actual profit after salary. Break even point would be only four years.

Just a tid-bit on statistics. Typically a business will take about 5 years to break even. Any business prospective to be considered valid will have a five to ten year break even point depending on the business.

One other thing to consider. The *hardest* thing for a business to build is a customer base. If you have a proven customer base, it too adds a *lot* of value to your business and so adds to it's selling price.

Here are some tips I like to suggest when thinking about selling your business:

Know the value of the equipment or inventory you have *if* you were to *sell* it.

Sample: If you own a piece of equipment that you paid $4,000 for, but if you were to sell it as a used piece of equipment and could only get $3,000 for it, use the $3,000 value. That is only fair to the buyer.

To get the value of your equipment or inventory is easy. We know you have been paying attention to this book and we know that you will pro-actively do the Balance Sheet which will be to make a list of your assets, and inventory and equipment are all a part of it. When you have done this, you will already have an easy and current picture of this "hard" value.

Next, you will want to build the profit structure as suggested in this series of books complete with job descriptions and company operations manuals. When you have run your business profitably for two years, it will give a prospective buyer a good and fair picture of what they can expect when they continue the business under the same profit structure. This will give you a good number for your Profit Value.

Next is your salary. When preparing to sell your business. take a healthy salary for at least two years. Do not worry about the increase in personal income taxes. Put the taxes in your budget. Pay for them again showing a true income after taxes to the potential buyer.

Using these three things (Asset Value, Profit Value and Income Value), I like to take the two year approach, which is: Total Asset Value plus two years profit plus two years salary. You can add to it whatever you feel is a fair value for customer base.

Sample:

Your company assets:	$ 120,000
Two years net profit:	$ 48,000
Two years owner salary	$ 120,000
Customer base value:	$ 12,000
TOTAL SALES PRICE:	$ 300,000

The buyer evaluation:

Owns in assets:	$ 120,000
5 Years Profit:	$ 60,000
5 Years Salary	$ 300,000
Avg Growth at 10%:	$ 40,000
Return on investment:	$ 520,000

Fancy schmancy calculations brings this to an average of 15% investment return .

GOOD DEAL! Easier to sell!

The important thing to remember is your business will *not* sell if you are not showing a good profit, good salary and assets free and clear.

When the time comes, we also suggest that at least six months in advance you contact someone who is in the business of selling a business to steer you in the right direction as to how to come up with a formula to calculate the selling price that will best fit your type of business.

Another Option: TRANSFER.

The business transfer is basically like selling your business to the current employees or key employee.

This can be done in a wide variety of ways. You can:

1. Determine the selling price and have them purchase the business outright by getting a business loan.
2. Determine the selling price and have them pay you in monthly payments determined by your current salary draw for X number of years.
3. Determine the selling price and have them pay a lump sum non-refundable deposit with payments on the balance based on a set amount.
4. Determine the selling price and have them make payment directly to you based on reduced salary draw and percentage of the profit.
5. Determine the selling price and have them make a lump sum non-refundable deposit with a guarantee minimum percentage of volume or percentage of the profit for X years.
   a. Sample: If average profit is $24,000 a year and you want 50%, they would pay $12,000 guaranteed regardless of what profit actually is, or 50% of profit if higher than $24,000 per year
6. Set up a set amount per month to be paid for X years for retirement income.

This is what I really like about the transfer option. You can set it up such that you *can* get a lump sum amount *and* have a monthly income for your retirement income.

For this option, it is always highly advisable to decide what you want. You write up a contract draft. You take it to an attorney and have them draft a final copy, then proceed with the business transfer.

Another option: SEMI-RETIRE

This is another good one for those of you (like me) who just love their work and really don't want to retire.

Sure, I want to slow down and enjoy more in life, but I have decided I will always do private consulting for small businesses who need my help. I just won't do it as much.

For this option, you may wish to find a buyer or existing management person in your company and work it out such that you are "Part Time" consultant / manager for the company. This involves you transferring the company by contract to the new owner, but you still work for them in whatever capacity you desire.

This way, you can work as much or little as you like and take a reduced salary *and* a percentage of the profit for an indefinite period of time.

Your life is active, you live longer, you keep doing what you love, and you can take as much vacation time as you want, and whenever you want. Sounds like a good retirement plan to those who really love their business and consider retirement spending "less time" with their business and enjoying life with the rest of the time.

For a final thought of this chapter and book…

Go ahead and get the "Guaranteed Wealth System" book and learn how to become debt free in record time and how to plan for your retirement with the same successful structure designed for your business. It will greatly help you retire the way you want and learn how to build wealth as fast as possible. It's on our website.

As for money management, please do NOT just put this in the back of your mind.

USE IT, DO IT. I KNOW YOU CAN because you have been such a good reader. Now get out there and get this money stuff set up, and stick to it.

BREAK! (football team huddle breaking to get into play theme there).

Now, on to book three where we talk about sales and marketing.

The Guaranteed Profit System
Book 3

Open The Door and Bring 'Em In

"A Sales and Marketing Guide"

By: Lynn H. Fife

Open The Door and Bring 'Em In: Chapter One
Generic Sales and Marketing Terms

So, you have your business in order, and you are ready to bring in more customers (or your first customers if you are just starting out).

Before we jump into this full tilt, let's begin with a few basic terms just to make sure we are speaking the same language. Let's start with sales, marketing, and advertising.

As I will define it here, advertising is an actual piece of paper or physical thing your customer can see. Marketing has to do with how that item gets in front of your customers. Sales is what you actually do to get the customer to buy your service or product.

Also, I will speak here, as in my other books, about two different types of businesses. There is the service industry, where you offer a service (for example, accounting, painting, resume preparation, etc.). The other is the retail business, where you are selling a product (for example, a candy store, bakery, restaurant, clothing store, etc.). Sometimes a business has both elements, such as a beauty salon where you provide the service of cutting hair and you also sell products such as the shampoo, etc.

As a term of endearment, I reference these two types of business as "servicers" and "retailers." I do my best to address both types of businesses. If you see something that doesn't relate to you, just skip ahead until you see the word that identifies your type of business. If you are a dual type business, then this whole dang book applies to you.

Now here are some generic terms we all need to agree on and use.

First up is "Open Market" vs. "Vertical Market."

Open Market means your product or service is open to almost everybody out there. The majority of the population can use your service or product. Let's take, for example, a beauty salon. Everyone needs to get a hair cut. Some do it at home, but a huge majority of the population get-er-done elsewhere. This is a great example of an "Open Market" company.

Vertical Market means your product or service is used by only a small portion of the population. Like my services. Since most of the population works for someone else as an employee, and this book is only good for people who run a business, there is really only a small portion of the population that actually can use my services.

Take it one more step. If you have a business such as one making a specialty tool for a sand blast shop, the only people who would buy your product is a sand blast shop. This is known as a "Limited Vertical Market." Or, let's say I made this book of interest not only limited to those running a business (a vertical market), but narrowed it even further to address only those who run painting businesses (a limited vertical market).

Easy to understand so far, isn't it?

Next is the term "Target Market."

It doesn't matter what type of business you have, all businesses have a target market.

Here's an example. The owner of an espresso stand asks himself, "Self. What type of person will be most likely to come here, buy coffee, even sit down for a while, hang out, and eat muffins? Why, people who have time on their hands, need a place to hang out, and don't mind spending $4.00 for a cup of great coffee plus another $3 on muffins or snacks. That's $7.00 per visit, perhaps two visits per day, for $14 per day habit, or (for five days a week / 20 a month) a person can spend $280.00 per month just to hang out here. Now *that's* the customer I want!"

So, this espresso stand owner thinks, "I think I'll send my flyer to a bunch of apartments in the low rent district!" Circle one: Good choice   Bad Choice

Smart person that you are, I am sure you circled Bad choice.

It is obvious that not all people are your "Target Market." Get it? Target means these are the people you want to target because they are perfectly suited to be your business customer.

We will spend a bunch of time on how to find and attract your target market later in this book. Remember, this section is just getting the basic terms down.

Next up is "Decision Factor." It just means, "This is the dude or dudette (California Valley coming out in me there) that makes the decision to spend the bucks."

This term will be very important later in this book when we discuss how to maximize your sales by focusing on the right person (decision factor) and telling them what fits their learning / personal attributes.

Oh. Here's a tricky little devil. "Sales Ratios." Sound's kind of "mathy" doesn't it. That's because it is mathy. Nonetheless, it is very important to know what sales ratios mean and their importance in your business.

Sales ratios are calculated based on the following:
1. How much money you bring in during a specified period of time (say $2,000 a week).
2. How many customers spent that money (say, 50 customers).
3. How many customers walked away without spending money (say 200 total customers minus the 50 sales you made, for 150 who didn't buy).

From these numbers you can do some simple math and get important information.

Example. Let's say the store is an art store. Using the above numbers, the store had 200 customers in a week, of which 50 bought something. The math (which we can do in our head) tells us 1out of 4 customers bought something. Or in sales ratio terms, you get 25% of your walk-in business.

The owner may ask, "Self, what can I do to increase the purchase of my goods?"

More math comes in. The art dealer looks at all the sales. We had $2,000 in sales for the week from the 50 customers. This math (also done in our smart little heads) comes out to $40.00 per sale. Verify that, and if its true, then it means that customers are willing to spend money on the $40 or less items. So you feature the "best" thing up front to get customers to come in, and once they are in, the items most visible will be the items that sell for $40 or less.

Next week's figures come in. We sold $3,200. We had 200 customers, and we had 80 customers buy something. The ratios came in different. We now got 40% of our walk in customers to buy something (because what they want the most is most visible) and we didn't have to rely on more customers coming into the store.

Can you see where these types of numbers are important?

But wait. I can hear some of you out there saying, "But I'm not an art store." Doesn't matter. Think about it.

Window Installer (How many bids they give vs. how many sales they get, vs. average sales?

Bakery? How many customers they have, average purchase price, what they buy the most of, how to plan for the next food order, how to increase, decrease what they make, etc.

Photo shop: Number of customers, what they buy, average price spent, etc.

It doesn't matter what type of business you have, understanding sales ratios can really help you when you learn how to put them together very quickly and use them. More on this later in the book.

Next terms up. " Prospect, Prospectus, Prospecting."

Said in a fun way, you can go prospecting with a prospectus to get a prospect.

Prospecting is the act of going out there and looking for customers.

The prospectus is the piece of paper or item your customers get that tells them about your business in detail. The difference between a prospectus and general advertising is that the prospectus will usually have more detailed information than say, a business card or other simple advertising piece.

The prospect is the actual person or people you are going after to do business with. You know, the customer. A prospect is a customer who has not yet spent money. If they have spent money, we call them…. Well…. Gold!

Finally, the term "venue" comes to mind. A venue can be a supplier you buy goods from or it could be a "way" of getting something done. Example. You are not sure how you want to distribute your beautiful, magnificent, and enticing flyer. You think, "I can direct mail it. I can hand it to a bunch of Boy Scouts to have them spread them over the neighborhood. Or I can have my employees pass them out to all their friends. I wonder which (ready? here it comes) 'venue' I should use."

Ok! That should get us all warm and toasty so we can move on to the next chapter which gets us into…

Oh heck, you can read. Maybe my not telling you will give you just a few seconds of suspense for those of you who actually like that kind of thing.

Ok. Next chapter.

Notes:

Open The Door and Bring 'Em In: Chapter Two
Just Who Is Your Customer Anyway?

Since you are already so smart you know the word "Target Market," I can tell you that is exactly what this whole chapter is about. Identifying your target market is probably one of the most important things you can do in your business.

We will start with the companies providing service—the servicers. OK. What company type shall we use this time? Let's pick a residential painting company.

Critical elements have to be identified here. First, does this painting company hire cheap labor and pay cash under the table (boooooooooo!) which means they pay less, don't have as much expense, so they can charge less?

I hope you realize that I am a full supporter of being 100 percent legal and legit. It's those people who do not operate legally who make our insurance rates go so high. I mean, if all the companies out there that are operating illegally would become legal and start paying for workman's compensation and general liability insurance, it would lower the rate because there would be a broader base. When more companies do not pay, it drives the rate up.

Anyway, back to target market for the painter.

It's easy to say, "I am a residential painter," but that is not specific enough. There are lots of ways to be a residential painter, and lots of different markets.

Example: There is the family trying to sell their home. These people don't want to spend a lot of money for property they will not keep.

Then you have people who have just bought a home who also may be on a tight budget but are willing to pay a little more for a longer lasting finish.

Then you have people who have lived in their home for a long time and the house needs painting for maintenance. These people are willing to spend more as an investment in their own home.

You have people who just want a change or to make the place look better, so they too may be willing to spend more. You have homes in the middle-income area and you have multi-million dollar homes, and the occupants are willing to spend different amounts.

Get the picture? Sure you do.

The point here is no matter what kind of service business you are in, *not everyone is your target market.* Think of the type(s) of service you offer and who would be most likely to hire you. If you have cheap low cost service with little or no overhead, you can attract those who want to spend less. Visa Versa for those of you who have a higher cost service with a higher overhead.

This concept of matching your target market to your business is talked about in the previous books in which we explained how to do an accurate budget and how to use your budget (expense needs) to determine your price. There's great stuff in those books. If you are not sure of this content, it is always a good idea to review the previous books in this volume. It will help you understand this concept.

Anyway. The point is, when you are running your business 100 percent legit and you know your overhead expenses, those expenses will pretty much determine the price you must charge a customer. Now the game is to find the customer who is willing to pay that price for your services.

Everyone knows you get what you pay for. Don't worry about those other companies who get the work by having the lowest price. They will just be out of business after a while, only to be replaced with someone else who will do the same. Your objective is to stay in business and grow your business to be a profitable organization.

For your Retailers now.

Retailers have two kinds of customers: people who need an item, and people who may not feel a "need" to buy your products, but can be persuaded to "want" to buy your product. In other words, go for the impulse, get the desire, plant the bait, reach out and touch someone, etc.

Here is an example of impulse buying. If you have a candy store, a person may not feel the "need" to make a special trip to your store just for candy (repeat customers exception). Thus, you open the door, put a fan blowing the chocolate smell out into the street so passers by can smell your goods and get that chocolate vibe going and get sucked right into your store. Your special target market is more in the line of "who *could* like my products" as well as "who *does* like my product."

OK. Let's tie both servicers and retailers together now. It doesn't matter what type of business you have, there are many aspects of target marketing that are the same. Here goes.

You gotta get into your customer's head.

Sound's easy and we all seem to know it, but what happens is this thing that gets in the way, this thing called "owners pride." That's right. You are probably proud as a peacock in full fanned out strut. You started this business. You think it's the cat's meow. You have done a ton of work on it, and you offer the best product or service around. You think you shouldn't have to do much to bring in customers.

Here's a secret. Every competitor you have says the same thing. It's like that saying, "You are unique, just like everybody else."

All businesses "claim" to be the best, and most of the businesses out there strive to be the best, but when it comes down to it, a prospective customer (not a repeat customer) will go with whoever comes up first and keeps their comfort level up.

So. What can you do to get more attention to your business? First, stop thinking like a business owner and start thinking like your customers.

Take a look in the yellow pages. Look at any section, any ad and see what is the biggest thing you see.

Right! The company name. More words like "Quality, Service, and Free Estimates." This is the business owner just screaming out their pride in their businesses.

Name recognition is very important, and we will discuss that a bit later. But when a person goes to the yellow pages, the company name is not usually what they are looking for.

Consider our painting company. If you have a customer with a very expensive home, they will be looking for "insured," "custom homes," "elegant," "care with your valuables," "bonded" and all those kind of words. What do they see? "Free estimates, low prices, budget" etc.

Thus, the answer is to take a few moments to get into your targeted customer's head.

Here's a hint on that. Imagine the type of person who would usually purchase your service or goods. They are sitting in their easy chair watching TV, then BAM! A commercial pops up and says "..." (This is where you fill in the blank that contains something you think would really get their attention).

Sample: If you have, say, a car wash business, your customer may want to hear, "OK, you know it's been a long time since you had the car washed, Right? I know, you don't have time or you keep forgetting. Not to worry, our Spiffy On Site Car Wash business was built just for you. We actually come to your location. We can give you a full interior and exterior detail cleaning or just a simple exterior wash. Give us a call now at (800) 555-1212..."

How does this differ from what the typical business owner does? They focus on what they are proud of, all the neat stuff the have to offer. "We have a car wash. We offer exterior cleaning with non-abrasive detergent, special chemicals to prevent spotting, liquid or hand waxing, interior detailing, Armoral treatment, leather protective treatments, vinyl treatments, wheel treatments, inside door jam cleaning, rain treatments for the windshield, and yes, we even have air fresheners..." and on and on and on.

As owners, we get all wrapped up on what we want to tell the customer and forget the reason WHY they would buy from us. When you shift gears and think of what *they* want to hear and what *they* want the most, then you will have much better success at attracting your target market.

OK. I'm getting too close to the marketing part of this book, which comes later, so back on focus to your target customer.

The point of getting into your customers head is to realize that different people want different things. For the painting company mentioned above, there are people who only want a coat of paint, because they know they will probably move within a couple of years, so a long-lasting paint job may not be a concern. All they want is to get a coat of paint up that will last say five years or so. They don't want to spend a lot of money because they may not have a lot of money to spend. Nothing wrong with that. It just helps the painting contractor decide if this type of customer is the right customer for their business.

On the other hand, there may be a customer who has been saving up for an exterior paint job and they don't plan on moving anytime soon. They DO want a long lasting paint job and they realize you do get what you pay for, so they want a fair price, not necessarily the low price.

In painting, the surface preparation is the key. One painter may take a garden hose and squirt off the loose dust, then go to painting. Looks fine but doesn't last very long. OR another painter could use a pressure washer followed by grinding off all old paint, feather sanding the edges, re-set all popped nails, dig out all old caulk and replace with new caulk for all joints and give a full prime coat before painting. Cost the same? I think not. Last the same as the garden hose job? I think not! Huge difference and it proves once again, you do get what you pay for.

In the latter case, the customer understands full surface preparation will bring the entire surface of the house to "close to new" as possible and will guarantee adhesion for a very long lasting paint job (10 years plus) when the top grade material is used. Worth the money? You bet. This is a different target market customer.

Both customers have their desired painting company. The tight budget customer is looking for a painting company who is lower cost and is OK with not doing full surface prep. Sorry to say but there are many painting companies who will take the job with minimum prep. But another company that only does the "high end" work will not be interested in the tight budget customer. Instead, they need to target those who would be willing and able to spend more for the level of quality work they provide.

So much for painting. Would this apply to any business? You bet. Candy store. Some people are on a no-sugar diet. If you feature "no sugar" candy, you have a target market to hit. If you have a tire store, you have some people who don't want to spend a lot of money on tires. You know, the ones who always come in and say, "What's the cheapest thing you got?" But you also have customers looking for the high performance tire and are not afraid to spend, say, $300 a tire. If your store is a high performance tire store, you would market to those types of customers and not worry about the "cheapest thing you got" customers.

I am sure you get the general idea. Just a few summary pointers here.

Make sure any marketing you do is properly suited to your target market. If you have more than one target market, like our candy store who can sell both the fully loaded sugar stuff and the non-sugar stuff, you will be best off having two different advertising things going on so you can attract both markets. A painting company can put out one advertising piece for residential customers and a different one for commercial painting.

When you focus on your target market, your results will be much better because you focus only on what *they* want to hear and not clutter them up with a bunch of general information they really don't care about.

OK. On to yet another exciting, motivating, exhilarating chapter in this book. (Hard to put it down huh)?

Open The Door and Bring 'Em In: Chapter Three
The People Business

You already know you are in the people business. This chapter is here to toss in a few interesting things about people that may help you get a better sale.

I like to think all people have two basic sides. These are just my own terms. I like to use the "inner person" and the "outer person." It is important to do a few little tricks to find out what type of person your customer is, because it will help you identify what will urge them to buy or, on the down side, what will turn them away.

Let's begin with the inner person.

- All people can think (well, some better than others, it seems).
- All people have the ability to "do." Yes, even those who, for example, may be in a wheel chair.
- All people can see or visualize things. Yes, even the blind can visualize things.
- Finally, all people have emotions. Yes, some stronger and more on the surface than others.

I label each of these four types as "Thinker", "Doer", "Seer", and "Feeler." While all people have all four abilities, one is the most dominate and another is a strong secondary.

Now, I would love to claim I thought of this stuff first, but alas, this is old hat. Been around for a number of years. Meyers Briggs has a whole book on it, and they even have a test that many counselors have used to help many people. I'm just summarizing using my own words. Let me get back to my view of it all.

Here's an example of, well, me. I think of myself as being a "thinker / doer" since I analyze things a lot, and I also enjoy hands-on doing. When I took the Meyers Briggs test, guess what? Bingo! Nailed it. (Only I found out I was off the charts "thinker.")

Most people have a good idea of what type of person they are, but do they think about how this relates to their customers? Good question.

First, the chart:

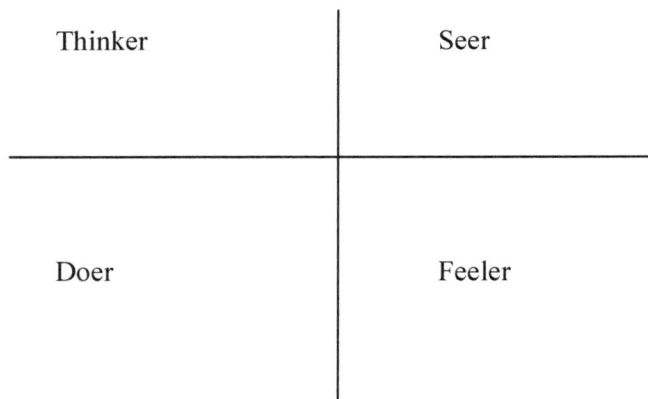

Thinker	Seer
Doer	Feeler

Let's take some examples. If you are a service company, say a house cleaning company, and you have a customer that calls with a bunch of questions, They want all the details and they are looking for lots of information, they are probably a "thinker" type person. Since they want all the details, so give it to them. They love you.

If on the other hand, you have a person on the phone that says, "This house feels so grungy. Can you help?" That sounds like a "feeler" person. Key word was "feels…" etc. They haven't asked for details, and if you start to give them all the facts, they feel like you are trying to up-sell them on a bunch of stuff they don't want. They feel pressure, and you probably have lost the sale. With the feeler person, you focus your conversation on stuff like, "When we are done, your home will feel sparkly clean, etc…"

With that as the basic example, let's take a little more time to discuss how to identify each of the four "inner person" attributes. Then you can apply it to your customers.

The "Thinker." This is the kind of person who has the need to understand how things work, why things happen; this is the fact-gatherer. When they think they have enough information, then they are comfortable with the purchase. This person may also like to come up with ideas or suggestions of their own. Their creative mind pops in. They like to analyze things, and they put a lot of value on logic. Mr. Spock of *Star Trek* is huge in the thinker profile.

How do you identify the customer who is a "Thinker?" Great question.

As with any inner-person profile, the key is to listen to what they say or how they react to you. That gets us just a little off on a side note here.

A successful business trick that is really no trick at all, goes hand in hand with the saying, "You have two ears and one mouth. The wise person uses them in the same proportion." With all customers, especially in the service industry, it is always a good idea to ask a bunch of questions of the customer, and listen to their answers, encourage them to talk. Think about it. If you ask a question, it forces an _____. That's right. An answer.

When you get an answer from the customer, it forces (or allows) what we all know as communication. If, on the other hand, you are so focused on selling your product or service, and you get in the habit of doing all the talking, you are not listening to your customer, not able to tell what sort of person you are dealing with. Most people think "selling" is "talking," but the great sales person realizes most sales come from listening.

So start here. Develop a bunch of questions in your mind that will help get the customer talking. When they talk and react to you, then you have a great shot at identifying their inner person.

What? You want some examples of questions to ask? OK.

- For the Floor Installer: "What would you like your new floors to be like when we finish?"
- For the Hobby Shop: "Are you looking for something that takes a lot of time or something that can be done more quickly?"
- For the Resume Service: "What type of image would you like to portray?"
- For the Glass Company: "Have you seen any custom window tints yet?"

Notice, these questions allow customers to let you know more about themselves and what they want. The sales person would NOT jump in there and just start telling customers about their products or services.

Can you imagine the frustration in customers who went to the Hobby Shop and the sales person started to show them every single possible hobby item in the store? Yikes!

OK. I think you get the idea of the question system. Now, let's get back to how we can identify the various inner person attributes.

For the thinker. The thinkers will usually gather a little information, then start asking questions. They are screaming at you (silently) that they want information because they are a _____ .

 Right! A thinker.

Remember how to keep a thinker happy? Right! Fill them with all the information they can handle. When they have enough, they will stop asking questions, and you have a much better chance of getting the sale because now they feel educated.

Next up, the Doer. When talking to the Doer, they may say something like, "Is there anything I can do to help in the process?" or "How do you do this part …?" Way easy! They are saying, "I'm a doer"!

So what do you do? Right. Get them involved. Example: If you are a floor installer, you can tell them they can save a few bucks by moving all the furniture out of the work area into other rooms. You have filled their inner need to do, and you get the sale.

Next we have the seer. No. Not the psychic person using the crystal ball. The other type. You know, the visual person.

When you fire your questions their way, they may say something like, "What will that look like?" Or, "What color does that come in?" Easy to filter this one because they focus on visual words like "look" and "color." For this person, we need to use similarly reassuring words like, "This will look absolutely wonderful"! Or, "That is the perfect color for this"! Bingo again, you have a customer who feels you are in sync with what they want.

Finally we have the feeler. This is the person who responds to your questions with stuff like "I'm really looking for something that will make this place a little more friendly and inviting." Or, "I hear this type of chocolate really makes your inner mind tingle with delight."

Notice the "feely" words. Yup. You got 'em. The words "friendly and inviting" and "tingle with delight" are all strong emotional words that let you know you have a feeler in front of you.
So what do you do? Right again (man, you really are getting this stuff). You let them know, "This particular style will really make this place feel like grandma's house." Or, "Just wait till this chocolate touches your tongue." Ca-ching! I hear the bell for another sale.

So much for that part of the inner person. Develop a habit of identifying the inner person of your customers. Eventually, when someone responds to your questions, your mind will be saying, "OK, is this dude a thinker, doer, seer, or feeler?"

With enough practice, you will develop a knack of getting the inner person down pat within a few statements. Then you will be able to think of what makes them tick so you can respond in a way that will help you get the sale.

Now. On to the outer person. How your customer appears, how they act, how they reveal themselves on the outside, what their outer lifestyle is. You can get clues from their outer appearance and actions that can help you make your sale to them.

For example: What type of car do they drive? What kind of clothes do they wear? Are they decorated with jewelry, or are they jewelry free? Do they practice immaculate personal hygiene? Do they talk with elegance or like me, sort of homey?

What these outer indicators tell you is whether they understand and believe the life long lesson "you get what you pay for," or are they looking for the cheapest thing (quality and price wise). If they drive a Cadillac, you know they enjoy a quiet, more luxurious automobile, thus would most likely enjoy more luxurious items from you. If they are not much into what others think of their appearance or for that matter, what other people think at all, then they probably won't want to pay for quality product or service from you.

Now, I don't want to get into a discussion on what is bad or good. What I have learned is that everyone does what they do and lives how they live for a reason that stems from their up-bringing and their own personal comfort level. They are not wrong or right. They are just different.

So why mention this? Yet again, another great question.

Example: If you meet a customer who is wearing a nice suit with polished shoes, this person will easily deal with the price of your goods or service. They are used to spending money for quality stuff. Assuming you have quality stuff, you have an easier / more comfortable sale.

If on the other hand, you have a guy who is wearing blue jeans with a hole in the knee and a t-shirt with a marijuana leaf growing on it, you may have someone who is more stressed about spending more money and may expect more than is fair for his dollar spent.

Disclaimer here. These are just general observations that may help you in some cases. I know there are always exceptions. I was working at a mansion and taking a lunch break outside by the pond. I saw a dude in blue jeans with a hole in the knee, scruffy hair, and a five-day growth on his face. I asked if he was one of the workers on the project. He said, "Well, yes, in a way. I'm the owner."

Blew me away. This "owner" was a multi millionaire several times over. His personal residence was on 1200 acres. Taught me never to assume the outward appearance to be a true indicator of the real outer person. So, just keep in mind, there are always exceptions to the rule.

How to benefit from all this in the sales process? Just remember, it is very important to adjust your sales methods to fit the customer.

Retail sales? Yes. This applies very much so. You may have a woman come into your store wearing a bunch of jewelry. I guarantee, if you physically stop whatever you are doing, take a gasp of air, point to her prize ring and say, "Wow! Can I see that?" Then you take a close look and say, "That's awesome," you most likely have a customer for life.

Get the idea. I'm sure you do. OK. More about the "people business."

We often forget that people are not experts in your product or service. They are typical people. And most typical people, they LOVE to be educated.

Do you know what the single biggest item that people spend their extra income on is? (Suspense build up with this dramatic pause). Education. No, really! Look. You bought this book, didn't you? People take classes in dancing, computer use, heck, tons of stuff. They are screaming for knowledge. Gaining knowledge makes them feel, well, smart.

The cool thing is, when you have a smart customer, they can make a smart decision on whose product to purchase or whose service to hire.

Let's dig into some examples here:

First, for the retailers: Let's use our chocolate store again. When you have a customer that is a thinker, and they ask a question on "the secret ingredient," lean forward in a half stage whisper and say, "It's the butter. Some of the most expensive stuff you can find. We have ours imported from Germany. Other places use the typical stuff you get here in the U.S., which is less expensive, but we have found it better to have the fantastic taste for a few cents more. Don't you agree?"

Now this customer has something to tell his friends. Next time any form of chocolate comes up in any conversation (like at almost any party where women chocoholics are located), your customer will say, "Did you know that that chocolate store downtown actually imports butter from Germany. If you haven't tried their deluxe fudge, you are really missing out." She's in the "know."

Let's use a plumber, for example. The customer needs a toilet replaced. All they know is there is this ceramic thing that sits on a hole in the floor. They think all there is to putting a toilet in is to remove the four nuts, lift the old toilet off, slap the new one on, and you're done. They will get prices from a few plumbers and take the low price each time, IF, that is, they are not educated on all the concerns that go on while installing a toilet.

This is where the smart plumber (like you) will take the time to help the customer learn about some of the different choices they have in toilets. You may say, "Well, Mrs. Arbuckle, there is a water-saving toilet that I like to call the "double flusher." This means you give it one quick push on the handle and it only takes two to three seconds to flush using only 1/3 the amount of water. This saves a bit on your water bill. If you hold the handle down for four to five seconds, the flush will be three times longer for those, well, let's just say "tougher" jobs a toilet has to do. The price is only about $30 more for this type of toilet. Would you like that type?"

The customer now has something new and interesting to tell her friends while promoting you, the really professional plumber whom everyone should hire.

Don't stop there, for crying out loud. Keep it going with, "Also, the installation process involves undoing and checking the existing water pipe and hose that comes out of the wall. I noticed you have the old style copper tube which, although it may be a little flexible, can easily break with repetitive disconnections as time goes on. We highly recommend the new flex hose which only adds about $10 to the price and will last much longer, leak free. Then, we have the wax ring that fits around the hole in the floor. Most plumbers will just use the old one. This is not recommended because much of the wax is removed and disturbed when we removed the old toilet. We highly suggest we install a new wax ring. This too is very inexpensive, adding about $10 to the install process and warrants a tight seal under the toilet, preventing possible leaks that way."

And now, the wrap up. The plumber would end with, "Of all the items we talked about, what would you like?"

The cool thing that is happening here is that you now have an educated customer. This customer knows that the price of services is related to quality and a long lasting product. When they get a lower price, they will know they are not getting what they pay for and may have future problems. If you do your job correctly, they will learn that all plumbers pay the same for parts and the labor is about the same for all of them. The only way anyone can lower their price is to give less quality.

Summary of this powerful technique: You have an educated customer who now understands WHY your price is what it is and whip is far more likely to hire you because you took the time to educate them.

What do you say we move on to the next chapter and talk about how to screen our customers for higher sales results?

Open The Door and Bring 'Em In: Chapter Four
Shifting For Nuggets

Welcome to our expedition where we are searching for gold. Golden customers, that is. We are going to screen out the not-so-great, probably-won't-hire-you potential customers, and sift for great potential customers who are willing and able to pay for your services.

Retailers, for the most part, look for great customers by using advertising and marketing methods that attract customers to *come to their location* to purchase goods. Servicers, on the other hand, must have advertising and marketing items that entice the customer to *call the service provider*. But what *kind* of customers does your advertising piece attract?

Imagine. You are a service company. (We will use retailer's examples later.) There are your potential customers on the phone with the statement, "We were thinking of (your service) and would like to get an estimate."

Your first response may be to grab a piece of paper, write down their information, jump in your vehicle to go out there and give them an estimate (or schedule a time for them to come in and talk with you).

But please keep in mind one important thing. Your time is worth money. Your time giving a price should be spent with customers who are more likely to hire you. Don't waste time with someone who will likely NOT hire you. Are you taking the time to find out which type of customer you are dealing with? I hope so.

What we want to do is *filter out* the customers who will most likely say "no" to us, so we don't end up wasting our time. After all, why would anyone want to take the time to meet with the customer, show them a service package, prepare an estimate, do a follow up call, only to hear those familiar words, "I didn't think it would be *that* much!"

Wouldn't it be nice to know in advance if a customer will say "No?" Man, could we save a bunch of time and get more stuff done. Heck, we could take on more bids from those people who do say "yes" and increase our sales ratios a bunch!

What we are recommending is this:

Take time to ask the potential customer a few questions while you have them on the telephone during your first call.

Here are some questions I like to use. I'll explain why afterward.

"Are you in the process of selling your home?"
"Are you getting other prices?
"When are you planning to get the work done?"
"What spurred you to call our company (why are you getting the work done)?"
"Have you ever hired this type of work done before?"
"If you have hired someone else, who was it?"
"Why aren't you using them this time?"
"Where is the work location?" (for service type companies)

Let's examine each of these questions.

"*Are you in the process of selling your home?*"

If the answer is yes, it means they do not want to spend a ton of dough on something they are trying to sell. They want the lowest price, and typically, that's not you. You stand a 95% chance of not getting the sale. So don't waste your time.

Hey! Wait a minute! What about that 5% possibility?

Yes. I know you "might" get it. But ask yourself a question. Would you rather spend your time getting six out of ten of the estimates you give, or would you rather get one out of 20? You always "might" get the strange one, but why waste time trying for a few when you can spend the same time getting a bunch.

OK. So, when they say "yes" to being in the process of selling their home, the worst thing you can say is, "Sorry, we don't do that type of work." You just told them you don't want their business, and you just gave your company a "stuck up" reputation. Not good.

Instead, you can say, "I understand that in the process of selling your home, you probably don't want to invest a lot of money for something you can not enjoy yourself, and I am guessing you want a good job for as little money as possible. Am I right?"

They agree, to which you follow up with, "We have an associate company that may be able to take care of you. You see, we focus on high quality materials, high quality labor, and are fully insured. This is very important to our customers who are investing in a home where they plan to stay. Our associate operates on a lower overhead structure and can do a great job for you for a better price. May I contact them for you and have them give you a call?"

I know what you are thinking. Something like, "Wait a darn minute there. What the heck are you doing? Giving my competition my business?"

Yup! Exactly so. Think of it this way. These people will likely get lower bids from your competition anyway and hire them. You have already lost the sale. What you do is this. You call the competition that usually beats your price. You say, "Often I get leads from customers, and I just can't take on the work. When I get them, would it be OK if I tell them to hire you?"

You will most likely hear a pause on the other end of the phone with the recipient in disbelief of what they are hearing. They may ask, "What's the catch?" To which you reply, "I suggest that you price the job however you normally do. When you get your total number, simply put $100 bucks on top of it to give me; that helps me pay for my advertising which brought in the lead in the first place. You only have to give me the $100 if you sell the job. This way, it costs you nothing. What do you say?"

They are delighted and agree to your terms.

Now, the important part. When you are still on the first phone call with the customer, finding out they are selling their home, ask them if it would be alright if you contact Contractor B and give them the information *and* if it would be alright if you call them back in a few weeks to follow up to see if Contractor B is doing a good job for them. You don't want to continue to refer customers to Contractor B if they don't do a good job. The customer will be very appreciative. Then *you* service the customer by contacting the other contractor.

Next phase of this system. When you decide to pass on this project, you call Contractor B and give them the information.

A couple of days go by, and you call back the customer. Ask them if Contractor B contacted them and if they have scheduled work. When they say, "Yes," you then call back Contractor B and say, "Hey, congratulations on getting the Arbuckle project. How did you want to pay the $100?"

Contractor B now knows you are keeping track, and he will be more than happy to pay you for each lead you provide where he gets the job.

What a powerful thing we have just discovered here. What it means is when you *know* you are not going to get the job, pass it to Contractor B and get *paid* for work you didn't do. After all, how much time did it take you to talk with the customer, pass the lead, and follow up. What? Maybe 20 to 30 minutes total? For a $100 bucks? That works out to $200 bucks per hour for passing on work you won't get anyway. What a deal!

Aren't you glad you purchased this book now? My, what value for your book dollar.

OK. On to the next customer screening question:

"Are you getting other prices?

When they tell you "Yes," they are saying they are shopping for prices. Time to get down to the nitty gritty a little early.

A little aside here. Did you know that most people don't like to talk about the money part of business? No, really! It's true.

We all grew up being taught by our parents / guardians that money is something you just don't talk about. Don't beg for it. Don't borrow it. Don't steal it. Don't ask anyone how much they make. Don't ask anyone how much they paid for something. Flat out, just don't you dare talk to anyone about money. It's just plain rude!

OK. That seed planted in our tiny brain has grown up with us. If you don't believe it, just ask yourself, "Hey self, do you ever feel a little uneasy asking for the deposit or final check."

Did you know that most people just prepare an invoice and "slip" it to the customer when they feel there is a lull or break, don't say anything, and rock back and forth on their heels waiting for the customer to pull out the check book. Sound familiar?

It's ok. It's normal.

I say, "Just get over it"!

So, here we are on the phone with a customer who has told us in a round about way that they will be shopping prices. I like to get to the point by asking," Did you have a budget in mind."

Now it gets interesting. Sometimes you hear dead silence. They are thinking, (visualize the balloon thought bubble here), "I don't want to tell them because then they will charge me that much and more." So they say, "Not really. We don't know how much this type of thing costs."

Perfect lead in. You respond, "Let me ask you a few questions for clarification of what you want, and I can give you a ballpark number to see if it fits within your budget." You took the lead. They are comfortable.

I know there are a few of you thinking, "What? He did it again! You *never* give out phone quotes"!

Hold on to those reins a bit. Just stay with me and have an open mind, and I think you will have yet another "wow" moment.

When you get the basic information, you should have a gut feel for an approximate price or price range. Let's say the price range is between $1,000.00 and $1,400.00. *Do not* tell them the low number. If you tell them the range, they only hear the low number, and if it comes out higher, they get upset. So you tell them, "It may be as much as $1,400.00 *or less* depending on the actual conditions of this project. We will know better when we discuss all the particulars of what you want. Does this fit in your budget?"

This is where you may hear the words, "Oh, my gosh! I didn't think it was that much"!

To which you respond, "I gather you are on a tight budget and we can certainly understand that. We do have an associate (you know what's coming, don't you?). Their name is Company B. Can I contact them for you and have them evaluate this project. They may be able to save you some money and fit your budget?"

You just avoided wasting a ton of time to hear those "Oh, my gosh!" words again.

Next question...

"When are you looking to get the work done?"

This is strictly to see if their expectations are sooner than you can provide. If they say, "We have an event this Saturday and need it done by then." You know in your heart that your schedule just can't handle it. You can let them know your schedule is full but would it be alright if you pass the information to your associate Company B, and there you go with another $100 bucks in your pocket.

That sounds a lot better than scheduling an appointment, taking a ton of time only to find out you can't meet their schedule, doesn't it?

Next question, please.

"What spurred you to call our company (why are you getting the work done)?"

This is where we hear all kinds of cool stuff. Let's say your customer says, "Well, we had some damage done, and we need to get some price quotes for our insurance company."

Ever hear this? Bet you have.

What does this really mean? Sorry to say, but quite often it means they want to get three price quotes and they want them *all* to be high. They submit them to the insurance company who in turn gives the customer a check. The customer keeps the check and does the work themselves. No work for you. Surprised? You shouldn't be.

What I like to do in this case is say, "Great. We can schedule a time to visit to come up with an estimate for you. We only charge $200 for estimates, but don't worry. When you hire us, the $200 is deducted from the overall price, thus the estimate will be free. We will need the estimate check ready when we arrive to do the estimate."

Usually, they will hang up the phone. No problem. You're done.

Option B. Remember Company B. You may want to shoot it his way, and who knows, they may submit the high bids, take the low bid, you lose either way, but Company B may not.

Next very interesting question.

"Have you ever hired this type of work done before?"

I like this because it lets me know if they have a clue what your service costs.

If they say they have never hired this type of service, we may want to go back to the question "Are you getting other prices" and give them the good 'ol ball park price routine.

If they say they have hired it out before, you can inquire as to who they used and why they are not using them this time around.

It is interesting how you can glean out, or sometimes out-right get the information that they will probably use the other guy, they just want to check the other guy's price to make sure it is fair.

This is where you can go into the "estimates cost $200" routine, as described earlier.

Either way, sometimes this question will give you the definite impression that they are not really serious in hiring you, and you once again didn't waste time with a most likely "no" customer.

Another great question.

"If you have hired someone else, who was it?"

Good benefit to this question. If they say, "Yeah, I used Company B before." You know they are expecting prices similar to Company B. You can proceed to the next question.

If on the other hand they mention a few companies that are similar to yours in professionalism and price, you know you have a good chance of getting the work and can consider the customer a good lead.

Next question:

"Why aren't you using them (the past service company) this time?"

Most likely they will say, "They went out of business."

Hint here. If the previous company went out of business, it is because they were not making enough money. They didn't make money because they didn't charge enough, just like we talked about in the first book of this Guaranteed Profit System series. Remember, 80% of businesses go out of business within the first five years. Number one reason, they don't charge enough. Why? They match the competition price. The competition? Goes out of business 80% of the time. See the circle here?

Anyway, what it means for sifting out customers is that the caller "may" be expecting similar prices and now is a good time to go into the "do you have a budget" routine as explained above.

Final Question.

"Where is the work location?"

Wouldn't it be lovely to know that they want you to travel over 100 miles *before* you set the appointment?

This would involve travel time and perhaps even per-diem charges. Just a hint so you can clue them in on the extra charge prior to driving forever to give a price and then end up not getting the work because they tell you, "We wanted to hire someone local and save the travel charges."

Whew! Lots of screening questions. Lot's more time involved than just jotting down their information and scheduling an appointment.

Beneficial? You betcha.

Just remember, the time you take on the phone will save you tons of wasted time scheduling appointments, preparing your estimate, only to hear the words "No thanks." This way you can hear it in advance and even make money by using the "Company B" system.

Way cool stuff there.

OK. Retailers. Wake up now! Time to talk about sifting and screening your customers for higher sales.

For Retailers, things are a lot different. Your customers will not use the phone. They will use their car to come to your place of business and look at your goods. Some of your screening can be done when the customer walks in to your store.

Let's start with the walk-in greeting.

Wait! Just a tid-bit of information. We all have this "thing" about strangers. Our parents taught us about strangers. If you have children, you probably taught them about strangers. What we heard is, "Don't talk to strangers. Strangers can be bad. If a stranger walks up to you, run away screaming." Etc.

This training sticks with us into our adult life. No, really. Just think about it. You have ten people who walk into an elevator. How many words are spoken? Right! Very few. We all stand there like statues looking at the light change from floor to floor. Heck, we don't even make eye contact.

How does this apply to business? Well, in the retail business, almost all of your customers are strangers, and you have this hidden thing going on that tells you, "Leave them alone. If they want something, they will ask." So we just let them be.

This is where the first type of screening kicks in. Instead of waiting for them to come to you, get in there and be pro-active. You go up to them, and after a typical greeting ("Good morning and welcome to our store"), say stuff like:

"Is this your first time here?"
"Do you live in this neighborhood?"
"Did you come here looking for a particular item?"
"How did you hear about us?"
"Would it be alright if I show you one of our new items?"

Note: I left out the ever so common question, "Can I help you?" This is the question that leaves your customer feeling that you are saying, "Let's get down to business and be done with it." Now, if you are very busy, then fine. Your customers will respect that. But, if you are slow, then give your customers more personal attention.

Really. People like attention. Some people more than others. Some people will soak in all the attention you can muster up.

Before we analyze the above questions, just one more thing to think about. When you ask a question, listen and look for your customer's body language or tone of voice when they answer. They may answer quickly and with a short tone. This is them screaming at you, "Leave me alone." They don't like anyone talking to them for fear of the "pushy salesman" experience. Then you can just go to the typical question, "Can I help you find something?" Or, you can say, "If you need anything, just let me know." I like the last one better. It says to your customer, "Ok. I respect your space. Live long and prosper." They feel good now.

If, on the other hand, they embrace your question with enthusiasm, you will get the feeling that these people are OK talking with you and would really enjoy your help in getting to know your products. That's when you give them all the attention they want. Make them feel you care (which you really do), and you will have long lasting repeat customers.

Alrighty then. Let's break down the above questions for retailers and see how we can glean some valuable information that will help you get more sales.

First question.

"Is this your first time here?"

This question will let you know if your customer is familiar with your product. They may answer, "Oh, yes, we come here all the time." At which point, they are telling you they already know what you have to offer. If they say, "No. This is our first time here", *and* they hold their interest on you. They are saying, "Show me what ya got." The freebees are really cool here. When most people get something for free, they feel "treated" and will want to come back.
By the way… Does the item you give away cause you to lose money? Not if you read the first book. We talked about how to track your "promo" items and how to put it in the budget. Your budget is used in calculating your prices so in effect, all customers are contributing a penny or so to help you pay for the promo items you give away. Yes, that's right. It's free when you plan and budget for it. More cool stuff.

Next:

"Do you live in this neighborhood?"

This will let you know how far people drive to come to your store. The farther away they live, the more you want to make sure they have a great experience in your store so they will tell their friends, and so on, and so on, and so on.

Same thing if they live around the corner. You can greet them with, "It's great to see you here. Did you know we have daily specials?" Note that with the close people we can say things that will get them coming back more frequently. After all, it's easy for them because they live close. If they live farther away, you can ask if they would like to receive an email or direct mail when you have a special sale event.

Just think about what might attract a person who lives close to your store compared to the person who lives farther away, and then, you can focus your conversation on what would attract them. Savvy?

Next up:

"Did you come here looking for a particular item?"

This is great because it lets you know if the customer just wants to browse around, be left alone, or if they saw an advertisement and came for a specific reason. If they came for a specific product, you have a probable sale and the opportunity to suggest other items for additional sales. In other words, your time is well spent getting to know this customer and helping them find what they want while telling them about similar things they may not know about.

If a person says, "No, I'm just looking around," I would think of this person as a one shot deal. To make sure you don't just abandon them, you could say, "Would you like me to give you a quick tour or our store?" If they say "No" again, then you know it's time to back off with a statement like, "Great. If I can help you, just let me know. I'll be over there." If they do accept your tour offer, then you know they are really more interested in your products and are not there just to kill time and satisfy their curiosity.

Next question.

"How did you hear about us?"

This is a good question because it will let you know if they were referred from one of your other customers. When people come from a referral, they are there to buy something. Their friend told them about something, and this customer wants one too. They are ready for and want your help. Time well spent. Good time to suggest other items for additional sales.

If they respond with, "Oh, I just saw your store while I was waiting for my husband to get his stuff at the hardware store across the street." This may be an indication they are just killing time, so back off and give them their space. Keep 'em comfortable.

I really like this next question:

"Would it be alright if I show you one of our new items?"

When they say, "Sure." They are screaming at you they are wide open to buy a bunch of stuff. Time well spent.

If you get the negative, "No, that's OK. I just want to look around." this again is a "back off" signal.

OK now. With all the customer screening questions, can you see a common theme? Yes. This is very similar to the Servicers world. The first purpose is to identify what your customer wants, so you can give them what they want. It could be your product, or it could be just to be left alone. You must make them feel comfortable.

The other purpose is to make the best use of your time. Just like the Servicer who does not want to take hours preparing an estimate for someone who will most likely say "No" anyway, you don't want to take a lot of time with a customer who will most likely not buy anything. Screening will help you make best use of your time, so you are giving attention to those who will buy over those who will not buy.

Now, I 'm not saying to ignore someone who is not going to buy something. They may and most likely will buy something later. The timing may not be right. This is where I leave it to your good judgment.

On to the other type of screening. Psychological screening.

We all seem to know this but many forget to apply it in business.

You know. It's when you go to the grocery store to get a commonly needed item. Like a gallon of milk. Where is the milk? Right. In the very back of the store. Why? We all know they do that so you will walk past other items and see the cookies, crackers, chips, dip and other "yummy" impulse buy items. It is very rare that people leave with only the milk.

If they would only put the milk right by the cash register, I could get in and out without spending more money. Good for me (probably more healthy for me), but noooooo. They make me walk all the way past those other items that automatically leap off the shelf into my shopping cart.

This is the other type of screening. You need to identify the items you sell that are impulse items. For example. If you own a guitar store, the guitars are on the back wall. You have a rack of guitar strings they have to walk past to get to the guitars. " Oh, yeah, I need to re-string my guitar." Bam! A sale is made. On the counter where they check out, there is the new Intele-tuner which tunes a guitar based on vibration instead of microphone pickup. On sale for only $39 bucks. Bam! 'Nuther sale. Guitar straps with the new side cut profile. Bam! New "mar free" guitar stand. Bam! And on we go.

Just take a moment to look at your store. Do customers go directly to your feature item, or do you have a bunch of cool stuff related to the feature item? Give it some thought, and let that type of screening take place.

Why do I call this screening? When your customer walks in the store, watch them. See if they are sucked in like an invisible magnet is pulling them toward a specific item. You now know what holds their interest. They may see the impulse item but the more impressive and expensive similar item is not so easily found. You have the upper hand. You know what to say and what to offer. You can show them the "wow" item and Bam! You just got additional sales.

OK. Any Questions?

Yes. This person sitting in the front row reading this book. What is your question?

"When a person asked to be left alone, how do you know they are not just casing out the joint, or they may be a shoplifter?"

Great question. Thanks.

This is actually a very important part of the "screening" process. When you talk with someone, you will get that gut feel. When or if you get *any* type of feeling that this person may be interested in shoplifting or that they are up to no good, that is when you stay with them. Even if they ask to be left alone. Back off but stay within ½ isle from them, letting them know you are watching them. If they look at you, just say, "If you need anything, I'll be right here." This makes a potential shoplifter nervous, and they will leave, most likely not to return.

Also, it's never a bad idea to get those security cameras. They have a fake set you can get for about $39 bucks each. They mount high and pan side to side to give the impression your store is under constant surveillance. Also, post signs in areas where shoplifting is most likely to occur that say, "Smile, you're on camera. Shoplifters will be prosecuted to the fullest extent of the law," or something similar. This will not offend the typical shopper but will send the message to the amateur and prevent a lot of potential loss.

Any other questions?

No? Great. Let's move on to the next chapter then. Shall we?

Open The Door and Bring 'Em In: Chapter Five
The Word According to You

Advertising! The starting point to all sales.

What we are about to discuss now pertains to both Servicers and Retailers.

We all know that advertising is getting the word out to your customers. But there is a whole bunch of stuff about advertising that many people do not realize. I learned the hard way.

Let me give you my quick story.

I invented something back in the 70's. It was to deal with the situation where a doorknob punches through a wall. The typical repair was to patch it with a piece of drywall, only to have someone punch it back out next time the door swung open. You reinforce it with a piece of wood, but this takes time, costs about $100 bucks to have a professional painter do it. The answer I came up with was a piece of heavy-duty plastic a little larger that a light switch plate with a piece of soft rubber in the center. On the back you have four wide strips of double-sided, self-adhesive, thin, high-tack tape. You peel off the protective strip from the tape and stick it over the hole. Yer done!

Great idea. I thought I would make up a bunch of these things and sell 'em. I had a friend who knew plastics, forms, adhesives, etc. I put together what I thought was a great advertising piece. I did a bunch of work trying to learn how to get the product picked up by a plastic manufacturer for mass production and marketing.

Well, I was an amateur. It flopped. I spent a bunch of money. Lost a bunch of money. And I learned my lesson. By the way, someone else came out with the same idea about two years later, and it made a bunch of hardware magazines. I hope they did well.

Next time around for me was with my software for painting contractors (Eagle Bid). I decided I was not an expert at advertising and I couldn't afford to lose a bunch of money again, so I hired a professional advertising company. I ask them how much they would charge to help me with the advertising. They said about $3,500. I asked how much if they taught me what they were doing as we went along. They said $8,000. I said, "OK." It was worth every penny, and I learned a bunch of stuff that blew my mind.

The first thing they taught me is that advertising is done in phases. The first phase is the brainstorm phase.

The consultant, his assistant, and another associate of mine who I felt knew something about my business, and I all sat down together.

The idea was to toss out names for the product, and to toss out advertising ideas and questions. Such as, what would the advertisement say? What would the pictures be? What would be the tag line? Stuff like that.

We all started out with some typical stuff, some serious stuff and a little bit of humor. As time went on, we started getting down right silly, crass, gross, and the party escalated. We actually were having a blast.

The consultant assistant was writing down everything that was said. I mean everything. Even the extremely stupid stuff.

At the next session (when we were back to normal), we went over everything that was said and gleaned out some pretty good stuff. Some of the stuff came from when we were being down right silly.

We decided to go with a cartoon format since the advertising was to be done for a magazine. We thought, when people read a magazine, what item always catches their eye? Well, obviously, the cartoons do. They just suck us in because we all like to chuckle once in a while.

We came up with a painter sitting in front of his desk which was made from a door sitting on a couple of 5 gallon buckets. He was in blue jeans, t-shirt, unshaven, pencil behind the ear, pictures hanging crooked on the wall, you get the idea. The caption said, "Don't laugh. His profits are way up."

The name for the product was "Eagle Bid." Why? Because lots of people have seen a picture of an eagle head on lots of things. It's familiar. US Post office for one.

It was amazing to me. I had people call me up when we first launched the software ad. It had only been on the market for a couple of weeks, but people would call and say, "I saw your ad in the magazine. I think I have seen you for several years now, and I thought I would like to get the demo disk now and take a closer look."

Funny? You bet. I found it very interesting that just from the eagle head icon and name Eagle Bid, people thought it had been around for a while because it was familiar. Effective advertising. You bet. Success with the sale of this software? You bet. It is still being sold today.

So. Let's break this down a little more to help you with your advertising.

Phase one is your brainstorm session. Gather a bunch of friends and ask them to come up with ideas on what they think would be a good advertising piece for your company.

Write down everything that was said. You can let everyone know it's ok to get silly and come up with anything that crosses their mind whether it be stupid, gross, or whatever.

In the back of your mind, please try to remember. One of the biggest mistakes people make in the advertising arena is that they build the advertisement around what *you*, the business owner, wants to say. We forget to focus on what your customers want.

Example: Go to the yellow pages and take a look at any page, almost any ad. These ads were mostly done by the business owner. What is the biggest thing you see? Right! The company name. A brief list of services or products. Words like "Free estimates" and "discount prices."

Really, now. Does your customer really care what the company name is? If I am looking for a carpet installer, and my home is worth over a million bucks, I want someone who will be careful with my valuables. Someone who can be trusted. Someone who can work with *my* schedule instead of making me wait "between 8:00 AM and 1:00 PM for an appointment," for which they don't show up and, instead, they call to say they are running late. I just wasted a full day waiting for an appointment. You know what I'm talking about.

So, we shift our advertisement away from what *you* want to say, and shift it toward what *the potential customer* wants to hear.

Instead of saying, "*My company* offers this, that and the other thing, call for a free estimate." I would say, "Making *your* home look and feel more elegant."

See the difference. OK. Keep that in mind for *everything* related to advertising, and you will do much better.

Moving on. Now that phase one of your advertising campaign is done and you have a bunch of stuff written on several pieces of paper, phase two is to determine exactly what format of advertising you want to prepare and how it is going to be marketed.

Side note here. You may have noticed there is a distinct difference between advertising and marketing. Advertising is the piece of paper or item your customers see. Marketing is the method you use to get your advertisement in front of your customers. At the moment, we're just talking about the advertisement piece. We will move on to marketing in the next couple of chapters, so hang in there.

Let's take a look at some of the different formats you can choose from. We have:

Flyer: This can be used as a direct mail piece, a poster on bulletin board, a flyer stuck on a window or post, or a countertop piece.

Direct Mailer: This is usually done on card stock on a size acceptable to the post office as a post card mailer (better mailing rates).

Street sign: For the Servicers, a sign you can leave in the front yard of your project while you are working there. Beware, some communities don't allow for it. For Retailers, a sign out in front of your store on the sidewalk or visible to people driving by. Some people purchase an old van and paint it up, leave it parked in a parking stall visible to drivers.

Brochure: This can be used to give to your customers giving them information about your service or products. The purpose is *not* to sell them. It's to introduce them to what you offer. The actual sell comes later. A big problem people have with brochures is they get extremely wordy. Lots of words, no pictures. More pictures, please.

Portfolio: This can be used to submit prices, show menus for a restaurant, give more detailed information about your company to a serious potential customer, etc.

Business Cards: We don't need to spend a ton of money on expensive business cards. In some cases you can make your own. In others, you can have a nice business card done relatively inexpensively. Just remember, the purpose of a business card is to give your customers your company name, address, phone number and license number (if required in your state). It also gives an instant image. We like it to be more professional. That's about it. It is not a portable billboard. Some people just cram a whole bunch of stuff on a business card, thinking the business card will sell their product. Save the sales for the proper time. The business card is just a source of contact information. Keep it simple. Keep it professional looking. This is where "less is more" comes into play. The less extra stuff you have on it, the more professional it looks.

Vehicle Signs: Your rolling billboard. You would be surprised how many companies tell me a lot of their business comes from someone saying they saw their van. This is very effective. Make sure they can instantly get *what* you do and a phone number. The mistake is people put their company name big and service or product small. If you see a van that says, "Bob Johnson Services," you don't have a clue what they do, and you don't have enough time to get it. If on the other hand, it said in big bold letters, "Office Furniture Moving," and in small letters it said "Bob Johnson Services," then back to big letters the phone number, you now have a much more effective vehicle sign. Note the focus is *not* on what *not* want to tell them but on what will interest *the customer*.

Internet: By far the most widely used form of advertising. Most of the businesses I have consulted tell me most of their business comes from the Internet. Most people have stopped using that thick telephone book. Heck, I don't even have one in my house. Most people have now learned that if they want anything, they can just go to the Internet, go to their favorite search engine, type in what they want followed by their city name, and bingo. Up on screen comes what they are looking for. Sometimes even a map showing the locations of their different choices.

I always like to click on the business that has a website. I get lots of great information and usually end up being pre-sold before I even jump in my car and go there.

Not to worry about the Internet. If you need help in that area, please give us a call. We have Excellent resources (very affordable) for design, hosting and even web site maintenance that will help keep your website on or near the top. Contact information can be found at the end of this book.

For your company, you can decide which of the above items you would like to use.

Once you have decided what to use, then you can start on the budget thing we talked about in the first book in this Guaranteed Profit System series. The budget will help you evaluate the expense and hopefully estimate the best use and benefit for your advertising dollar.

Next. Phase three. Understanding what makes a good advertising piece and applying it to your advertising item.

We have already given the first and most important part of making a good advertising piece. That is, focus it on what the customer wants. We don't need to pound that in any more.

An equally important aspect of advertising is remembering that the typical, average, normal person's thinking level. It works like this.

When you are reading this book, your mind has shifted into "college level thinking." Your brain is turned on. You are focused. But even with the mind turned on and focused, the average mind will only remember 30 percent of what it gathers the first time around. That is why it's a good idea to re-read this book. It will help you remember a whole bunch more.

It's like watching a movie for the second time around. You always catch stuff you didn't see before.

Moving on. If you take that same individual whose mind is turned on reading a book, and put them, oh, say, in a car, does their average thinking level decrease?

I can hear some of you laughing out there because you know it's true. Fact is, the average person, when they go into "coast" mode (driving or watching TV), their thinking level drops to that of an eight year old. Yes, about a third grade level.

Now, if you have a hard time buying this, just look at any TV commercial. You know. The one with the frog with his tongue stuck to the beer truck bouncing down the highway? You've seen it. That type of stuff is effective because it entertains the mind of a third grader. If you turned on your college level thinking, would that still be funny? I doubt it. You would most likely call it stupid.

Your customers do not walk around, drive around, or sit around thinking at college level. They are most often in coast mode, which means they are thinking at a third grade level.
If you want to get their attention, you have to entertain or attract the third grader in them. Good Example: "Have fun taking pictures. Great pictures every time with our easy to use digital camera." Can you see how even an eight year old would be tugging on mommy's skirt saying, "Can I have one? Please. Oh, Please."

Bad Example: "Introducing our new technology, high definition, auto-focus digital camera featuring automatic multifunction photographic color balance" and on and on we go.

See the difference. Here again, we as business owners get caught up on all the neat stuff we have, and we forget the customer's viewpoint.

So, keep your advertisement simple, to the point, attractive to third grade level thinking, with lots of pictures, if possible. Remember, the main focus is to attract the customer *to* your business. We are *not* at the point of selling them. We do that when they arrive at our business (Retailers) or when we meet them for an estimate (Servicers).

On to phase four. The layout and design.

Here are a few hot tips that will help you generate a great advertising piece.

First on the list is color. Most people know the best eye catching colors are yellow and red. I'm not saying to make your entire advertisement red or yellow, but instead, if you have a featured, eye-catching item on your advertisement piece, these colors work best. Enough said on that. Pretty easy.

Next on the list is placement. While most people think of things in squares, your ad can really stand out if you think outside the box. Just a quick example. If you have an ad that has a box line around it, most people just stuff things inside that box without having anything to break it up. Something like this:

Our Service Company	(800) 555-1212

Offering quality service since 1970 ; We offer:
    This thing here
    That thing there
    This other thing here
    And of course this thing
        Call for a free estimate.	

Note again, this company is focused on what they want to tell the customer. Let's just change it up a bit and say the same thing differently only with a little more flair and focus on what the customer wants. It may look something like this:

Spring Cleaning!
Yuck!

Let us:
Make it easy for you by doing this thing here
You don't have to do that thing there either
We also can do this other thing here for you
And of course this thing really saves you time.

Call: Our Company (800) 697-5413

Use the yellow color inside the circle and whatever color you want inside the box area.

See the difference. Placement of boxes, circles, text, etc. all make a huge difference in both eye appeal and effectiveness. Also, notice the company name and phone number are the last thing on the ad. What comes first is what the customer wants.

Next on the list. Forget the page folds

If you are preparing a tri-fold brochure, here again we get stuck inside the box. Really. Take a look at almost all the tri-fold brochures that are out there. You open it up and there are three columns of information. Everyone stays within the column. It looks far better, more professional and has less limitations for your message and content.

Here's an example of what I mean. The lines in the middle of the page running perpendicular represents the paper fold. You can see how I have ignored them and just used the whole page as my canvas. Take a look:

Words words words
Blah blah blah blah blah

More words here…
Blah blah blah

Our Company Name (800) 555-1212

Unlimiting and very effective. Also note, lots of pictures, less words. Remember, the third grader likes pictures and doesn't like to read lots of big words.

Now. For the most important thing… Content! Ta Da!!! (Trumpet sounding off)

There are five basic elements of content. We will list them in order:

1. The Grabber: It does just what it suggests. Its purpose is to grab the attention of the reader. Like the example on the previous page, the grabber was "Spring Cleaning... Yuck!." It got their attention; now they want to read more. A grabber can also be a picture. Example: If you are providing computer training, you can take a picture of an open laptop computer with a guy sitting in front of it with his elbows resting on the table and his hands holding his head. The picture alone shows frustration with computers and works well as a grabber. Summary of the grabber: To get a person's attention and get them to want to read more. This applies to *all* of your advertising items. Yes. Even your vehicle sign. Take a look at what you now have and see if you can do something to enhance attraction.

2. The Funnel: Now that you have their attention, you need to get them thinking about your products or service. One great example (and I am *not* suggesting you use this). I had one client that had an ad in the newspaper that said:
Get ready... this is a little bit of a shocker.
SEX & MONEY!   This is the grabber.

We can't help you with the sex,   This is the funnel.
But we can save you lots of money... etc.

Great example, isn't it. I think you get the idea from this sample. The main point is to get them *out of* the third grade thinking mode and turn on their college level brain so they can get your message.

Take a look at your advertisement and see if you have a smooth funnel. If not, you may want to work on it a bit. It will help transition your customers to your message, and you won't lose them by attempting to get right into the subject matter.

3. The Body: This is where you get to give them your main message. Remember, you are still entertaining a mind that is not turned on to college level thinking so keep everything simple and to the point.

Examples: A. "Summer Sale, 50% off most items." Or:
        B. "Color consulting."

Bad Examples: A. "Great savings on t-shirts, pants, swim suits, underwear, shoes, socks... blah, blah, blah...."
            B. "We help you select the right color for your project using our color wheel and photos to help you get a clear picture of what you want... blah, blah, blah."

Just remember, the purpose of the brochure or most advertising pieces is to give your customers an idea of your products or service. You get *far* more sales when your customers call or come to you, so don't try to make your advertising piece "sell" the item for you. The sales come later when you have them live and in color in front of you.

4. Contact Information: Ok, now you have their interest. How do they get your product or service? This is the generic part of the advertisement. If you are a retail place, and people need to find you, a good idea would be to put a quick and easy map showing major cross streets. Or, you can say "In the Alderwood Mall."

Don't forget to make your website easy to remember. Check into different URL addresses. Example: If your product is "dishes," then check the web to see if the URL www.dishesforyou.com is available. Too often I see companies that have websites that are almost impossible to find. Like: www.rrodreserviceco.net. Let's face it. No one will remember that one.

Make sure your phone number is easily found and easily readable from a distance. Just common sense actually.

Finally…

5. The Tag: This is the final statement on your advertisement. We have two types of tags. One is suggestive and the other is pro-active.

Suggestive tag would be your slogan. Something like, "We know what you want. We have what you need." Hey! I like that. I think I'll use that on my web site. Oh. Already did.

The pro-active tag would be something like: "Call during the month of May for $25 off any order."
Can you see why that is pro-active? It makes the reader want to call you right now because if they wait, they will miss out on the $25 offer.

Which one to use? Good question.

I have to leave that up to your judgment. As a general rule, if you have a seasonal business or a product that you want to greatly reduce stock, then you would use the proactive method to encourage them to purchase now.

If, on the other hand, you have a business similar to a restaurant, the suggestive tag would be more effective. Its purpose is to put something in their mind that they will remember and recognize so that the next time they want to go out and eat, they remember your slogan, "When you want something uniquely delicious…"

OK. I think you get the main idea of the key elements of putting together a good advertising piece.

One final thing you will always want to do. When you have your advertising piece mostly done, it is a great idea to have everyone you know take a look at it. *Do not* tell them this is something you came up with, or it is your design. People don't like to criticize *your* work but they are happy to tell you the truth about someone else's work because they are not there to hear it. Let them know, "This is an ad that was presented to me. I don't want to say anything good or bad about it. I want to get your honest opinion. What do you think?"

Separate the fact that you did the design, layout or text. Listen to what they say because they are *not* experts in your business. They *are* expert customers and their opinion counts. That's why you get lots of people to look at it. Go with what most people say. This will greatly help you fine-tune the final piece.

So much for Advertising. Now that you have this magnificent piece of advertising work in front of you, how do you get the word out to your customers?

That, my friend, is the next chapter.

Open The Door and Bring 'Em In: Chapter Six
This is a Test… This is Only a Test

Can you guess from the chapter title that this chapter will be about marketing? Well, it's actually about test marketing, but that's close enough. I just like the catchy title. Hope you do too.

Marketing venues are pretty much the same for Servicers and Retailers. Actually, all the marketing venues we discuss can be used in both markets. The only difference is their effectiveness, which you will be able to determine at the end of this chapter.

Let's just jump in here by mentioning the various things you can consider.

Typically, it would all start with your budget. What can you afford? If you have read our first book in this series, you would already know that your customers will pay for the advertising as long as it is in your budget AND you use your budget to assist in your pricing.

There is that thing called, "going too far," though. You can over extend yourself with too much money spent on marketing, while not allowing time for your advertising to work for you. Example: You decide to do everything we suggest. Costs a ton of money. You get a loan. Marketing doesn't work as fast as you want. Sales don't come in as much as you need. Poof! You're out of business.

So, let's go through some things, and you will see there is a bunch of stuff you can do that costs very little money. We'll have a little fun here. After each thing I mention, there will be a few words behind the item. They will be, "Great, Good, Average, Not So Good, and Bad." We will also have a second line with the words, "Expensive, Somewhat costly, Inexpensive, and Almost Free." Your mission is to circle one word in each line that best represents your immediate feeling about the marketing idea. Make sure you circle your impression *before* you read our comments about it. After you read about it, you can go back and see if you changed your mind.

Here they are:

A. Direct Mailer:

Great	Good	Average	Not So Good	Bad
Expensive		Somewhat Costly	Inexpensive	Almost Free

Did you circle one word on each line indicating your initial response? Cool…

Here are some facts about direct mail.

Approximately 65% of all direct mail sees the inside of a trash can instead of seeing the eyes of the intended reader. Guilty! I am one of those.

Another fact. Of those who *do* look at all pieces of mail they get, 90% will see what it is, think "same old thing" or "another advertisement, seen enough of them." And then it hits the trash without being opened. This works out so that approximately only three out of a hundred people will actually open your direct mail piece or take time to read it long enough to find out what you are advertising.

Another fact. Just because people see your ad does not mean they will automatically purchase from you. The average *response* from a direct mailer is about one out of a thousand purchasing because of the ad. That is actually considered pretty good.

These are "average" statistics, but just because they are average doesn't mean we have to do "average" direct mail. After all, direct mail is really expensive to pay for printing, postage, bag, tag, sort and handling fees. Average piece can cost about $.40 cents each (printing expense and all). For 1000 to be mailed would cost $400.00 spend for one sale. If your item is $10,000.00 that may be a good thing. If your item is $200.00, you lost money.

Just a side note here. I hear it all the time from my clients. They say, "If I spend $2,000 for this advertisement, I only need one sale for $2,000 to break even."

Wrongo! Remember, your advertising budget may represent (in a very aggressive advertising budget) 10% of your income. That means, every $1,000 spent should bring in $10,000 of business. Anything less, you're losing money. So those are some things to consider before you jump into a direct bulk mail type of marketing.

If you are smart (as we all know you are), you can learn about this thing called "demographics." When you send a mail piece, you want it to go to only your prime target customers. Example: If you are a house painter, you do not want your mailer to go to people who live in apartments. You don't want people who have houses that are only worth $50K or less. You don't want people who make less than $xx,000 per year because they won't have money for that type of thing. Get the drift?

With demographics, you can ask almost any address database service (the people where you can purchase a mailing list) to provide you with specific demographics. With our painter above, he may say, "I want only people in the 76000 zip code area who make over $100,000 per year who have homes worth $200,000 or more and who are between the ages of 30 to 55. Exclude everyone else." Your chances of succeeding with your direct mail just got better.

Let's take direct mail to the next level. You have past customers who already have said yes to your product or service. They will be highly likely to purchase from you again. This is where you can do your own in-house direct mailing. Make your advertising piece and mail to your customers to keep you fresh in their mind. Even if they are not ready to purchase from you again at this point in time, they may know of someone who is looking for your product or service. This type of direct mail is far less expensive and far more effective.

Summary: Direct mail could be Very Expensive and give Bad Results with just a blanket, bulk mail campaign. It could be Somewhat Expensive by hitting only your target market (demographics) with Slightly Better Results, or it could be Inexpensive with Average Results when you focus on past customers.

Want to guess which one I like best? (Hint. Least money, best results).

Right! Next we have: . Newspaper Ad:

Great	Good	Average	Not So Good	Bad
Expensive		Somewhat Costly	Inexpensive	Almost Free

Let's face it. People do not go to the newspaper to look for products or services. They go there for the news, sports, or (my inner child) the comics. If people are really looking to purchase items or services, they will go to the Internet or Yellow Pages or a friend who just bought a similar product or service.

So, let's shed a new light on this. Each newspaper has a staff of people whose job it is to write articles each and every day. That's what the main purpose of a newspaper really is. To give the reader something to read.

Now. Visualize this writer sitting in their office each morning thinking, "What the heck am I going to write about today?" All of a sudden, their fax machine goes off, or their computer goes, "Bing" with a new email. It's a (dramatic build up here) *Press Release.* "Cool… Here's something I may be able to use," they say. They get all excited (well, maybe. That depends on the press release content).

That, my friend is where you can get some huge exposure for your business. You go through the paper and find the section that would best apply to your business. Example. If you have a chocolate store, your section would be in fine dining, or the food section. For our painting company, that would be the home improvement section. For the resume preparation company, perhaps the education section or employment section. Not so hard so far.

Next, you simply look at the name of the person who wrote the article. Usually, you can go on line and type in the newspaper name and the writer's name and you may go directly to the right spot where you can extract a phone number, fax number, and/or even email address. Bingo. You have the contact information. You can also call the chief editor and ask to whom you would send a press release for a specific department.

Now the seemingly hard part, but really the easy part. You get to write the press release.

Start by reading other articles and get a flavor for the writing style of the person who writes articles for the particular department you are interested in. Some may be obviously flaring, such as "Announcing the grand opening of one of the finest restaurants ever to hit planet Earth…" Or, they may have a more subtle tone such as, "Arlington has a new restaurant that features… etc." When you get a feel for their writing style you can apply the same tone to your press release and make it more easily acceptable by the writer.

Now, I know it seems awkward to think that you could actually write an article, but really. It's no big deal. After all, look at my writing style. English majors all over the country are grinding their teeth every time they see my work, but hey, I have a bunch of books out there and have gotten hundreds of press releases published. 'Taint no big deal.

All you need to do is sit down and write about something as if you were explaining it to a new employee.

Example: For a roof cleaning company, their newspaper section would be in home improvement. The focus would be for the reader's benefit, so you would focus on explaining how a homeowner would go about cleaning a roof and why? Your press release could read like this:

"If you have a wood shake roof on your house, you may not be aware that this type of roof can last up to 50 years when properly maintained. The sad thing is, most people replace these beautiful roofs after only 20 years or less. Here are some things you can do to greatly extend the life of your roof. First, go and rent a pressure washer from your local equipment rental store. You want one that will put out at least 2500 psi. Most may come with what is known as a "flat tip." If you can get a "roto tip" it will make the job much quicker and easier. …"

Good stuff so far! Make sure you throw in some stuff that let's the customer feel they may not want to do this work. Stuff like, "Remember, steeper pitch roofs can be very slippery, so be careful when walking around up there. You may even want to rent a safety harness just in case."

At this point the wife is thinking, "NO WAY! My hubby is not getting up there. Maybe we need to hire someone to do it." Ka-ching! The sale bell goes off.

For the retailer. An example would be in the food section of the newspaper for a candy store. A press release may read, "We have just discovered a new form of chocolate truffle which is imported from France. La-Truffe uses a unique chocolate that is somewhere between the light chocolate and dark chocolate we are used to. They dust it with a very light chocolate powder, which melts instantly upon contact with your tongue. This mouth watering delight is hard to find, but definitely worth your search… etc."

The important thing for a press release is this. The newspaper writer does not want to flat out give you free advertising. Every one of your competitors would want and expect the same. The writer wants *good information* that will either entertain or inform their readers. Thus, your focus is *not* on your company, but instead on the features or education about your product or service.

Here's the plug for you. At the end of the article, add, "for free (or more) information about this (item or service), call Your Name at Your Company (800) 555-1212.

Typically, a writer does not want a ton of readers calling them with a bunch of questions. They want to pass those questions on to you, so they will most likely print you at the end as a plug for you and a release for them.

Another hint. Anytime you send a press release, you need to send a bunch of pictures.

Does this really work? Good question from yet another reader of this book.

Let me just say this. We had a company we consulted with that did exactly this. They were a new business opening up in town. It went for about two months with nothing being done. Then, one of the family members called up the owner and said, "Hey, I really like your ad in the newspaper. That must have cost you a fortune."

The owner went to the newspaper in the social section and saw a full page, full color article about their company. The phone started ringing more, and the business had a huge jump-start. Sure it works. All you have to do is put forth the effort. It's better than doing nothing and getting nothing. Right?

We had another client who got a call from the newspaper editor who wanted to set up an interview, come to their place of business, take photos and do a feature article on them. Happens all the time.

One final tip on press release. Use this format:

At the top of the page:	Press Release
Next:	Contact Info. (your name, address, phone, email, fax, website… etc)
Next type:	Article: (then just jump into your article content).
At the bottom:	End - 30 -

The – 30 – at the bottom is understood by many writers as a code that lets them know they can use your press release however they want. They can edit it, change it, use it whenever they want. Don't be surprised if they call you for a phone interview or to get more information.

Evaluation of newspaper marketing:

If you do it like everyone else and pay for an ad, it is very expensive with not very good results.

When you write the press release, it can be almost free with huge results. Cool huh?

Next up on the list of marketing stuff:

C. Trade Publications / Magazines:

Great	Good	Average		Not So Good	Bad
Expensive		Somewhat Costly		Inexpensive	Almost Free

First let's define what we mean by trade publications. I'm guessing we all know what magazines are (poor taste in humor there).

Trade publications can be newsletters, bulletin boards or magazines that focus on a specific topic that is related to your product or service. If you have a hunting goods store, you have tons of hunting and fishing magazines out there.

If you are an interior designer, same thing. Seems no matter what you sell, there will be some magazine out there with a focus on that or something very closely related.

Marketing in this area?

This is going to be easy squeezy. Just read the stuff about newspapers and the exact same thing will be true with trade publications and magazines.

Yes, they too have writers who are always looking for good stuff to write about. Don't forget pictures. Take lots of pictures and send 'em.

Evaluation. Same as newspaper ads. Could be huge response with just a few bucks thrown at it.

Another one:

D. Radio Advertising:

Great	Good	Average		Not So Good	Bad
Expensive		Somewhat Costly		Inexpensive	Almost Free

First. Some terms for typical radio advertising. You have "prime time" or "drive time" which means the time where people are most likely to be listening to the radio. This time is obviously more expensive.

But wait, we all know radio advertising can be expensive. Let's take a look to see if there is something else we can do that is much more affordable.

The first obvious thing is non-drive time or even slow time announcements. Hey, homeowners, adults, teens, etc. listen to the radio at work, at home, in the car, on a date. They are still out there. Your response may not be as good but the cost can go way down.

Also, on the good side, many radio stations will offer to use one of their radio personalities to help you write and make your announcement. Most do not charge for this service since they know you will be using it to pay for airtime. Something to check into.

Here's a hot thing I like. There are tons of talk shows and more and more people are tuning into the talk shows because they are tired of listening to twenty minutes of music and forty minutes of advertising. Talk shows hold interest and seem to make time fly faster for the long commuter.

Different radio stations talk about different things. There are "do it yourself" talk shows. "Home and Garden" talk shows. "Care for your Pet" talk shows. You would be surprised how many there are.

Now, if you think about it (and I know you are), let me ask you a question. Would your service or business have any type of relationship with some of these talk shows? The "home improvement" talk show opens tons of doors for residential service related businesses.

If so, all you have to do is send them the same press release you sent the newspapers and trade publications with an added note that you are interested in appearing on their radio talk show as an expert guest in (whatever you do).

My wife and I did this with her faux finishing school. What they did was ask us to provide them with typical questions we get from our customers. They added a few of their own. We went over the questions and answers before we went on the air. That greatly helps the radio personality learn about our business and helps them ask good questions, knowing good answers are coming. Reeeeeeeel Smooooooth.

We went on the air, spent about fifteen minutes talking with the host, then opened up the phone lines for questions. We took about forty-five minutes to answer questions from people who called in. It was a blast. This happened on a Saturday and the next week, we saw a bunch of people come into her school saying they heard us on the radio.

Cost. Nothing but press release time and telephone follow up time. You can do it to.

Evaluation of radio advertising:

It can be expensive with average results if you purchase drive time or it could be almost free if you use the press release, talk show interview system. Way cool.

Next up:

E. Internet:

Great	Good	Average	Not So Good	Bad
Expensive		Somewhat Costly	Inexpensive	Almost Free

151

Ah, yes. The information highway. The most widely used source for purchasing in today's economy. Man. If you are not on the Internet, it's time we talk. No, really. Give me a call and I can help you get there for not that much money.

The steps:

1. Get a URL (Internet key so that people can easily find you. Like www.yourcompany.com. The URL is the center part between the *www* and the *com*.

2. Design your web site. MS Publisher has some templates to choose from. If you want something that will really make you stand out, you can start with a website of templates found at www.templatemonster.com. You can view their templates and pay an average of around $60 for some great looking templates. The template is just the overall look your website will have. The design is where you come up with the text and the pictures. There are lots of web developers who can help you there. Some are excessively expensive, taking advantage of the novice, while others are fair. I usually charge about $50 to $100 per page, assuming the customer comes to me with information about their company and pictures already on a flash drive or CD. If I have to start from scratch, it could get more costly.

3. Find yourself a great host. Someone who rarely goes down, and who will be there to help you edit or change your website. We really like the company "Out Of Nowhere" found at www.outofnowhere.net. They are very reasonable and will take good care of you. Heck, I use them for all my web needs.

4. Plan on doing regular website maintenance. This is where you go to any search engine and try to bring up your web site by using key search words. These are words that your customer will most likely type in the search box if they are looking for someone like you. Example: If I were looking for a carpet cleaner, I would type in, "Carpet cleaner, Arlington, TX." You want your company to pop up within the top five to ten. Any more than that and you will most likely be overlooked or missed. How do you keep your name up on top? Have your host do maintenance for you, which involves them making a few changes and re-submitting your website. The newer websites typically get posted up top until newer ones replace them. Keep a good eye out for this and get the most out of your host / website dollar.

What is the actual expense you ask? That all depends on how much information you can provide and how much work you can do yourself. If you use MS Publisher for your own design you can do it yourself and have your host put it up for you for as little as $300 bucks. If you have someone else do the design and you have all the information on what you want. It will cost an additional (approximate) $100 per page. Hosting is usually around $20 a month and maintenance is done only as needed, or you can schedule for regular maintenance for around $40 a month. Overall cost: Initial one time to set it all up, from $350 to $1,000. If you found someone who wants to charge you several thousand bucks, find someone else, for crying out loud. Disclaimer. These numbers represent 2008 economy. Subject to change obviously.

Effective you ask? Well, everyone knows almost every house in the US and in other countries have computers and most people have learned to surf the web. Not being there is really missing out.

What makes a website effective is good, easy-to-find information. Don't get caught up with a bunch of words. Keep it "bullet style" simple. Easy to navigate. Easy to get information. Only as much information as needed to get customers to call or come to you.

Evaluation: Overall expense per month is very inexpensive and could have great results when your website is clean and easy to navigate. We have had many clients tell us that most of their business comes from the Internet. Get 'er goin'!

F. Email:

Great	Good	Average		Not So Good	Bad
Expensive		Somewhat Costly		Inexpensive	Almost Free

I know. You think that's the same as Internet. Well, kinda. It's similar, except with email we can be more pro-active.

No! I'm not talking about spam. I hate spam. I get well over 400 each day. I had to turn my security system up to the point where I can only get email from people I have sent an email to.

What I am talking about is a newsletter or "true opt-in" email list. Either case, it's where your customers really ask you to send them stuff. I hate it when people take email addresses so they can send their advertisement and the customer did not specifically say they wanted it. That is abuse of their email. Well, to me anyway.

If you are a retail store, you can let your customers know that you frequently have items that go on sale. Ask them if they would like to receive an email when you have these special sales. If they say "yes," you have a true opt-in customer, and then you can do your bulk email to them. They *want* it.

If you have a service industry, you can prepare a monthly or quarterly newsletter that will have some valuable and desirable information. Example. For our painting company in earlier chapters, they could have an article on how to check for seasonal house movement, what grade of exterior caulk to purchase, where to purchase it from, and pictures of how to apply it. Owners love and welcome this kind of stuff. They give you permission to email the newsletter. You have a true "opt-in" customer.

This is free marketing and can have huge results. These customers have already purchased from you, are happy with their purchase, and will most likely purchase again. All you need to do is make sure they remember you and are encouraged to use you or buy from you again.
Evaluation: Very low cost, almost free with potentially great results.

G. Friends and Family:

Great	Good	Average		Not So Good	Bad
Expensive		Somewhat Costly		Inexpensive	Almost Free

Now I'm not talking about multi-level marketing stuff where you get a list of all your family and friends for the purpose of trying to sell the product or service.

Now wait. I am *not* putting down multi-level marketing companies. There are a few great ones out there for which, if your company is a multi-level marketing company, this book is perfect for you. As a matter of fact, if you are looking for a great "spare time income" multi-level marketing opportunity, give us a call. We have found one that I think is fantastic, honest, straight forward and provides the best training and support I have ever seen.

Oh. Sorry. Back on track with contacting friends and family.

This type of marketing is really very simple and completely free. I have a client who started their business in the service industry. They did nothing but contact friends and family. All they said was, "Did you know I have this new business that I am doing now? If you know of anyone who could use me, please let me know." She asked for a list of their friends and asked if she could mention their names as references. She would call her family member's friends, or even the friend of a friend and say, "Hey, I was talking with Robert Arbuckle about my new business. I do (what she did). Now I know you may not need this type of thing, but all I am asking is if you know of anyone who does, can you send them my information?" When they said yes, she asked for the address where she could send some business cards. She then sent business cards to everyone she could.

Standing in the grocery store, the person in front of her always got a friendly conversation. If there was a toddler in the cart, she would say, "Which isle did you find that cute thing and do they have any more?" Just a fun opener. She would say, "I'm (her name), and I've just started a new business. If you know of anyone who could use this type of thing, could you have them give me a call? She would hand them about three to four business cards. Most people said "Sure." That is the only thing she did to market her company. Within only six months, she was backlogged for three months out. Had plenty of work and in some cases had to turn away work to Company B. (Thought we were done with Company B, didn't ya)?

Evaluation: Cost is almost free (cost of business cards or flyers) with possible great results. All it takes is a total non-fear of strangers. Get over it. They're just people.

H. Door Hangers:

Great	Good	Average		Not So Good	Bad
Expensive		Somewhat Costly		Inexpensive	Almost Free

Are we starting to hit more of your discomfort level? Come on now, it's really not that bad.

I know. We all hate those door hangers. Some neighborhoods will not allow for it, and it could be a flag for a potential house thief. I mean, it flags the house that no one is home. Be careful with this one. You don't want to have your name on something people really don't like or that promotes house theft.

As with all things, we can stop and think a little outside the box and become creative in a way that will be accepted. Take for example a landscape company. When they are in a neighborhood servicing a client, they can prepare a door hanger or let's just call it a flyer that promotes their company. As they drive through the neighborhood between say 4:30 PM and 7:00 PM, they can watch for people coming home. When they see a live person, they can offer to give them a brochure and ask if they would like an estimate for taking care of their yard.

You will be surprised how many people will be receptive.

Here is where the numbers come in. If a landscaper did this every night for one week, they may meet, say, only one person every five minutes. That's 12 people an hour. That's about 25 people for their two and a half hours canvassing. That's about 125 contacts per week or 500 contacts per month. Advertising statistics show that with personal contact marketing, the average interested percent will be somewhere between two to four percent (depending on your trade and appropriate season). We'll call it only three percent.

Do the math now. What? Getting tired? Math wasn't your strong point in school? Ok then, three percent of 500 contacts per month would yield 15 new customers per month.

Assuming our landscape company is just doing basic mowing for a fee of around $35 per client allowing for ½ hour work and drive time, they can handle about 12 clients per day or about $420 per day income. Thus, it would only take three to four months of sincere effort to canvas a neighborhood before our landscaper can completely fill their schedule, and then they won't have to canvas any more. Word of mouth will take it from there. Assuming no helper is needed, that would give them a total gross income (before business expenses) of around $9,000 per month. Take out minimal business expenses (I'm just guessing $2,000 should cover it) and they have a personal income of $7,000 per month or $84,000 per year.

The secret to getting over your "stranger, danger" fear is to keep this in mind. The worst thing they can say is "No." Heck, everyone in any form of sales knows when you hear a "No" that means you are one step closer to the "Yes." Make a game to see how many "No's" you can get, so you won't have to worry about hearing it.

You know. Pay your dues. Work hard at marketing, and the results will come. (Sounds like a take on "Field of Dreams" doesn't it?")

OK. Now you can see how some form of door hanger or flyer can be effective. Even in the retail market. You should always have flyers and pass them out to strangers in parking lots, post office, grocery store, anywhere people are gathered. What can it hurt? Just make sure you do it legally. Example: Don't do it outside a baseball stadium. They frown on stuff like that.

Evaluation: Door Hanger / Flyer can be inexpensive and very effective when you overcome your fear of talking with total strangers.

That should get you started on the marketing thing.

Now would be a good time to get yourself a cold drink. Take a breather. Clear your head using whatever method works for you. You know. A walk around the block. Dip in the neighbor's pool cause they're not home. No wait. Scratch that last one.

Before we leave this chapter, there are just a few more things you should keep in mind with regards to marketing.

There's this thing called "test marketing." It really has more to it than just the idea to "test" something. Here's how it works:

First, you need to decide which of the above items will help you the most and be most effective for your type of business. Don't just pick one. Pick as many as you feel will be effective.

When you do your first advertising piece as explained in the previous chapter, run it by a whole bunch of friends and get their feedback. Remember, as a business owner, you are thinking of what you want to tell your customers, but we need to focus more on what the customer wants and not what you want to tell them. Sounds like an echo from the past, huh?

That is why you run it past your friends or even a stranger who may be a customer. When you get their feedback, you will realize some of the language you use is understood by you because, well, it's your business, but your customers may not understand it. They will tell you, "I don't get it." They are screaming at you to change the wording to something a third grader can understand as if they are hearing it for the first time in their life. Clear is better. Gets more response.

Now that the first round of testing is done (having your friends look it over), then you put it out there and see if it works.

Statistics show that an advertising piece must be exposed to a customer about six times before you can determine if it is effective or not.

Interestingly enough, when a person sees something for the first time, if it doesn't reach out there and grab their attention, or even if it does, it registers once for a few brief seconds, only to be replaced with tons of other stuff that passes through the mind in the course of a day. When the mind sees it repeatedly (average, six times) then the mind seems to remember and register it far better.

What this means to you is this: Don't get discouraged just because you spent a ton of dough on a marketing campaign only to have no sales. That's normal. Give it another shot over and over again. After about six to eight times, if you still have no success, then your advertising / marketing idea probably does in fact stink.

This is when it is time to buck up, think about changing what you are doing, and have another go at it until you find success.

Or in worst cases, as a good friend of mine once said, "You gotta keep pushing and pushing. When you can't push no more, then shove it."

Basic meaning, don't get too tied up in an idea or advertising piece that is your creation. Your baby. Sometimes, ideas are just bad, and you have to accept it. That doesn't mean give up. It just means find something different. You only give up if and when you discover that no matter what you do, it just ain't gunna work.

This is a great chapter to review. Has lots of ideas to get the word out and get your customers coming to you.

Open The Door and Bring 'Em In: Chapter Seven
Making Contact is Fun!

Advertising pieces look marvelous. Marketing is under way. Customers are starting to pour into your business. What now? Just wait for them to throw money at you?

This is where we get to the fun stuff. Well, it will be fun once you learn how to overcome your inner fear of strangers and get more comfortable with what to say to your customers. That will make the entire encounter enjoyable for both you and your customers.

First, let's get a little more into the minds of your customers.

Here's a question for retailers: When customers walk into your store, do they like to see (you choose):

A: Display shelves neatly organized with products easy to find. Prices prominently displayed. Personnel who look neat, clean cut, perhaps evenly uniformed.

B: Stuff just put on the shelves wherever, no prices (you have to ask someone), and people wearing blue jeans with a hole in the knee, a t-shirt that says, "Go away, I'm busy," a four- day beard, and they can smell something "funny."

I realize the above was a little on the obvious side. OK, a lot on the obvious side. But it does portray a common-sense picture of what your customers really like.

If they walk into a store that feels dirty, and the employees look, well, un-presentable, then they may not want to return. If, on the other hand, they walk into a store that is clean, and the people are pleasant looking, it creates an immediate mental image.

Yes. Image is everything. It can either create repeat business or scare away business.

The advice here is to take a close look at your operation to see if it meets the standards and the impression you want to give your customers.

Servicers: This applies to you as well, only a little differently, since you don't have a store for people to walk into.

You have about ten seconds to make your first impression. Your customers will see:

A. A: A truck that is about 20 years old, paint chipping off of it, rust showing through, dulled paint finish. A person with blue jeans, the hole in the knee.... Etc.

B. B: A clean looking vehicle with the company logo painted on it. A person wearing slacks, a shirt with a collar and with the company name embroidered on it, filled with a person that has a clean appearance.

Same thing, huh?

So, what do *your* customers see? Do you need to re-evaluate your overall appearance? Gussy up a bit? Good idea.

That's just personal / physical appearance stuff. What about the non-physical stuff? You know. The conversation part. What do you say to a customer?

We already gave a few tid-bits of information on that earlier in this book. Let's take a few moments to expound on it.

Back to Retailers: Remember. Your customers came to the store for a reason. They are either looking for something specific to purchase, or they are just browsing around to kill some time.

Being ignored is one of the worst things customers experience. You know the feeling. When you go into a restaurant, get seated, and no one comes to even take your drink order for about ten minutes. You already feel like walking out even if you *are* hungry.

Same is true with most of your customers. Greet them. Even if you are with another customer. Just quickly acknowledge their presence and say, "Hi, I'll be with you in just a moment."

When you are free to talk with your customer, say something like, "Hello, is this your first time here?"

Usually, they will take the ball and run with it. They will tell you what they are looking for, or just tell you they are browsing. Ask them if they live in the neighborhood. Is there something specific they are looking for?

If they want to be left alone, so be it. But keep your eye on them in case they do shift into needing your assistance.

Here is a little thing I learned from a garage sale service company. They said, at one of our garage sales, we watch everyone. If they even so much as touch something, that tells us they have an interest in it. We know there is a good chance they will walk away with it. We make mental note of what they touch, wait for them to touch about three to four items, then we go back to them. We pick up one of the items they touched and say, "Make me an offer, even a silly offer."

If the item has a sticker on it for one buck, the person may say, "$.50 cents." The host says, "Sold"! Picks up the next previously touched item and says, "Make a silly offer on this." The customer says, "$.25 cents." "SOLD" Then we say, "Now that you know the rules, take another look around. Our objective is to sell all this stuff, and it will go fast because of our 'silly offer' system." The customer then goes back to stuff they have already seen and starts picking up stuff and calling out, "Two bucks for this?" "SOLD."

Side note here: If a customer sees a sticker for say $20 and offers $.50 cents, the sales person says, "I said make a 'silly' offer. Not a ridiculous offer. How about $15 bucks? You know you want it."

Anyway, I know retailers have set prices so the bargain hunting system above won't work.

What we *do* learn from all of this is that if a customer touches something, they are interested in it. They may buy it. Some people just need a little impulse encouragement. That's when you would go over there and say, "That's one of our most popular items. Are you thinking of that for yourself or for someone else as a gift."

Continue with words like, "That is an Excellent choice." "They will love it." "It looks great on you." "May I suggest something similar."? Oh, here's a good one: "Did you know that item is on sale?" "SOLD"!

Most important, just keep an eye out and take the opportunity to help your customers make the choice to buy.

Restaurant, candy store, bakery, or similar type of retail business: Same thing except you may not have a bunch of product displayed on shelves. If you do, make sure those shelves are positioned so people have to walk past them to get to your counter.

Ever since McDonalds has been around, they have taught their employees to say, "Would you like some fries with that?" We all know this as suggestive selling. Heck, we are so used to it, when we go through the drive through window, we give the order and without even breaking pause, we say, "... and, no thanks, I don't want anything else." You've done that before, haven't you?"

So, let's be just a little more subtle and / or informative. Example: Let's imagine a bakery store. You walk in and hear the person behind the counter say, "Have you seen our new Bavarian crème raspberry muffin? It's absolute awesome."

Anytime you have anything new, your customers need to know about it. They will not know, and they will not purchase if you don't tell them. So go get 'em.

You Servicers don't have customers walking in a store looking for stuff on a shelf; you are called by the customer to offer a service.

I think the best way to introduce working with customers in the service industry is to use the example of our painting contractor. That's something we can all relate to, and it gives a great example.

The customer calls and wants an estimate for painting. They are thinking, "Painting is just putting the stuff that's in the bucket onto a surface. Heck, I could do it, but I just don't want to get up on a ladder or clean up the mess it makes. I think I'll hire it out. It shouldn't be that expensive. After all, anyone can do it. It's not like hiring a doctor to do an operation..." and on it goes.

The typical painting company will go to the customers house, take a look around, do some calculations, then BAM! The customer falls over when they see the price of a couple of grand. You just lost the sale.

Let's live this experience over, and see if you can see what the secret is to getting a whole lot more sales.

The painting contractor meets the customer and asks if they will walk around with him to get a feel for the quality they want.

The painter says, "I see there is moss growing on the side of your house. If we put paint on the moss, the paint will not have good adhesion, and the paint will fail in a very short time. As little as six months. We have choices here. We can 1.) take a garden hose and hose off as much as we can. There will still be a residue and the paint may not stick properly but it will last perhaps one year. I regret to say that some of my competition actually does this to save cost and come in at a lower price. Choice 2.) We can power wash the surface prior to painting. This will remove all the surface moss and make the paint stick much better. However, there are still spores inside the wood that could allow the moss to grow back. You see, moss likes three things. Moisture, food source, and an absence of light. Paint cuts off the light, the wood is the food source and the moisture trapped in the wood provides an Excellent re-growth that can occur under the paint after we paint it. For that reason we go to Choice 3.) We can apply a product called Jomax which is a Mildewcide that will kill the moss spores, preventing them from growing back. We do this as an injection while we are power washing. Now, most painters will only Powerwash and not do the chemical injection, because it costs less and helps them get the job because of a lower price. But the difference is about an added three to five years more life of your paint job by doing the Mildewcide."

OK. Here's my favorite part. "Of those three choices, which would you like?"

The customer asks, "What's the price difference." Painter: "Garden hose about $50 total. Pressure wash only about $300 total. Pressure wash with chemical injection, about $400 total."

Customer picks choice three for a longer lasting paint job.

This continues with the choices of the quality of paint. They can get paint that costs $15 per gallon that lasts two years, $20 a gallon that lasts three to five years (what most painters use to keep the price down and give a lower price), $28 per gallon that lasts five to seven years or $35 per gallon that lasts 10 years plus.

The customer picks the quality they want.

Let's get deep now. Evaluate what is going on. Let me assist (that's my job, after all, I understand).
1.   The customer is being educated.
2.   The customer is being given choices
3.   The customer knows the price difference.
4.   The customer knows what most companies do to come in with the low bid.
5.   The customer understands the difference between low price and quality.

Think of it. Can anyone purchase materials for less than you can as a service contractor? NO!

The *only* way anyone can lower their price on the material side of the project is to:

_____ (this is where you write in your response).

You may have written in something like, "lower the quality of the material," or, "Cut corners," or "buy cheaper stuff that I don't want because I want a longer lasting or higher quality product." Well... that last one was a bit too long to shove in that short little space, but you get the idea.

Right. The fact that everyone knows deep inside, but we forget when it comes to hiring out work, is "You get what you _____."

Right!

Let's go just a tad deeper. Isn't it the same for labor?

No really? Think deeper. Sure it is.

Oh, I can hear you skeptics out there saying, "But wait! My overhead is higher than my competition, and I have to pay more for labor than they do because I am legal and they aren't."

Although that sounds like a great argument, let's explain that to your customers in a way that *does* make sense.

First point to make to your customers. You can ask, "Is it important to you that the company you hire has insurance?" If they go, "Huh," or something similar, you can explain, "If there is any type of accident that happens on your property and the contractor does not have insurance, your home owners insurance kicks in. Your rates go up (if you don't get cancelled) for a very long time because now you have a claim." Then ask them again if insurance is important.

You can let them know that many contractors do not have workman's compensation insurance or general liability insurance because it costs too much, so they lower their price and take the risk. Funny thing (well, not so funny depending on which side you are on). They are not at risk. You, the homeowner, are. That's why we are fully insured as required by law. Besides, the insurance expense is really not that much compared to the overall cost of the job. It may only add $100.

The other concept that I really like and works every time is this: Are you ready?

The smart contractor (that's you) can explain, "When I started this business, I had a choice to be like most companies by putting an ad in the paper and getting people to work for me for as little as they are willing to work for. Think of it this way. I can pay $8.00 an hour or $$20.00 per hour for my labor. Will the $8.00 per hour be skilled (accurate, clean work) or not (sloppy and often missing stuff)? Will they be fast or slow (obviously slow)? Now, the $20.00 per hour laborer. Will *they* be skilled or not (obviously skilled, accurate and clean work)? Will they be fast or slow? (Obviously fast since they have years experience)?"

First concept achieved. Keep it a goin'.

"With a low paid laborer, I can charge $25 bucks an hour but it takes them 100 hours. How much is that? (Obviously $2,500). My other choice is to hire the high paid laborer, but I have to charge $50 bucks an hour, but it now only takes me 50 hours because they are much faster. How much is that? (Obviously $2,500 again). Summary: you can have slow, sloppy, problematic work, *or* you can have a fast, clean, complete *and* out of your life schedule in ½ the time for the same money. Which do you want?"

You see. You are educating this customer with common sense, with this concept: The *only* way anyone can lower their price on the labor side of the project is to: _____.

Same as with materials. Cut corners, be illegal, hire lower paid, less qualified workers, and the list goes on. All of which are not a good choice for your customer, and you get to explain that in a way your customers will agree.

Final summary of the above education process; it does not matter what your service is. When your customers understand that that material prices and labor expense is carved in stone for everyone who does, in fact, give you the quality you want, then the price you give them is the *right* price. Not the high price or the low price or any price in between.

When you are successful at educating your customer to that one concept, they will not need to get another price. Why waste the time? Now, this is so important, I want all of you Servicers to re-read this entire section where I started with "For Servicers" in bold print earlier in this chapter. The more you get the concept down and start using it, the faster your sales ratios will explode to a new height.

Now, I don't mean to brag or anything, but when I started using this technique, my sales ratios went from 25% to 80%. That's right. I get about eight out of ten estimates that I do, simply because I take the time to educate the customer. It doesn't matter what your service industry is. Follow the technique as it relates to you and your trade.

Example: If you are a house cleaning service, DON'T just tell your potential customers that the cost is $150 for the initial house cleaning and $100 each time thereafter. Take time to educate them on choices. Such as, "For the initial cleaning we have a few choices, we can 1.) Just vacuum and sweep the floors and dust off the flat surfaces only. This would only take us about 1½ hours at a cost of $50.00. Or we could 2.) vacuum, sweep, dust horizontal surfaces, mop floors, clean sinks, toilets, showers, vanities, kitchen countertops, and appliance outer surfaces, which takes about three hours for $100.00. Or, we can 3.) vacuum, sweep, etc. etc. etc."

And you go on, with the fact that your house cleaning service had a choice to hire low paid help or high paid help, etc. Same concept as for the painter above.

Will this technique work for a paralegal document preparation service? Why not?

The customer has the choice of purchasing a template from you for about $25 bucks, that they can edit and change themselves, or 2.) they can have you take the template and put in their personal information, let them do the addendums, and you can file it for them etc. etc. for about $75.00 or 3.) etc. etc. etc.

Same thing with labor. You can hire low paid labor who type slow and you pay less per hour but it takes longer or you can hire high paid labor who are fast typists where you pay more per hour but it gets done faster, etc.

Same thing.

This is really powerful stuff, and I will be honest with you. It is very difficult to get these systems down pat. It took me about three years before I became comfortable with it. But I got it to the point where it was like polished glass. Reeeeeeeeeel smooooooooth.

The first thing that will help you with these concepts is to get over your fear of talking with strangers. They are just people. They called you or came to your store to talk about and / or to spend money. So just do it.

Honestly, the more you do it, the more comfortable and natural it will become.

I can't stress enough that using this system will take the stress out of sales.

So. Now that you have the sale, what else can you do to maximize profit and perhaps get even more sales?

Man. You have the best questions. Let's dig into the next chapter for that one.

BREAK! Go relax and we'll get back to more great stuff when you return.

Open The Dorr and Bring 'Em In: Chapter Eight
The Spin Off

Congratulations. You have a bunch of good customers who love your product or service. They had a good experience with you. Why not make them even happier by giving them even more? That makes you happy, too, with the extra sales.

What is "Spin Off?"

Another fantastic question.

In the business world, Spin Off basically means to offer something else that is or may not be one of your feature products. Here are some great examples:

Coffee Shops can sell travel mugs, muffins, or a true spin off--cooking aprons.
Beauty Salons can sell shampoo or a true spin off--art hanging on the wall.
Painting contractors can sell wallpaper or a true spin off--window cleaning.
Fabric stores can sell looms, quilting braces, or a true spin off—candle-making kits.

The whole idea is this. You already have a business set up. People are already using your service or coming into your store. If they *never* purchase your spin off item / service, you have lost nothing. If they *do* purchase the item, you now have extra sales, meaning extra profits, meaning happier spouse, meaning better home life, meaning quicker retirement! WOW! Didn't know it could go that far, did ya?

There really is not that much difference between Retailers or Servicers when it comes to learning how effectively to add spin off's to your company, so let's just jump into it. Shall we?

This is similar to advertising in that you start with your brainstorming session.

Sit down with anyone you feel comfortable with, and ask, "Can you guys / gals think of anything that you have seen that is way cool that I may be able to sell in my store?" OR, "Can you think of anything else I could do with my existing equipment to provide a service that you may want from time to time."

I had a consulting client that did restoration work. His business was seasonal. He was swamped in the summer doing exterior renovations to historical buildings. Winter, he was back to eating macaroni and cheese, laying off employees and wondering how soon he could start up for the next season.

He got to thinking, "Hey, I've got these big ol' trucks here. We could beef up the suspension and adapt them with snowplow equipment. When the snow comes, and I know it will, I will be jumping up and down with joy instead of getting all bummed out."

As with all new things in business, there is an up-front expense.

Oh. Sorry, I just have to go off on a side note here. It has to do with people and their typical thoughts about money.

We all know it takes money to make money. Why then does the typical person, especially a business owner, always say, "I don't have the money to do that?"

Guess what. They are right, and they never will have the money to do what they want. All businesses start out with an investment. Same thing with anything you want to add to your business. It will require an investment.

Whatever the expense, when you plan for it, put it in your business budget (like we all learned in the first book in this series), then the customer ends up paying for it, and it ends up costing you nothing. But the first step is sacrifice. If you have to sell something you don't use that much (ski-doo in the back yard growing spider webs), or if you have to take out a second mortgage on the house, or if you have to get another loan from Mom. Do it. But it is only safe when you do the budget thing and put the expense in your estimating and pricing as fully described in our first book.

So, don't worry about the expense. Once you have done the evaluation (coming up next) and the prospectus looks good, then the expense is just a technical thing that needs to happen to make the new item or service come to pass.

Back on track here, then…

This renovation company took on snow plowing in the winter. It only took two winter seasons before the snowplow equipment was paid for. The wonderful thing was, he didn't need to lay off his workers. They became snowplow drivers in the winter. He established routes with neighbors, people with long driveways, etc. He just did the marketing thing we suggested earlier in this book; he went door to door looking for people to introduce the concept.

His service was simple. He explained to people that when it snows more than four inches, he will automatically come out and plow their driveway. Charge was $10 each time. They were billed monthly. If they didn't pay, he stopped plowing. He took a $100 advance deposit that was held in the event of non-payment. I think you get the idea.

His last report was that he gets to keep all his people working, his sales volume drops a bit, but even after paying his employees, and himself his set salary, he is able to put an additional $10,000 per year in pure profit just from his plowing business.

Great spin off.

Another person I know worked with a courier service. She liked to do crafty things. Christmas, she took a ping pong ball and wrapped a doily around it in a cone shape, stuck a pipe cleaner halo on the ball and put angel wings behind it. A Christmas tree decoration. She also made a couple of other Christmas decorations from ideas she had, took pictures, and made a flyer to pass out in the office.

Report: She made a net profit of around $1,200 just in the month of December.

What? Did she stop there? What do you think?

She made it a seasonal thing. She had things for Valentines Day, 4th of July, Saint Patrick's Day, etc. Over the year, she ends up with about $8,000 per year pure extra profit.

Get the idea.

Service industry people have tons of stuff they can do with their equipment. If you are in the residential service market, and you have ladders, you can clean windows, clean gutters, clean roofs, spot touch-up house caulking, window glazing, and the list goes on.

Now, I can feel a couple of you twigeting out there (is that a real word?). You are probably thinking, "How do I go about evaluating a spin off? I mean, I don't want to dump good money into junk that won't sell."

Great question. And again, in keeping with our theme of "my, what value," here's some tips on that:

It starts with a little research.

Get on the information highway, the Internet, and find out what the item or service you are thinking about typically sells for.

Go to the Internet again, only this time, look into all the details of the expenses to purchase this item or items needed for the service. Key words, "wholesale, supplier, or factory direct."

Once you have gathered as many facts as possible about your spin off item or service, then go to a spreadsheet program. I like MS Excel.

YES! It's another free download from our website as explained in Book one page 7. Download two different things. One is a manual worksheet done in MS Word that is called "Marketing Worksheet" (How original). The Excel version is called. (wanna guess?) Yup. Excel Marketing Worksheet. Anyway, go ahead and download these thing and you will see how they can help you in the marketing evaluation process.

Start building the worksheet so that you can enter all the expense items and have the worksheet show you different scenarios. Take a look at the worksheet below to see what I mean:

Expense Item	*Cost*		Evaluate	Result
Part A item	1.50		If I purchase this qty:	100
Part B item	.75		My total Cost is:	$ 725.00
Part C item	.25			
Part D item	.50		If I sell This Many:	90
			Sell them at this price:	$20.00
Shipping to me ea.	.25		My gross sales will be:	$1,800.00
Packaging per unit:	.15		My Profit Is:	$1,075.00
Ship out cost each:	3.85			
			It takes 15 min. per item:	.25 hour
Total cost per unit:	$7.25		I make ? per hour	$47.78

Looking at the above, I'd say, "Let's do it, dude!!"
Now, if you're not sure how to use Excel or another spreadsheet, then it's time you schedule that in your on-going educational process. It really is not that hard once you learn it. It typically takes me about four hours for a person new to MS Excel before they are off and running with it full speed.

The important thing is that you know what you are getting into before you jump into it.

The worst thing you can do is figure out it cost you more to produce than it is worth the time.

We had a person look into making ink refill kits and wanted to sell them on eBay. They went out and bought the ink, bottles, labels, syringes, storage bottles for the bulk ink, funnels, rubber gloves, the whole shebang. It ended up costing them about $16.50 per kit. They went on eBay and saw a whole bunch of listings (literally hundreds) with no bids on them asking price for the "buy it now" feature for $17.95. Great profit of only $1.45 per unit, huh? Not!

Had they done the research, they would not have gotten involved. They still have a garage full of ink refill kits. Oh well. We all make mistakes. Our benefit is that we can learn from this one.

OK, now that your research is done, it's time to spread the word. Remember, you already have existing customers.

For the Retail market, you can prominently display this new item right by your cash register for all to see. Each time you ring up a sale, you can simply say, "Hey, did you see this?" "SOLD"!

For the Servicers, you can do a direct mail to your past customers. It will be a reeeeeeeel cool looking flyer (following the advertising tips you learned in this book). It can say something like, "Introducing our latest service… blah, blah, blah." No, wait. "Blah, blah, blah" may indicate it's boring so let's change that to, "etc. etc. etc."

If your customer is in your office, have a flyer on your desk and give it to them. If you are in your customer's home and will be returning the next day, you can leave a flyer in your work area for your customers to discover. When you collect your final check, give them a flyer and let them know you have this new thing or service.

You will be surprised at how much and how often you sell your "extra profit" spin off item or service. What do you have to lose? Nothing.

As a quick review, just give it some thought. You already have the business set up and going. Why not take full advantage of having a business and maximize its profit potential?

Well? Why not?

Hey! I got great news for you. Did you know you have even more business income opportunity just waiting for you? It's called…. Nah. I'll wait till you turn the page to the next chapter.

Isn't the suspense fun?

Open The Door and Bring 'Em In: Chapter Nine
More Extra Free Business

Let's start this chapter with a few basic historical statistics.

First. Did you know that the average "successful" business hits the "break even" point at or about their fifth year in business? (Remember 80 percent of new businesses go out of business before that, so the ones left after five years are just starting to break even.

"Break even point" means they have made back the amount of money they spent on getting into the business. Example. If it cost, say $50,000 to purchase inventory, buy equipment, sundries, everything you need to start your business, then it takes about five years to earn that back, from that point forward, the earnings turn into higher profits.

Next statistic: It takes between three years (Retailers) to five years (Servicers) for your customers to become familiar enough with you that they will tell their friends about you so that your sales increases just from sheer word of mouth.

Next item: After about ten years, it is possible for a company to be successful and profitable with only repeat business.

Yes. I know of several companies that do not have an active advertising or marketing plan. Their business is 100% word of mouth and repeat customers. Wouldn't *that* be wonderful?. You betcha.

Put all this stuff together and it brings up the question: is repeat business important?

Now, if you don't know the answer to that one, we need to talk.

From a business management viewpoint, we call that "follow up."

Believe it or not, the area of follow up is the one that is ignored by most companies, especially the ones that go out of business.

Did you ever wonder why we all know it's important, but very few are active in follow up activities? Me too. Here's the deal.

Remember the "stranger danger" problem we all grew up with. You know. We don't like to talk to strangers because we were taught not to right from the get-go. Like the elevator example we gave in the first book. Right! You put ten people in an elevator and how many words are spoken? None! Why? We don't like talking to strangers.

This really is the root of why people don't do any follow up. We think we are pestering, begging for business, becoming a pushy salesperson, blah, blah, blah.

The other thing is, our human nature says, "the customer has already come here or hired my services. The sale is done when I collect the money."

Buzzzzzz! Wrongo! The sale is just beginning. It is far from over. Well, that is, if you want repeat business. This is where follow up comes in.

There is a difference between Retailers and Servicers in the way follow up can be done effectively. Who should I start with this time?

(Coin toss going on here).

Retailers: There are a bunch of things you can do to follow up with your customers.

Examples: We all go to restaurants, right? We all notice differences in restaurants. Some, you go in there, get seated, get your drink order, place your meal order, get your meal, get asked if you want desert, get the check, pay the check and leave. Same old story time and time again.

Then you go to other restaurants where it is just a little different. You start off the same--get your drink order, place your meal order, and get your meal. But, here is where some better restaurants know the importance of follow up. They have the waitperson check back with you every few minutes. You know. That's when they come up and say, "Is everything alright, or can I get anything else for you." Water is checked every couple of minutes. You are asked if you want more bread. The soda beverages are re-filled without even asking you.

Then we go back to the typical routine about the desert after-sell, but before you get the check, the manager or owner of the restaurant walks around the store and says, "Hi, I'm the manger, and it's my job to make sure your experience here was a good one. How was everything tonight?" They may even engage in conversation: "Is this a birthday celebration?" And on they go.

Now, I don't know about you, but that extra service, constant follow up, and especially the manager coming over-- WOW! I really like that.

Did you know that when something goes wrong (retail or service), if it is a minor thing, most people will not tell you? They, too, have a fear of talking to strangers. If it is a minor thing, they don't want to make a fuss over something small. They want to avoid a confrontation when the overall experience was really ok. So they clam up.

But. Wait until they talk to someone else about their experience. They will remember what went wrong. They will say, "Yeah, that place is OK, but their bread really stinks." You just lost a customer and have no clue why.

When the manager comes around and tells you his job is to make sure everything went well, the customer is more likely to come out with it. They may say, "Everything was great. The waitperson was fantastic and very attentive. Just a quick question about the bread. Is it supposed to be that hard?" The manager will become very concerned and perhaps offer to take off the price of a desert.

That gets us into the other type of follow up. That is the "problem" follow up. That's right. Problems always happen. People make mistakes.

When it comes to a mistake that makes a customer dissatisfied, the rule is, "You lose ten customers each time you have one dissatisfied customer." Or, "You have to have ten great customer experiences to make up for one bad one."

This gets into the psychology of people again. When something good happens, we remember it, but we don't go out of our way to tell people about it. However, when something bad happens, well, *now* we have a story to tell everyone.

No, really, when people are telling their life experiences, are they usually good ones or bad ones? Or more clearly asked, are most of them about good stuff or bad stuff that happens in their life?

Right again. The bad overtakes the good in this case.

I am sure you can see how important that applies to your business.

Here's another true story that will give you a hint on this type of customer experience. See what you think.

I know a woman who was in a minor car accident and had severe back pain from it. After four weeks, she was finally able to get out and around. Her husband asked where she would like to go out to eat. She picked restaurant "X" (Sorry. Must be careful putting names of businesses when you author a book). They called ahead and told the person answering the phone that she had been in an accident and could not wait for more than a few minutes, so could they make a reservation? The restaurant said, "We don't take reservations, but I can put your name on our list now, and if you can get here in about twenty minutes, let me know you were the ones who called in, and I'll get you seated right away."

This was great, except for... here it comes. They arrived there and flagged the hostess as instructed. She recognized them and said, "We'll have a table ready for you in just a few seconds."

Well, twenty minutes went by, and by this time, the woman (who had been standing and sitting on a backless bar stool) was in so much pain they had to leave. The man went to the hostess and said they had to leave because of his wife's pain and expressed disappointment that they had been ignored. The hostess asked them to wait for just a few seconds while she got the manager. The manager was given the quick story.

Do you know what that manager did? Want to guess? Go ahead. Put something in your head and see if that's how it turned out.

Here's what happened. He said, "We're very sorry for this inconvenience. Next time you come here, give us a call in advance, ask for me, and we'll make sure all goes smoothly next time."

Sound like a "blow off?" Well, as it turned out, it wasn't. About three weeks later, they called and asked for the manager. He remembered their names and asked what time they would be arriving. When the couple arrived, they were walked immediately through the crowd of waiting people, ushered to their table on which stood a dozen fresh-cut roses. The manager told them the roses were for her and that tonight's meal, drinks, appetizers, desert and all were on the house.

Do you think this couple went back? Do you think they told all of their friends? Duh!

So, just remember, when any of your customers have any kind of a bad experience, it is far better to eat whatever expense it takes to go above and beyond what is expected to make sure your customer walks away with a "WOW" experience that they will tell their friends about and give you a lot better chance of growing your business with repeat customers and referrals.

There is another form of follow up, but we have already talked about that in our marketing chapter. That is the follow up of getting your customers' email addresses and asking them if it would be alright to let them know about up-coming sale events or to send them discount coupons, etc. When you *do* get that information, make sure you keep it and use is as much as possible to promote your company. You know, keep you in their mind often.

Let's shift gears here to the Servicers now. It is a little different for you.

Typically in the service industry there is the item of price. Right? In other words, you give a price or an estimate or a bid or whatever you want to call it.

So, with our follow up for the type of business that prepares an estimate for their customers, it actually starts on the telephone when the first call comes in and asks for the appointment for someone to come out and look at the project.

In the earlier chapters where we talked about screening, but here is another item you may want to add to your first phone conversation. When you are about done *or* at the point where they ask if you give free estimates, you reply with, "Estimates are not free." Then listen for the hesitation and silence for a second or two. Then proceed with, "Now don't get me wrong, we don't charge for an estimate. However, they are not free. They cost us money in the value of our time to come and visit your project, take measurements, come back to our office and prepare a bid package for you. It costs us about $200 (or whatever you feel is more accurate). All we ask in return for the value of our time is that in the event you do not hire us, just let us know who you have hired and for how much. This will really help us with our marketing and we won't have to charge you the $200. Would that be alright?"

They have been prepared for the next phase of this type of follow up.

When you *do* meet them, when you have done your greeting, measurements, etc., just before you leave you can remind them once again about what you told them on the phone. It may sound something like, "If you remember on the phone, I mentioned that estimates are not free in that they cost us about $200. And, I mentioned that in the event you decide not to hire us, just let us know who you did hire and at what price. This makes it so we won't have to charge you the $200, and it will really help us out in the marketing. Would that be ok?"

Cool, they heard it twice and are in complete agreement. The final time is when you present your estimate.

At this final meeting when they do understand that the material part of the bid is carved in stone as well as the labor (you smooth salesperson you), and they say no to you because they want to get other estimates, that's when you remind them, "Remember on the phone about our agreement. In the event you decide to hire someone else, that's fine. All we ask is that you let us know who it was and what the price was. When would be a good time to call you back," or "How much time do you need to get these other estimates?"

Point: Set the appointment for your follow up call.

It can actually get a little fun here. You call them back a week later (or whenever they ask you to call them back). You ask them if they have made a decision to hire you yet. If they say they decided to go with someone else, you say, "Great? Who did you go with and what was their price?" I found that most of the time there is no hesitation on their part to tell you because of your previous agreement. If they do hesitate, then I remind them of the agreement, and if they choose not to tell you, I ask would it be all right if I mail the invoice for the $200, since that was the agreement.

What? Did you just read what you think you just read?

Yeah, but don't take that to the point that you do it all the time. You will develop a feel when and how and if you should go that far. Obviously, we don't want to give our potential customers a bad feeling about us. Besides, like I said, it is really not that common, almost rare, that a customer will not be more than willing to give you this information if you have asked them twice before and they have already agreed.

There is another thing that you will find happen with this follow up system. Your customer may say, "We've decided to go with XYZ Company who gave us a price for $1,800. Your price was $2,700.00."

Now, I really like this because what they are screaming at you is, "This other guy said he would do the same, we bought his story, we are about to get taken, and we don't really have a clue." It's true. They are about to get cheated. Remember. The way you did your estimating and sales approach as we described earlier is designed to educate the customer that material expenses are the same for everyone. The only way to lower the price is to lower the quality of material or cut corners. The only way to lower the price on the labor side of the bid is to cut corners and sacrifice quality. Your customer is getting cheated.

Your choice: Hang up and let it slide / let them get cheated, or you can let them know in a very subtle way that they are going to get cheated. To prepare yourself mentally, just put it in your head where you can say to yourself, "Self. I don't care if they hire me or not. Well, of course I want their business, but the most important thing to me is my customers get great value for their dollar spent. If someone is going to cheat them, I want to warn them as a favor to them. Even if they don't hire me."

With this in mind, you can take the second option above and let them know in a subtle way. I like to say something like, "Oh (dramatic pause). When you have problems, just give me a call and I'll come over there and fix things."

I have done this literally hundreds of times and about 95% of the time, I get the same response. I hear from them, "What? Is there something we should know about XYZ Company?" I assure them I cannot say anything bad about another company. That would not be ethical. I do remind them that our estimating techniques are to figure out exactly what the material cost is for the quality they have asked for. I remind them that the materials are carved in stone and no one can get the material for less than us. I also remind them of the labor they have requested and remind them that the only way anyone can lower the price on labor is to cut corners, *and* most customers will not know it until as little as a few months later when the problems occur that would not occur if the work was done right in the first place. I end with, "You see, Mr. & Mrs. Jones, the price we gave is the right price. We know there is no company out there that can do what you have asked for a price that low. We know you *will* have problems when you discover the effect of this other company's cutting corners. When you do, we would appreciate the opportunity to come back and do it right the second time. If you change your mind about hiring XYZ Company, please let us know so we can get you on our schedule."

You will be surprised that about 20% of the people who had said no will change their mind and end up hiring you.

There have been many times when, about two weeks later, I have gotten a call from a customer who said, "You were right. We started checking the quality and XYZ Company came back by trying to charge us extra. We fired them and decided to go with you since you were all-inclusive in the first place. We just feel more comfortable with you." Ka-chin! SOLD!

Here's another thing that can happen: Your customer may say, "Well, we called about ten other companies and we are having a hard time getting past the companies who are out of business or a phone machine."

Great! What an opportunity to sell. You tell them, "I am not sure if you realize that 80 percent of businesses are out of business within the first five years. That's why you find so many out of service phone calls. As for those with a phone machine who don't return calls, that tells you what you can expect if you hire them. You will have a hard time getting in touch with them. Did you want to just go ahead and schedule us to do the work?" SOLD!

Here's yet another one: Your customer may say, "We have scheduled three other appointments, and they have either put us on delay, or they didn't show. One gave us a 'window' of six hours that we were supposed to sit home waiting for them and miss work. We just couldn't afford that so please just give us more time."

Great! Another opportunity to sell. You tell them, "This is a typical common problem when gathering estimates. It tells you what you can expect when it comes to the actual service you will get if you hire them. We pride ourselves on being prompt and complete, which is what you can expect when we do the project. Did you want to go ahead and schedule?" SOLD!

Can you see how very important it is to follow up with every single bid you give? When you do take the time, you are giving your customers the message that you *do* care, you will be there for them, the job will be done correctly and professionally. It established your professional reputation and ends up in far more work.

OK. Let's take a little breather here.

Shifting gears just a little bit but still staying on the subject.

Some of you Servicers work with general contractors or you work as a subcontractor to another contractor. Whatever the case, the idea of follow up still applies.

In a contractor's office, they are bombarded with a whole bunch of stuff to get their project done. They may be getting several bids from several different trades. Thus, they don't like to spend a bunch of time giving every person who gives them a price bid results (who got it and for how much).

That doesn't mean we let it slide. Let them know estimates are not free and all you ask for the value of your time spent is bid results. Mention it three or four times. Now, contractors *do* want your price, so they will *tell* you they will give you bid results, but when the time comes, they seem too busy or unreachable.

Follow up starts with your method of giving bids in the first place. Many contractors just fax or email you an invitation to bid. You fax or email back. You get the project plans, specifications or scope of work. You prepare a bid and fax or email it back to them. You sit back and wait to be blessed with the job. Nothing happens. You find yourself giving ten bids to get one job (by the way, that's average).

Evaluate the above. Many businesses have become a technical / automated office. When they use the fax or email and you respond with the same, you are nothing more to them than a machine with a number. Thus, setting up your follow up requires we get back to the good old days of personal contact.

That's right. When you get your invitation to bid, call them and set an appointment to go to their office, pick up the documents, shake their hand, etc. When you get back to your office, make another phone call with questions. When you submit your bid, follow up with a phone call, and ask if they got your bid, or if they have any questions. This means you make about four or five personal contacts per project. By the time you have done four or five projects you have made what… 15 to 20 personal contacts. You should know their spouses name, if they have kids, do they like golf, etc. You are now MORE than just a machine and a number, and it opens the door to get more bid results and the opportunity to negotiate with them, so you do end up getting a lot more work.

So, back to our bid submission: When you do give them a bid, remind them of their promise, and ask them about the last project you bid (bid results). After about four to five projects, you should have developed some type of relationship with them, due to your personal contact as mentioned above. This is where you can say, "You know Tom, we have given you five bids now, and as I mentioned a while back, estimates are not free. They cost us money to do the measurements, calculations, and provide you with our professional bid package. The way we look at it is, we are about $1,000 into our pocket trying to get your jobs. What is it going to take to get one?"

Many times I hear, "Well, you've just got to shave your numbers." This is where I can explain about materials and labor being carved in stone, 80% of my competition will be out of business because they don't charge enough or they are illegal (which when it comes to OSHA or insurance on commercial project can be a serious thing). Then (the fun part), I ask them to go back to the other jobs I bid on, look at who they hired, take their price and add all the change orders they added and compare it to my price. It's a game that is played. The bidder purposely leaves stuff out so their price will be low, and they know the contractor will not catch it. When the job is in progress, the contractor discovers items are not included, and they end up paying for change orders.

The important thing here is that you establish a personal relationship so you *can* discuss these things and end up getting more work instead of just being a number. If they keep coming back with, "You're just too high," and you know they won't even take the time to consider the truth in what you say, then it's time to move on. Stop giving them bids and find a contractor who is more reasonable. You will find them. They are out there.

Great stuff there, huh?

Ok. Now, on to yet another great idea that will help you sell more work and establish creditability with your customers.

Retailers and Servicers alike can appreciate this next section. It is all about warranties and how we can take advantage of a warranty program.

We all know (or should know) that the law requires you to provide a warranty to your customers. Even if you don't have a written warranty, you are required to warrant your services (for Servicers) for one year, or for retailers, that your product is all that it is represented to be. Example for retailers, if you sell a yo-yo, your customers are to expect that it works correctly and if made of wood, does not have any splinters, etc. If there are any defects, you are required to make good by either giving a refund or replacement that meets your customer's expectations. Although there are not any specific time limits, the law uses the term "reasonable" a bunch. Meaning, your warranty must be for a reasonable amount of time as it relates to the item.

For Retailers, it's easy. When a customer is not happy with your product, and they are reasonable about the return time / process and the returned condition of the product, then the best thing you can do is to replace it or give a full refund with a smile.

Did you catch that last part, "with a smile?" That may be the hard part. Just remember the age-old business-owner expression that goes hand in hand with, "The Customer Is Always Right"… which is: "Whoever makes the mistake, eats it. If it's you, eat it with a smile." I like to add, "Eat it with enthusiasm." Give them whatever it takes and in some cases, even more, to make sure you end up with that oh, so important, happy customer who will spread the word in your favor.

Here's something for you Servicers. Retailers can take advantage of this too, so don't go away.

In the service industry, you have just finished a project where your customers may have spent quite a bit of money. Just like the retailers in electronic goods, you can offer an "extended warranty" for the work you just provided. Example: Our plumber in the earlier chapters can say, "We just finished installing your toilet. The amount comes to $450.00. It comes with a one-year warranty. We offer an extended warranty that will take that up to three years for only 10% of the purchase price which is only $45.00. It covers any fitting leaks, seals, or any related hardware. Would you like to take advantage of this?"

Now, the reason is this. It is not so much for putting an extra $45 bucks in your pocket for work you may never have to do. You take it to the next level. You say, "This is a pro-active warranty where we will call you back and ask you to do an inspection. If there is anything that needs attention, we will be out there to fix it at no expense to you."

Did you catch the marketing hook there? Right you are. You get to call them every year for three years. They WANT you to call because it is a free service. Each time you call, you are now in their mind again. If they have anything else they may be thinking about doing, they will ask you, "By the way, since I have you on the phone, how much will it cost to replace a vanity sink?" SOLD!

Same thing for painters. Your extended warranty will be for 10% of the project and it will include an annual inspection by *your* painter who will look for cracks, re-caulk them, and do any touch up painting from typical house movement. While you are there, don't be surprised if the customer asks for a price to paint something else. SOLD!

Yet another great idea. Aren't you glad you bought this book?

OK, then, I think that is quite a bit for your sales and marketing. Please do yourself a favor and go back and re-read this entire book. Fact is, the average person only remembers 30% of what they read for the first time around. When you re-read it, it will bring that up to 70%.

Also, use the stuff in the first book. Especially the pro-active business plan where you can make a list of all your advertising needs, complete with all the steps to keep you on track. Use this pro-active business plan every week to help keep you on track. And as always, if you have any questions or need one-on-one personal help with this or anything in your business, just get in touch with us via our website: www.evergreentech.net We are there to help you. Your success is our success.

Now, on to the wonderful world of employees.

The Guaranteed Profit System
Book 4

Where the Good Employees Are

"How to Find and Keep Good Employees"

By: Lynn H. Fife

Where The Good Employees Are: Chapter One
Your Choice in Employees

Welcome to the wonderful world of employees. This is the world where it can be a dream. Well, either a nightmare or a sweet dream, your choice.

Our mission for this book is to help you learn about the great things, and the potentially dangerous things about hiring employees.

So, your business has grown to the point where you need (or already have) employees.

When it comes to hiring employees, you basically have three choices with the "type" of workers you hire. The term "type" refers both to the effect on your company and your employees. First choice is what I call "legitimate employees". The second type is known as "subcontract labor", and the third choice is called "piece rate" labor.

Ok. There is actually a fourth type of employee, which is the "illegal employee".

A funny thing happened on one of my consulting jobs. I mentioned to a client that the way he was handling his labor was illegal to which he said, "Ya know Lynn, illegal is just a sick bird". Get it? Ill eagle. He proceeded to tell me that, "I'm a small company. No one will ever know. I'll never get caught". Yea right!

So then, what type of employee is best for your company? Well, let's take a look at the three types and you will be able to decide for yourself which is the best fit.

Let's start with the typical and common illegal company. Note the words "typical and common". I am not sure if you are aware of this, but approximately 20 percent of the Retail industry do not follow labor laws completely, and the shocking statistic of about 60 percent of the service industry do not follow labor laws completely.

Oh sure. They "think" what they are doing is just bending a few rules, but they don't realize how serious bending the rules can be. We'll talk about that a little later. First, let's take a look at why so many companies fall into this "fudging" temptation.

The *why* part: It all boils down to price. Almost every employer out there thinks employees are one of the largest expense items in their business. They think, "I need the help, so let's put an ad in the paper and see if I can get someone to work for me for as little as possible. That will keep my employee labor expenses down".

Well now. Believe it or not, that is one of the first biggest mistakes in the employee world.

Let's back up just one step. Remember how many companies go out of business in the first five years? Right. 80 percent. They go out of business because the think and act as typical business owners. Our objective is to make is such that your business does not go out of business and we do that by helping you think and act different.

This is one of the thought process changes that need to be made. Here it comes…

Learn to think employees are *not* just a bunch of "money makers" for you. They are people. You are in the people business. There are laws for a reason. I know we think the labor laws are just there to protect the employee, but actually they are there to protect both. They are there to promote a good and fair working relationship between an employer and employee.

OK. Let's go back to the illegal company (which we don't want).

We'll pick it up with the concept of how employee labor expense affects your price.

With a legal employee, you have a bunch of taxes and insurance expenses. You have federal income tax, employment tax, social security… etc. Some states have a state tax. Most states require workman's compensation insurance. All of these things add cost to your price. Just as a rule of thumb, these taxes and insurance items will add about 1/3 or more of what you pay the employee in an hourly wage. Example: If you pay $15 per hour, your taxes and insurance will be about 1/3 of that or about $5.00 per hour.

Some of you are thinking, "No, Mine is about $2.50 on a $15.00 person". It is very common that you may be missing the workman's compensation insurance, which can be a biggie.

Again, this is an error in accounting. Because it is "insurance" we put it as an overhead item, however this workman's compensation is based on payroll dollars. If your employees work more hours, you pay more insurance. Since it is not a set amount and will vary from month to month, then it becomes what we call "Labor Burden".

Labor Burden is all those taxes and insurance things we talked about above.

Anyway, for those of you who are thinking, "how do I know what my tax rates and insurance rates are for my company"? I regret this book cannot tell you since each state is different and the rates for taxes and insurance constantly change. The best thing to do is go to a payroll company and ask them for ALL the items you pay for, with relationship to an hourly employee.

So, if a company is legal and paying all this stuff, as much as $5.00 per hour more and the competition does not operate legal by paying cash under the table and they do *not* pay taxes or insurance, their price will be lower.

That is the temptation. We are still stuck thinking we need to match or beat the competitions price. Remember, they *will* go out of business. The legal company will always have higher prices than the illegal company. The choice for success is to do *everything* 100 percent legal.
Here are some things that fall into the illegal category:

- Pay employee cash
- Don't take out any taxes
- Don't carry workman's compensation insurance
- Do not pay any extra for overtime (more than 8 hours a day or 40 hrs a week)

Those are the biggies.

So, let's shift to a brief description of what a legal company does with regards to hourly employees:

- Pay employees via pay check prepared by a payroll company or in house software

- Pays taxes on each pay day
- Pays workman's compensation insurance regularly
- Pays time and a half for overtime

Now, there are a bunch of other legal issues with employees and we have dedicated a whole chapter on that, so we'll wait until then to discuss that.

What? Oh, yes. There's another question from a reader.

What? You say, your mechanic friend told you that you can pay "piece rate" to your employees and you don't have to pay taxes or insurance on them.

Really? I have heard this a whole bunch, which is why we are going to get into that very thing right now.

The piece rate concept is actually a mix of hourly employee and subcontract labor. Let me start with subcontract labor then we can better understand how the piece rate comes into effect. We'll touch on the piece rate later in this chapter.

Subcontract labor is a very dangerous thing if you do not do it correctly. The danger lies with the federal government and taxes. We all have to pay taxes. Even your employees have to pay taxes.

Here's how subcontract labor *really* works. Legally that is.

Subcontract labor means one business is being hired by another business to do work. It is legal only when you have one legitimate business doing work for another legitimate business. Can you pick up the key word? Right! Legitimate.

Let's get to the rules of being a legitimate business.

> You must carry your own general liability insurance.
> You must be responsible for your own workman's compensation.
> You are in business to service all potential customers.
> You do not do work for only one person or business.
> You wear your uniform. Not the uniform of other companies.
> You do not drive or exclusively use equipment of one company.
> You do not fill out a time card or go through another companies payroll system.
> You work for a set contract amount regardless of how many hours you spend.
> Each project you work on is done under a contract specific to that project.
> You have no representation or authority of the companies you work for.
> You do not purchase materials or any other item for the company you work for.

There are a few more little things, but these are the biggies.

Look them over again. If you have employees that you are "calling" subcontract labor, then ask yourself, "Self. Can the people working for me as subcontractors say "yes" to *any* of those items listed"?

The government is very clear. If there is only _one_ of those items above where you are in compliance with your employees, then you are responsible to pay taxes regardless of what you "claim" their employment status is.

Danger! Danger! Red alert!

Here is what could happen, and often does happen to help many companies go right out of business.

The IRS really doesn't have time to audit all companies in the US. They like to focus on the big companies because when they find something, the get bigger dollars for the auditor's time.

But wait. Once you have been in business for five to seven years, then the total amount of sales you have done over the five to seven years may easily exceed the million dollar mark. The IRS is now interested in an audit because when they do find something, they can now get seven years of back taxes, penalties and interest making their audit worth while.

They check the sales. They see an increase. Sometimes they see a substantial increase. But they don't see an increase in your payroll. You explain you use subcontract labor.

They ask for time records. You show them time cards. Or, if you have been sending in 1099 (like your supposed to), they check into them to see if the subcontracted labor has been filing as a business.

Guess what. Your "subcontract labor" people don't even have a trade name registered. They don't have insurance, and when the IRS calls them, they say, "I work exclusively for XYZ company", *your* company. BAM! They got ya. The IRS politely, and with a smile, explains to you that the employees you have do not qualify as subcontractors because they don't follow the subcontract labor exemption as noted above in this chapter. You now have to pay all the taxes you should have paid for each hour they worked for the past seven years. This easily reaches $250 grand or more. Congrats, you are now out of business with garnished wages for the rest of your life.

Moral of this story is:

IF IT'S NOT 100 PERCENT LEGIT, DON'T DO IT.

On the positive side, i.e. legal side of subcontracting, there is a proper way, and an appropriate way to have subcontract labor. After all, there are businesses that are obviously legitimate subcontract labor base. One of my side businesses, for example, is a great case.

I still like doing faux finish work (fancy schmancy decorative painting).

Once in a while, I get a large job where the customer wants a lot of work done in a short period of time. I need help, so I go to my database of people who attended my wife's faux finish school. I know they are trained since they went through her class. I call them and find out who is running a legitimate business (insurance and all).

When I call them, I let them know I have a project. I give them the specifics and let them know, "It will take about 3 days and your subcontract amount will be $840.00. Do you want to join me on this project"? They say yes. At that point, I let them know I require a photo copy of their general liability insurance and workman's compensation insurance to make sure they are current. We fill out a project contract and we go to work.

If the project gets done in only two days, the subcontractor still gets the same dollar amount. If something goes wrong and we have to re-do a bunch of areas, the subcontractor still gets the same dollar amount.

This is how you do legitimate subcontracting.

What? Question in the front here? The question is: "Can I make my employees work for a set amount and give them a project contract and pay them a set amount like you just suggested"?

Well, there are tons of requirements included in that scenario. Remember the list above? You can't just do only one thing mentioned on that list and think it's legal. You have to do *all* the things. Such as, they can't wear your uniform. You must introduce them to your customers as subcontractors. They must work for someone else besides you. They must have their own legitimate business and send you an invoice for all the work they do. They can't drive your vehicles. They must have their own general liability and workman's compensation insurance… etc.

So the answer to the question is, "Sure. As long as they follow *all* the rules of being a subcontractor".

OK, I think we are all clear on the subcontractor thing. What about that piece rate thing?

The piece rate type of worker was developed from farmers a long time ago. They didn't want to pay someone a buck an hour who can pick four crates and pay the next guy the same buck an hour who can only pick two crates an hour.

So the labor department set up the piece rate type of labor for farmers so they could pay a specific amount per unit. I.e. $.25 cents a crate. Of course, that rate may have been used 50 years ago. Today, obviously it has gone up to whatever the market allows.

Continuing on. This piece rate does not only apply to farmers. It can apply to other types of businesses.

The danger is, it is only allowed for very specific types of businesses. Just because the piece rate is allowed to some businesses, does not mean it is allowed for all businesses. As a matter of fact, it is highly illegal for any business to use it who does not fall into the piece rate exemption as defined by the labor laws.

Example: The automotive repair business is a piece rate allowable business. It stemmed from common situations that occurred in the 30's through the 60's.

If a person's car was making a funny noise and blowing black smoke, the average driver didn't have a clue about auto mechanics, so they took it to the garage. If the garage was not so reputable (which many were not), they could tell the driver the expense to repair it was several hundred dollars when in fact it may be only an adjustment on the carburetor. They could and often did literally cheat their customers for hundreds if not thousands of dollars.

Well, the public was not stupid for too long. They got the government involved and said, "We have to do something about this garage mechanic theft problem".

The government came up with the piece rate exemption for auto mechanics which basically says: If a mechanic replaces an alternator in a Ford F-150 pick up, the time it takes a certified mechanic will be X amount of time. Period. It limited how much they could charge for labor and made all of us drivers more confident that the auto mechanic could not over charge us for labor.

Now, the auto mechanic owners would have reason be a little upset. They would say, "What if my mechanic takes twice as long. You make me pay him for all the hours he works, but only allow me to collect ½ of what it takes my mechanic to do the work. I'll be out of business in no time".

Piece rate kicks in here. The government made it so the owner pays the mechanic a set dollar amount for the work being done. In other words, a certified mechanic should be able to do the work in say 30 minutes. They get paid $15 bucks (works out to $30 an hour) no matter how long it actually takes them to do the work. If they get it done in 15 minutes, they can make $60 an hour. If they get it done in 2 hours, the only make $7.50 an hour. This makes it fair for the business owner and the vehicle owner.

What about the mechanic? Well, if they are a true certified mechanic and can do the work under the average amount of time allowable, they make good money. It's a great deal for the talented mechanic. For the lousy mechanic, it's not so good. After all, isn't that the way it's supposed to be?

What about *your* company? Can you use piece rate labor? The only way to find out is to call the authorities who will attack you if you are not running a legitimate business.

That's right. Call the department of labor and industries (Or the Department of Labor, or the Workforce Commission… whatever they call it in your state). Let them know what your business is, and ask them if you qualify for piece rate, or just flat out ask them how to set up your employees. They will be a great guide. When you get the instructions from the source, you know you are doing it correctly.

Enough for the "piece rate" topic. That brings us to the typical legitimate employee.

Almost all retail businesses and most service businesses are required by law to set up their employment with the legitimate employee type.

Why? Good question.

The law clearly states that you can not use subcontract labor or piece rate labor if you:

- If an employee is considered full time or part time labor for your company.
- If your employee is paid by the hour.
- If you schedule your employee to work specific days and times.
- If you have an employee wear your uniform or company shirt.
- If you have your employees fill out a time card or punch a time clock.
- If your employees are not set up as a legitimate business subcontracting work.
- If your company does not qualify for piece rate exemption.
- If your employee(s) have authority to sign as a representative of your company.

As you can see, most companies fall into the legitimate employee category.

There is one more break out type of employee you could have. That is the "Salary" employee.

The biggest difference between hourly and salary is, the salary person is not on a time clock. They can work as many hours as it takes to do the job. They get paid a set amount regardless of how many hours they work.

Labor laws are kinda sticky in this one too. Basically, a salary person is to be a *key* person in your business, meaning, they must be a manger or supervisor who has authority to fully represent your company, hire, fire, sign contracts, spend money… etc.

As you can see, a typical employee who comes to do every day work for you and they do not have the authority to spend money or hire/fire people, they are not eligible for salary status.

It is obvious. The salary status was allowed because a person in a management person could not be limited to 40 hours a week. If the job requires more time, the management person gives it more time without extra pay.

There is a small danger here and that comes with bending the rule temptation. The temptation is to call your employees an "assistant manager" and put them on a salary so you can work them 50 to 60 hours a week and not pay overtime. Many companies do this only to discover they can get in a ton of trouble with the department of labor.

If the employee learns that they are not a true management person. They can not hire or fire anyone nor can they spend money, and they learn they are entitled to overtime pay for all the overtime they worked, it is only a matter of time before it catches up to the owner and the employee walks away with a bunch of money and the business owner goes out of business.

Here's a story to illustrate this point. I love stories, don't you?

A company told me of a true situation where one of their employees walked into a bar after work looking very tired. Their friend at the bar said, "Man, you look beat. 'Sup"? The person responded, "Just had a long day. Started at 5:00 this morning and had a 10 hour day". His friend said, "I hear you, but at least you get the extra money for overtime". The employee said, "Nah. My boss doesn't pay overtime".

The friend's eyes opened wide and they said, "Listen, here's some things you should know. It is a federal law that they have to pay you overtime which is time and a half for every hour over eight hours. Or, if you work more than 40 hours in a week. You've been there for over seven years right? That will come out to literally thousands of dollars your boss will have to pay you *and* he can't fire you because you can file anonymously. Here's what you do. You keep your own time card record for two months. Write down your exact start time, lunch breaks, end time and overtime. Do *not* tell let your boss know what you are doing. After two months, call the department of labor and industries. Tell them you don't wanna get fired but your boss is not paying overtime. They will let you know they will audit all employee records and your name will not be brought up. They will want *your* record of the time card as proof as to what you actually worked". The employee came back and said, "'K. What's the number". Two months later the claim was made.

This employer had eight employees.

When the department of labor came in for an audit, mysteriously, the time cards had been lost except for the most recent two pay periods. The auditor showed the time cards kept by the anonymous employee and let the employer know, "for the past two months there has been an average of six hours per week in overtime that has not been paid. Since you have no records, we must assume the same has been true for each employee that works for you. We are allowed to go back seven years and calculate all the overtime you should have paid to the employees. You will be required to pay all the overtime you failed to pay directly to the employees, and (are you ready for this) you owe taxes on all that money for the past seven years and (yes it get worse) there is interest and penalties on top of that".

Bummer! The employee who turned him in had been working for about 12 years. He got a check from the owner for a little over $15,000. All of the other seven employees got checks ranging from $12,000 to $4,000. By the time all was said and done, the owner got nailed for around $280,000.00! Yikes!

Out of business? Ya think? By the way, can he file bankruptcy and get out of paying it?

No! He had to sell everything he had, go out of business, and had his wages garnished and probably still is to this very day.

That, my friends is what illegal gets you. Sick bird? Right!

When the employees learn their rights, they will turn you in for a few thousand bucks in a heartbeat. Don't kid yourself. When it comes to employees, stay 100 percent legal.

Where The Good Employees Are: Chapter Two
Learning Labor Laws

Wow. That last story was a scary one, huh? I'm glad it didn't happen to me. Well, this chapter is all about how you can make sure it never happens to you.

Most people think that labor laws extend only the point of paying the employees properly. You know, taking out taxes, paying taxes… that kind of stuff.

Well, it goes quite a bit further than that. This chapter is here to fill you in on some of the labor laws that frequently cause problems for owners.

Let's ease into this with some of the labor laws you may already know.

Time records (for those of you who have hourly employees): Technically, the law says the employee is to fill out their own time card. It is a written statement from *them* on the amount of hours they work for you. It doesn't matter if written by hand or by time clock.

The time card is supposed to show:
Employee name
Work period (from what date to what date)
Date of each day worked
Time they started work
Time they started their lunch break
Time they ended their lunch break
Time they ended work
Employee signature verifying *they* filled it out

Tricky stuff here.

It is oh so common to hear an employer say, "I can't get my employees to fill out their time card correctly. There's always stuff missing on them. I have to guess before I can make their paycheck".

Actually, it's not legal for you to fill out any part of their time card. After all, the time card is *their* testimony of the hours worked.

Let's take a look at what some… Ok, many employees do, and why they do it.

The employee gets to work at 9:10 AM but no-one seems to say anything. They also are supposed to work until say 3:00 PM, but they leave about 2:50 PM because no one will ever know or say anything about it. What time do they write on their time card? Right! 9:00 AM and 3:00 PM and they just got 20 minutes free pay. That is outright stealing. But, oh well. Who's watching?

Or, the employee shows up at 9:15 AM and knows the boss sees them come in late. They hurry to work and "forget" to record their start time. End of the week comes, the start time is not written, the person doing payroll looks on the schedule and sees 9:00 AM, or the boss knows they usually start at 9:00 AM so that's what gets written on the time card for them. They just got an extra 15 minutes.

Now it may not sound like much but it adds up.

If you have only 4 employees who fudge only 12 minutes a day on average, that works out to only one hour per week, or 4 hours per month or times four employees works out to 16 hours per month at an average wage of say $10.00 plus your burden of another $3.00.

When I do the math for you, it would cost about $208.00 per month or $2,496.00 per year that you just gave away because you fill in the blank spaces for your employees. They got that much extra money for showing up late and leaving early. For that kind of bucks, you could have gone on a cruise!

Makes you just wanna just hug those employees, doesn't it?

OK, So most owners learn to baby-sit the employees time card. "Now remember to have me initial your time before you leave today", which they rarely do.

Let's get back to the law and see how you can effectively handle this problem without having to baby-sit them.

Remember, the law says the employee must fill out the time card, and you are not allowed to write on it since it is their testimony of the time worked.

The solution starts with your company policy. Written, presented in a training session, and signed in agreement by your employees.

This written company policy section says, "All time cards are to be filled out by each employee". They are to write their name, dates of the pay period, the exact time started to the minute, their lunch start and end time to the exact minute and the end time to the exact minute.

The company policy continues with, "The time card must be initialed by the manager / supervisor / foreman / lead person in charge at the end of each day. In the event the time card is turned in and it is not complete in any of these areas, when the employee comes to pick up their paycheck, instead they will receive their time card with red circles indicating where the time card was incomplete or inaccurate and the employee will wait until the next pay period assuming the time card is turned in again after being corrected and is accurate".

Is that really legal? Sure is. Remember, the law says you *must* pay your employee for the work they did. The law does not say when you have to pay them. In most states there is a 30 maximum total period. This means your employees can work for two weeks and turn in their time cards. You cannot hold their check for more then 30 days.

So, YES. You can hold their check. Besides, if the information on the time card is not correct, you can not prepare their check in the first place since you are not supposed to write on their time card making it complete for your payroll.

Staring to make sense? Great!

Just remember, the time card is *their* record. It's the same thing as if you were to call a store and tell them so send you an item that is advertised for $100.00. On the phone you confirm the price of $100.00. The company sends the product and in the product packaging there is an invoice for $150.00. Do you just pay it? I don't think so. You would call them and ask them to send you a correct invoice. You don't pay for it until you get the correct invoice.

In the above situation, if the company told you to go ahead and pay only the $100.00 you owed and they would "fix their books later". Guess what happens?

Right! The company will show a balance due of $50. They will continue to hound you for it.

It becomes *your* mess to clean up *their* accounting.

This example teaches us to wait until we get an accurate invoice, *then* we pay it.

It's the same thing with a time card. The employee time card is their invoice to you. If it is not accurate, you don't have to pay it. When it is accurate, then you pay it.

The point here is:

First have a company policy. In the company policy, have the section on time cards. How to fill it out, what is correct and what is incorrect. Next, let them know if their time card is not accurate, they will not get a check on payday. They will have to fix their time card and wait until the next pay day to get their check.

Can you hear them squeal?

It's really no big deal. The employee will never have to worry about getting paid on time if they *do* care about being accurate on their time card.

By the way, any intentional misrepresentation on the time card (writing 9:00 AM instead of the 9:10 AM) is theft and should be noted as theft in your company policy. If/when they are caught, there will be no acceptable excuse. They will be terminated for theft and it will not look good on their employment record.

Our first book talks about writing company policies and the first book has the free downloadable forms that you can use as a guide. This will be greatly helpful to have your company policy complete before you introduce new rules or guidelines to your employees.

We also offer a completed company policy online on our website www.evergreentech.net. From the home page, just click on the button below the picture of our Guaranteed Profit System book that says, Free Downloadable Forms – Click here". Enter your personal security code found at the bottom of the table of contents and you will be taken to our online optional items section as well as the free downloadable forms that come with this book. I highly recommend the Employee Company Policy. It will save you hundreds of hours attempting to create something that is already done. Check it out.

Now, back on track.

Employees will always test the system.

Just like those cute little toddlers. They gotta test everything.

All it takes is firm adherence to your own company policy to let them live the actual experience of opening a paycheck envelope only to discover their time card marked up and see no check. I guarantee, it will only happen once.

Be prepared for, "but I have starving kids... need to make the rent payment... etc". Yes. You are very sorry for their financial stress, but alas. It *is* the law that I cannot fill out your time card. It was not you, the owner, that didn't fill out the time card correctly.

Perhaps the employee can take responsibility to do it correctly from now on. Their financial stress is a result of their own action. Not yours and they will just have to learn to live with the consequences of their action.

So. Do you think I said it enough ways? It's really a no brainer, isn't it?

Here's some actual dialog you may want to use.

I would say, "I'm so sorry. I'll tell you what I can do for you. I can look at your time card before you turn it in at the end of the week, and we can go over it together for errors. This way you will never have to worry about not getting your check on time. When it comes to giving you a check now, even when you have failed to turn in your time card accurately? Again, I'm sorry. It is actually a law that I cannot modify your time card for you, and we cannot prepare a check when the time card is not complete. It has incorrect information, so we cannot prepare an accurate paycheck. When you were hired (or in a previous meeting), you were trained, shown, and signed your name to agreement to our time card company policy. I know with this incident, and with your future accuracy, it will not happen again". Smile!

It's fair. It's firm. It's legal and it will eliminate a bunch of your time card accuracy problems. You no longer will be able to say, "I can't get my employees to fill out their time cards".

OK, enough time on that issue.

Next up is the law on breaks.

Here again, you may already know this but there may be a few readers who may not know the actual law on breaks.

In most States, the law for employers using hourly employees is basically this:

When your employee hits the four hour mark, they must have a ten minute break paid for by the employer.

When your employee hits the five hour mark, they must have a 30 minute break which is not paid for by the employer.

When your employee hits the 7th hour, they must have another ten minute break paid for by the employer.

Safety measures:

Sometime within the first four hours, give your employee a ten minute break. They are still on the clock.

Sometime within a five hour period, let them break for lunch. They are off the clock and must write down the time they started lunch (or use the time clock to punch out). The also must write down their time (or punch in) when their lunch break is over.

Sometime in the later part of their shift and sooner than one hour before they are off, give them another ten minute break. This assumes of course, they are working an eight hour day.

Questions?

I see one here: "If the employee only has a four hour shift, do I need to give them a break"?

Nope. Technically, you have to give them the ten minute break no later than the four hour mark. If they only work four hours, they hit the mark. Go home. No break required. However, as a good boss, and depending on the work involved, you many want to give them the break anyway. Example: If they are working outside in the sun hauling stones for a landscaping company, you may wanna give them as much of a break as is needed to keep them hydrated and healthy.

Another question?

"My guys want to combine their two ten minute breaks into one 20 minute break, skip lunch and go home a half hour early. Can they do that legally"?

Not only no, but heck no. Again, go back to what the law requires. It *requires* they take a 30 minute lunch break after five hours work. It would violate the law to "skip" lunch, so, sorry, no leaving early. No skipping lunch.

Side note: There have been companies who do take a 20 minute break in the morning after about three hours, then take the half hour lunch break after five hours, then work to the end of the day. This is OK since they have had the required, two each, ten minute breaks within their eight hour shift. So, I understand from my Labor and Industries source, that it's OK.

Again, if you are in doubt of any variation of how you work your breaks, the best source is the Department of Labor (or whatever they call themselves in your area). Find out what they say for your state/area/government and do what they suggest. Ya can't get in trouble that way.

Here's the next important labor law.

Discrimination:

This is becoming more and more sensitive. I think I'll start this one with a short story.

I had a painting contractor client in 1996. They had a woman come in for an interview. The woman said she had 15 years experience, was a foreman for another company and knew all the ropes with painting and all painting equipment. She wanted $18 bucks per hour.

The employer hired her and sent her on a job with another foreman who was to watch her and report back on her actual skills, attitude, etc.

Within two hours of her being in the job, the foreman called and said, "get this person off of my job. She spent 30 minutes masking off a door that usually takes a brand new person 10 minutes. She didn't know the first thing on how to set up our airless sprayer. Her brushing skills are that of a first year painter. Evidently, she lied through her teeth when she told you she was foreman quality".

When asked about her attitude, the foreman reported back that she was actually pleasant and willing to do what she was told.

The owner called her back in the office and let her know the report. He found out that she really wasn't a foreman, she just said that to get a higher pay. He told her he would be fair with her and allow her to keep the job but he could only pay her for her value as a first year apprentice at $11.00 per hour. She said, "I can't live on that! I'm outta here"!

Do you wanna guess what happened next? Right. Within two weeks, the owner got a discrimination lawsuit where she was claiming he cut her pay because she was a woman.

Here come the lawyers!

Oh. By the way, if you ever have *any* situation where you would like legal advice and legal representation, be sure to contact us at www.evergreentech.net. We have the *best* legal service that cost an average of $50 per month that gives you free legal advice from the top attorney firm in your state. They not only tell you what to do, but in many cases, do the work for you. Like having your own personal full time attorney for only $50 a month. Please give us a call and take advantage of this fantastic program. My personal feelings on this program? You are crazy to have a business and *NOT* have access to an attorney or legal representation.

OK, back to employee discrimination.

In the story above, fortunately, the owner had her application where she lied about her experience, the written testimony of the foreman and the open offer for her to come back to work for the value of her actual experience.

It took *months* of effort to do it themselves, but they finally got it cleared up.

So, how *do* we protect ourselves against this type of thing? Great question!

We will cover this extensively when we get to the chapter on screening and hiring. But for now, here's more on discrimination.

Basically, discrimination is where you make any decision in your company with regards to an employee where that decision has any whatsoever connection with race, sex, creed, color, religion, age or anything of a personal nature.

To avoid any question or problem of discrimination, just remember to make all of your judgments on actual personal skill of the person as it relates to your business.

Example: If a person "says" they know how to use a computer, it is your responsibility to test them to see if they in fact can use a computer for the purpose intended by their job description. This is where the screening process comes in (discussed later). It does not matter if they have a college education, if they are in a wheelchair, if they are deaf or anything else. Can they do the job they are hired to do?

Now in some cases, like in big business where you are handling large accounts, you may want your applicant to be properly trained. A college degree in a specific field may be required because is it needed for the work the applicant will be doing. Thus, it is legal for them to require a college degree.

If however, the person is going to work in a fast food place flipping burgers, then a college degree is not needed for that type of employee to do their job, thus it could be considered discriminatory to not hire them because they don't have a college degree.

Discrimination takes place in two areas.

First area is at the point of hire.

You, the owner have the burden of proof as to why you didn't hire a person. An applicant can "claim" anything and give you a world of trouble if you don't protect yourself.

How you protect yourself during the hiring process is to flat out tell *all* applicants, "We do not have a position at this time. We are simply gathering applications for possible employees in the future".

There isn't a law anywhere that forces you to hire someone when you flat out don't need them. Thus, it shuts the door on any discrimination suit.

Where owners get in trouble is they say, "Yes, we are looking to hire someone as soon as possible. Can you come in for an interview today."

With this scenario, you have told the applicant you *do* have a job and you *are* interested in them. Now, you have to prove *why* you didn't hire them. When you say, "Well, they just didn't have the pleasant smile I was looking for".

Sorry, you are not hiring a model for which that is a valid item. The person could sue for discrimination on the basis you didn't hire them due to facial imperfections / or physical limitations and they will win. You cannot refuse people work because their face doesn't smile the way you like it. And on it goes.

Are ya clear on the discrimination thing? I'm sure you are. If not, I would continue to ramble on a bit more on it.

OK. On we go to harassment.

Harassment is very close to the discrimination issue. Let's expound on that now.

Typically, harassment is most common when it is preceded with the word "sexual".

Sexual harassment as defined by law is, "When a person feels they have been personally violated by another person with unprofessional conduct in regards to physical matters".

Let's say that in plain Americanized English.

If a person goes up to another person and says, "You look very attractive today". The recipient can either, 1. Take it as a compliment, feel good about them self and get on with their day with a smile. Or 2. They can feel like the other person is trying to seduce them, get embarrassed and deep inside, wish they would stop saying stuff like that.

You cannot say to person 2, "Get a life". You also cannot say to person one, "You are opening the door to potentially terrible things". Neither one is right or wrong. It's just a personal choice.

For person 2 above, the situation is in fact sexual harassment. But note. The harassment indication is established by the recipient of the statement. In this case, person 2.

What about the sender? When does it become a legal issue in the workplace?

This is where the law is very specific. In the above case, if the recipient makes any statement to the sender that they are not comfortable and they wish them to stop, we have just entered into phase one of sexual harassment.

If the sender repeats the incident, then they are guilty of sexual harassment and are subject to a legitimate lawsuit.

Should it turn into a lawsuit, the burden of proof is on the recipient. They must document the day, time and details of the warning they issued. This is best done when the recipient goes to management, or if management IS the problem, they go to a fellow employee/worker. A statement is written and witnessed by the management person or fellow worker.

In either case, the complaint is to be presented to the offender. Preferably with their signature signifying they have received the complaint notice and been given a directive not to repeat the offence.

When/if the incident re-occurs, the same is true. The recipient is to document the incident and file it with a manger or if management is the problem, they can go to the department of labor and industries and file the complaint, get an attorney, and file suit.

The law is also very strict about this issue. Management cannot fire anyone for filing a sexual discrimination suit. Period. Matter of fact it is very hard to fire an employee once the have filed a legitimate suit.

Another type of sexual harassment does not require a warning or second incident. If for example, a woman is working on a job site in the construction field and a construction worker gives out a loud wolf whistle and shouts, "Hey baby, you're hot, do you wanna spend some private time with me"?

WOW! Is that stupid or what? That is a one time flat out clear case of sexual harassment. It does not need a warning. The person can go directly to the sexual harassment lawsuit.

So, just in summary: It's always a good idea to have mention of a harassment policy in your company policy. Train your employees it will not be tolerated in any form, playful or not. It will be subject to immediate termination. Etc.

Well, that's my feelings on it anyway.

Another form of harassment may not have anything to do with sex. It can be unjust harassment. Example: You have an owner who has hired an employee. That employee started to date the owner's sister. The owner doesn't like that, so they start giving the employee all the dirty work. Hauling trash, cleaning toilets, cleaning the floor corners on hands and knees with paper towels and a toothbrush... that type of thing.

This too is not legal. All the employee needs to do is file a claim that he is the one being harassed and can prove he is being asked to do unpleasant tasks that no other employee is required to do. The tasks are also not defined in any written job description for the position the employee holds.

Yes. You can land in a huge pile of dung for doing that type of stuff.

Remedy. If you don't like someone for any reason, it's up to *you* to figure out why, and to work it out with the other person in a professional way such that you can work together successfully.

If it is a performance issue, you, as the owner can set specific written job descriptions defining expected (reasonable) tasks for all employees and it will be up to the "problem" employee to comply.

If they do not comply, then you can terminate them for failure to perform in their job. If this is the case, make sure you have three written specific incidences for your protection.

Oops. I did it again. I skipped ahead to an item that is in the termination chapter.

OK… I'll put the reins on this one this time. You'll just have to wait till the last chapter on termination to get "the rest of the story" (for you Paul Harvey fans).

Next item for legal stuff is the issue of overtime pay for hourly employees.

The specific law for most states in the U.S. is this:

Standard overtime is one and one half the amount of their regular pay.

If an employee works more than eight hours in a day, they are to be paid overtime for each hour over eight hours with smallest allowable increment of 15 minutes.

If an employee works more than 40 hours in a week, they are to be paid overtime for each hour over 40 hours with smallest allowable increment of 15 minutes.

An employer can have workweeks defined as four days of 10 hours. If so, overtime is payable for more than ten hours in a day with smallest allowable increment of 15 minutes.

An employer may *not* mix a 10 hour day schedule with an eight hour day work schedule in any given pay period. They also cannot switch back and forth at will. The work week must be selected and established as "typical work week" for the company.

That's it in a nut shell.

Simplified, it means, for full time employees, you have a choice to work them four days a week for 10 hours a day or you can work them five days a week for eight hours a day.

Any time they put in over the eight hours a day or ten hours a day is automatic overtime. If they only work 15 minutes overtime, they get time and a half for that 15 minutes worked.

It *is* legal for an employee to volunteer to put in five or ten minutes each day without recording it so long as it is voluntary and not required, but once they hit 15 minutes, they are entitled to overtime pay.

Making that one clear: When I was a painter, if I spilled paint in an attempt to clean up quickly at the end of the day, and the clean up required me to spend about 30 minutes to clean it up. I didn't feel right making the owner pay me overtime for 30 minutes because of my mistake. I willingly gave the 30 minutes and did *not* record it on my time card. This is legal.

Now, I could have gotten overtime since I had the legal right, but, my work ethics would not allow my subconscious to take advantage of my boss that way.

Do our current employees feel the same? I doubt it. Only those who have true values would do that. Those are the ones you look to give raises to and promote within your company. None the less, if an employee did not have the same ethics, they would be paid overtime.

Make sense? Sure thing.

Here are some more examples of overtime pay to make it clear for all those questions I can hear screaming over the psychic wavelengths.

Employee works six hours Monday and wants to make it up on Tuesday to get in a full eight hours. So on Tuesday, they work and extra two hours. At the end of the week, they have a total of say 38 hours. Do you pay overtime?

Answer: Yes. You pay the two hours overtime for the ten hour day they worked on Tuesday plus any other time where they worked more than eight hours in the day.

Employer says to the employees… "We are working four days this week at ten hours each to comply with the allowable ten hour days multiplied by four days for your 40 hours. Next week, we will go back to our usual five day work week at eight hours a day". Is this legal?

The answer is: Heck no. Why? Because the law says you cannot shift back and forth. Your company establishes what is "normal" for your business and that is what you stick with. In the above case, if the normal work week was eight hours a day and, if the employees do work four days for ten hours each, the owner would have to pay two hours per day overtime. Example: The employee time card would have to read 32 hours regular pay and eight hours overtime pay for a total of 40 hours in the week.

Ooooooo. Here's another tricky question. "If I tell my employees there iso be absolutely no overtime without permission, but they still sneak in the extra two to three hours a week, do I still have to pay them the overtime"?

Whadda ya think?

Your inability to control employees does not mean you don't have to pay them overtime.

What you can do in that instance is put your overtime policy in writing in your company policy. The employee is trained, understands and signs his agreement to the policy. When they violate the policy by getting in unauthorized overtime, you write them up on a warning slip. Three warning slips, they get terminated for violation of company policy. Borderline theft.

So, Lynn, when *is* it a good thing to pay overtime?

That one is easy. If your customer (in the service industry or retail industry) ask you to do work that is not part of your normal week (like Saturday night), you can let them know these are off hours and, yes, you can do it however the law requires you pay your employees overtime pay. The amount will be X more.

When the customer is giving you overtime pay, then you can pay it without it hurting your profit structure. Matter of fact, it actually helps it when you do it that way.

Yes, in retail, that works too. Let's say you are a hobby shop and your customer wants one on one lessons. The only time they can come in is on Saturday Evening when you are usually closed. "Yes, I can ask Julie to stay late and give you some one-on-one training, however the law requires I pay her overtime. Your rate will be $XX per hour. Would that be OK"? When they say "yes", the overtime is paid by the customer. Not your profit picture. Cool!

Enough on overtime. Let's talk about other items that my end up taking away some of your company profit that relates to your employees.

Here's one for the service industry (retailers can take a quick nap here). With some service trades you are going to the customer's place of residence or business. If their location is a long way away, the issue of travel time pops up.

The law in most areas basically says, if you require your employee to drive more than one hour drive time from either the employees home or the employers office location (which ever is closer to the job site), one way, in non-traffic jam conditions (or about 50 miles), then you must pay them one way travel time which is to be *part of* their regular working hours.

Lot's of commas in there. Let's break it down.

First one is the one hours travel time from either your office *or* the employees home which ever is closer. Let's look at some examples here:

If your employee lives 15 miles to the North of your office but your job site is 55 miles from your office, the closest point to the job site is your employees home. You have your employee drive from their home to the job site. No travel time because the distance from their home to the job is only 40 miles. *But*, if you have the employee report to work at your office each morning, the job site is now just over one hour drive time (over 50 miles) so you must pay them one hour drive time.

The next job you have is 40 miles to the south of your office. The same employee above lives 15 miles north of your office. Do you have to pay him travel time because the distance from his house is now 55 miles from the job site? No. That's where the clarification "which ever is closer" kicks in. Your office is closer to the job site and does not require travel time to be paid. You cannot control where your employees live and it is up to them to get themselves to work on time regardless of where they live.

Again, for the service industry (which usually has higher pay then retail industry), this is common knowledge with employees and they just get used to it.

So much for travel time.

Here's something that is quite cool actually. The question often comes up, "Can I make my employees come to work early so they actually start working on time"?

This is a great question for both Servicers and Retailers. Somewhere in our past there were many businesses that went to the department of labor and industries with this problem: They said, "Our employees show up at exactly 8:00 AM and in the first several minutes, they get their uniform on, wash their hands, check the schedule, smoke a quick cigarette, then go to work. We shouldn't have to pay for them "getting ready" to work".

The argument was heard by governing authorities and laws were passed such that a company can have a company policy (in writing) that requires a person to get to work at least (whatever time is reasonable not to exceed 15 minutes) during which time they are to get ready to work by (whenever).

When you have this item in your company policy, train the employees and get them to sign in agreement to follow this policy, then you can require them to get to work X amount of minutes early so they can prepare to go to work and actually start work at the precise start time.

Servicers. Close your mouth. Yes, you can do this.

Hey! Have y'all picked up some key words that have been used with almost every legal issue? Hint: Something about a C_____ P_____ where you write it, train on it, and have your employees sign it.

More on that later. Just a warm up on how important it is to have it. It is for clear employee understanding, your protection and mostly to promote a great working relationship between you and your employees.

Just for fun and to expound on the "get to work early" thing. Hey, you Servicers. Ask yourself, "Self. 1. What time do my workers show up on the job? 2. What time does the work actually begin? 3. What are they doing those first 15 to 30 minutes"?

I'm willing to betcha the answer is, "1. Exactly on time or a few minutes late. 2. about 15 to 30 minutes later. And, 3. Getting ready to work".

So with your new company policy in place, they get there 15 minutes early and get ready to work so the actual work is actually starting at the start time. That would save you at least 15 minutes each day per man. That's 1.25 hours a week. That's five hours a month. With a company of ten employees, that's 50 hours a month. At an average wage and burden of $25 bucks per hour, that's $1,250 per month or $15,000 per year you will save simply by getting serious with a rule used for retailers nationwide.

Why not? Now, I don't wanna spoil anything later in this book, but we do discuss this very thing when it comes to your employee benefit program and how you can actually get your employees to *want* to come early.

Yea right! You're not buying it! Well, not yet anyway. Just wait. You'll see.

Either way, I like this policy because it gets us closer to the good 'ol fashion work ethics of 50 years ago when an employee worked eight hours (and often more) for eight hours of pay. Doesn't seem to be the same any more does it.

There are a few other items of labor laws that get into the hiring process and termination process, but we have entire chapters dedicated to those very things, so let's all take a break here, stretch your body, blink a few times, shake your head and shrug your shoulders a few times to loosen up and we'll be ready for the next chapter.

Break!

See ya back in a while.

Where The Good Employees Are: Chapter Three
Finding Good Apples

It absolutely amazes me. All over the country, no matter what trade, I hear the same thing. "It's hard to find good employees!"

What? You said the same thing?

Well, we all can agree to that.

Toss your hands up in the air and say, "That's just the way it is. You gotta sift through a ton of dirt and gravel to find the ounce gold."

Or, we can take a different approach when it comes to finding good employees.

It starts with the employees themselves.

They are people. They can think (although sometimes we wonder). They are working for you for a reason.

So what is that reason? To _____

Yup. For the same reason you are in business. To make money. They too have a dream of getting rich and retiring some day.

With that as a basis, let's break it down to both sides of the coin. Your side as the owner, and their side as the employee.

What do *you* want as the owner? What do *they* want as the employee?

See if you agree to these points:

You want:
- Willing to work for as little as possible
- Neat and clean appearance
- Honesty
- Hard Working
- Looks for things to do without having to be told
- Dependable transportation
- Shows up for work early each day
- Calls ahead if they are late or sick
- Really cares about their job. Ready, willing and able to learn

OK… Now let's see what they want:
- Top pay for the work they do
- Put in time, get a pay check
- Do only what the boss asks and nothing more

- I do my job but don't like to break a sweat
- Don't mess with my evenings and weekends
- Get money for beer at the end of the day
- A friendly boss who likes to joke around
- I really want to do something else, but this will do for now
- Get out of jail on the work release program
- If I'm late, they will figure it out
- If I get sick, Oh well. They can do without me for a day

Look Familiar? Sound about right?

That's because it is typical, normal, they usual thing. With most companies, there is a distinct difference between what the owner wants and what the employee wants.

So how can you fix this so both the owner and employee get what they want?

Great question.

First thing, you gotta stop thinking like the typical boss and start thinking the "Guaranteed Profit" way. Here are some thoughts to get you going.

Why is it that major corporations have a very long line of college graduates just waiting for any opportunity to come to work for them? Is it because they pay more?

You would think so. But in the "highly professional arena", a person would consider the job a great job if it had low pay, no benefits, anyone can get a job here, it takes no special talent, no education or continued education available… etc. NOT!

So what does the highly professional person look for in a "great" job?

Here's a list for ya.

- High pay or at least fair pay for the work being done
- Medical insurance benefits
- Profit sharing opportunities / bonus
- Vacation pay
- Sick leave
- Holiday pay
- Great working environment / personal desk
- A feeling of being part of a truly professional team (self worth).

Now hold on to your socks. I know what you're thinking. You are thinking, "Yea, but all that stuff cost a bunch of money, and it's not like we *are* an ultra professional business. I'm just a small business."

That, my friends, is the "typical thinking" we are trying to get rid of. When you think like a small company, you will have small company problems. When you start to think like an "ultra professional" company, you will have the same success as the ultra professional companies' experience.

Let's look at more things that are typical with most small companies, only this time, lets start with the employee viewpoint.

We'll have a little fun here. Let's do it in a format where you can circle what you feel will be their first choice. Now remember, you are thinking like an employee now.

Do you want (circle your choice):

Hourly wage to be:	High	Above average	Average	Low
Cash bonus:	Monthly	Once a Year	At random	Don't care
Two weeks per year vacation pay:	Heck yes	OK		Don't care
Medical insurance benefits:	Yes	Maybe		Don't care
Six days a year holiday pay:	Absolutely	OK		Don't care
Two days sick leave per year:	Sure	Maybe		Don't care
On going training to help you get raises:	Excellent	Maybe		Don't care
Career opportunity into management:	Great	Maybe		Don't Care

I see most of your circles are leaning heavily to the left side of the choices.

You are right and you are still thinking, "But Lynn, you're forgetting all this stuff costs money. I would have to raise my prices through the roof."

Hold on to that thought. We will explain how much if not all this stuff could end up costing you very little or even nothing.

"Oh, I just gotta see this!" your thinking. Right? Just hang in there. You'll see.

Before we get there, let's continue with this same thought process except for the owner side.

This time, I want you to be honest and circle the choice that best represents what *most* small business owners do. Note: Not what you do or what you think they should do, but what they really do:

Do most small business owners (Circle your best choice):

Pay an hourly wage that is :	High	Average	As little as possible
Cash bonus:	Monthly	Once a Year	At random
Never			
Two weeks per year vacation pay:	You Bet	Sometimes	Can't afford it
Medical insurance benefits:	Yes	If they want it.	Can't afford it
Six days a year holiday pay:	Yes	Sometimes	Can't afford it
Two days sick leave per year:	Sure	Maybe	Are you kidding?
On going training to help you get raises:	Yes	Occasional meeting	Nope
Career opportunity into management:	Yes	Maybe	None available

Now lookie there. All the circles magically shifted to the right.

So what does that prove? Oh, nothing much, only that the typical business owner is not even close to offering what a good employee would be looking for.

No wonder the typical business owner says, "It's hard to find good employees". Just look at what they are offering prospective employees. Low pay, no benefits whatsoever, all you get is a J.O.B. here.

Is the light going here. Let me take off the lamp shade and make it perfectly bright.

If you want to find the great employees, you have to offer things a great employee would be attracted to.

We will talk about how you can afford all this stuff in later chapters. I will tickle you here a bit. Just remember, all money comes from your customers. Extra benefits means you need extra money. You find extra money in increased sales (retailers) or increased labor production (Servicers). That's your hint. We have whole chapters on how to do exactly this later on in this book giving you even greater value than you ever expected. How can you stand it?

So. What this all boils down to is this. You start finding and attracting good employees by changing the way you think about what you offer.

The next step is to develop everything you need to start to offer these wonderful things to your employees. Example: Yes, you want to offer medical insurance, so that leads to a task to look into what types of insurance programs there are available.

We have a whole bunch of great tips for insurance, bonus programs and the like in later chapters so hang in there for the specific details. We gotta start with the foundation and build up.

In deciding and developing what you have to offer, we like to use our "pro-active" business plan method as discussed in detail in our first book in this series.

Quick review: Make a list of the items you would like to offer. Then, for each item, make a list of tasks that need to be done in order to complete the item. Use this "to do" list in a weekly meeting (with yourself if you are the only one in management) and schedule specific days and times for each task. This really is a great system to get stuff out of our head and into the world of reality. Things seem to get done a whole lot faster.

Now that you are working on those things, it's time to look at other concepts that will help you attract the type of employees you want.

IMPRESSION! When a person comes into your place of business looking for a job, what do they see? Do they see employees in uniforms? Do they see a professional looking store / environment?

Remember…. The goal is to let the prospective employee feel that they are competing for a job with other applicants. We do *not* do the "are you breathing… You're hired" method of screening. So, at least make sure your company image is that of a very professional one. It will start the prospective employee thinking the right way.

Now that image is in place, let's go and find these prime people.

Typically, where is the first place a small business owner will find an employee?

Right! They take out an ad in the local paper.

This bothers me for a simple reason. Think for a minute. Who is sitting at home, flipping through the paper looking for a job? The good employee? The "not so good" employee?

If the person is a great employee, they would be working.

Now, I know they may be a great employee and may just be looking for a better job with better working conditions and benefits. Bingo. You have a shot at them. Statistics show that about one out of 10 people who respond to a newspaper ad are not the ideal employee.

So, go ahead and put an ad in the newspaper. That will get a bunch of response but expect only about one out of 10 responses to be what you are really looking for.

Of course, your job offering is right there among all the others. What is going to get the good employee picking up the phone to call you. Ah yes. The "grabber ad". (Specifics on the term "grabber" defined in book three of this series).

Check this out:

"(Your trade) person wanted! We pay higher wages and have full benefits. We are looking for (brief description of what you want... i.e. five years experience in (whatever), valid drivers license... etc). Must be drug free and able to work in a non-smoking environment..." etc.

How many phone calls do you think you will filter with the "drug free" note? Right! That gets rid of a bunch of possible undesirables.

How many phone calls do you think you will attract with the "higher wages and full benefits" comment? Lots. That is where you will start the screening process (next chapter).

So, other than the newspaper, where else can you find them?

Another great question (you are so good at questions).

Here's one that works for some Servicers. Wherever you purchase your materials (paint store for painters, plumbing supply for plumbers... etc.), this is a good place to start.

Think of it. If a tradesman runs out of a material item or needs a part, where do they go?

Right. To the supplier.

And, who goes?

The worst employee, or the crew lead/good employee?

Right again. Usually the best employee gets to leave the job site and drive to get the needed item(s).

When they hit the supply place, they usually get some help from the salesperson behind the counter. While waiting, they browse around and hit the coffee machine area where there may be a bulletin board. On the bulletin board is your large, bright neon colored sign which reads... Wanna guess?

Right! It reads the same as the newspaper ad above. The phone starts to ring with more qualified employees.

Another great source is just visual observation of people around you.

That's right. I was in a grocery store one evening and I saw this girl bagging groceries. She had absolutely no wasted movement. She moved quickly and efficiently. She had great customer contact / communication skills. I got to thinking, "Self, wouldn't it be great if I had that same enthusiasm in my workers?" Then it hit me. "Hey! She's right there!"

I went up to her and told her I was really impressed with her work ethics. I asked if she had ever considered painting. She kind of shrugged and said, "No, not really." I told her the starting pay was $12 bucks an hour and after a few years, she could work up to $20 to $24 per hour. Her jaw dropped and she asked me for my card. Two weeks later she was working for us.

The story goes on. Two years later she was a foreman and five years later she was working as an estimator making $60,000 per year salary. All because someone noticed the value of work ethics and gave her an opportunity in a company that believed in employee growth and success.

The same can happen to you. If you see someone you like, make them an offer. The worst thing they can say is "No." The best thing that can happen is they go to work for you and you get the benefit of having a great employee.

Oh. Here's another place to find good employees. You have employees already working for you, right? You can let them know you are looking to hire someone. Let them know, "If you introduce someone to the company, they pass our screening process and work out for 90 days, then I will give you a $100 bonus".

The phone starts ringing off the hook.

Also, don't forget your family, friends, neighbors, or anyone else you may know for that matter. The good thing about family, friends, neighbors… etc. is you don't have to give them the $100 bonus. Still a good source of leads.

Notice. I said family and friends are a good source of leads. I did *not* say it is a good source for employees. Let's talk about the, "other family members" thing.

What? Did he just say I should hire other family members?

Well, I must admit this is a dangerous thing. There is a rule known as the three "F" rule. Which is… Family and Friends will Foul you up.

Now don't get mad at me here. I am not saying a family member can be a great choice. There are many family businesses that are working out just fine.

Here are some things you can ponder with respect to this item.

It is very true. The relationship between a friend or a family member is very different from the relationship between a boss and their employee. After all, family and friends are more comfortable and feel they can get away with more because of their "special" relationship with the boss. This is where the danger lies.

It really is a gray area whether or not to hire family and friends. I have consulted with many businesses that are family businesses that run *very* smooth. One of the common denominators with all family businesses is this. Each family member understands work is work. Home is home. If you cannot separate the two, you can't work here.

Many people have sought professional counseling in this area and have learned how to separate the two. It does go against our nature and takes a special kind of person / people to make it successful.

If you are not sure if you or your friend / family member is capable of working together, then ask yourself a question. If your family member or friend gets peeved at something that happens at work, are you willing to sever your relationship with them?

If the answer is, "no", then you need to hire someone else explaining to your friend or family member that your personal relationship is far to valuable to get in the way of work.

Ok… enough on that. I think I am ready for a mental break and a new chapter. Whadda ya say?

Where The Good Employees Are: Chapter Four
Impressionable Interviewing

Your phone is ringing off the hook with tons of interested people just waiting to work for you. Well… it could happen when you have the best job offering, that is.

In this chapter we will talk about how important it is to screen the applicant over the phone. Proper screening will save you a lot of time and even more in reduced stress because you will get rid of the, well, let's just say, "not so good applicant" up front.

The telephone rings. You hear a voice on the other end say, "I saw your ad, and I'm interested in a job…".

Here's where you start the process.

First thing you can do is just open the door and let them speak. Say, "Tell me about yourself."

Have a pen and paper ready so you can scribble notes to yourself on what they said.

Notice. You did not ask them any specific questions and many times the person will volunteer information that will give you hints.

Oh, here's a great example: We had an employee that said, and I kid you not… "I'm looking for a job that will pay me $15 an hour. If you pay me $15 an hour, you will get $15 an hour worth of work out of me. If you pay me $10 an hour, you will only get $10 an hour worth of work…"

Is that a winner or what?

NOT!

You see… the feeling you get from their first comments about themselves often times will give you a feeling about their attitude, education level, ability to talk to strangers, etc. Many times you need not ask anything more.

As soon as you get that inner feeling, "this person just does not feel right", then don't hire them. Just tell them, "We don't have any openings right now, but thanks for your interest." If they ask, "Can I come in and fill out an application?" Just say, "Yes you can, but we do not have any positions available and it may be a waste of your time."

There is a legal thing that says if you have an ad, you cannot deny someone the opportunity to fill out an application. Some people are out there just filling out applications so they can stay on unemployment. Oh well, that will happen.

OK. Back to the phone.

When you do have a person who gives a good first impression, now is the time to ask them specific questions. Here's a bunch of questions I like that follows the labor laws quite closely.

1. Where have you worked before?
2. How long did you work there?
3. Why did you leave?
4. Are you legal to work in the U.S.?
5. How do you plan to get to work?
6. Are you looking for full time or part time?
7. What pay are you looking to make?
8. What are your skills as it relates to (your business)?
9. Are you looking for a temporary position or long term employment?
10. Are you currently employed?
11. If we were to hire you, how soon would you be willing to start?

These are great screening questions because we can extract some good stuff from them.

A side note here… When asking these questions, be sure to write down their answer. We will use this later when or if they come in for a personal interview.

If they do come in for the personal interview, we can ask the same question and see if we get the same answer.

If you get different answers… what does that tell ya? Right… They may not be truthful in some things or most things or anything they say.

Do you wanna hire this kind of person? I don't think so.

Let's look at the above top ten questions one at a time.

1. Where have you worked before?

This will tell you what type of experience they have. It may be related to your business or not. It will give you a hint on how much time it will take to train them into the position you want to hire them for.

2. How long did you work there?

If they have worked at the same job for a long time, you know they may have been a good employee. Compared to a person who has a new job every month (because they can't hold a job).

If they tell you only two months or so, ask them about the previous job and how long they worked there and so on until you have at least a two year history. This will give you a feeling for their dedication to work. It will also let you know they may be a less desirable employee because they can't keep a job for a reason that you really don't need to experience.

3. Why did you leave?

This is a fun one. We hear all the time, "My former employer and I just didn't get along…", or "they cut back on my hours and I need more full time work." Can you hear the hidden message?

If they couldn't get along with the boss (because they were always breaking the rules), what makes it different with you. Which employee gets their hours cut? The good one or the bad one? Do you want to discover the same for your company?

Some good things to hear are, "I have always wanted to work in the (your field type) business and have been waiting for an opening in that type of work…", or, "I just graduated college and am looking for work in (your business type)."

I think you get the idea. Just listen and extract what it could mean. It can either be a positive possible meaning or a negative possible meaning. If you just get that gut feel that there is anything not positive, then trust your inner feelings and let them know there are not any openings right now. You eliminate the possible problems without having to discover them.

4. Are you legal to work in the U.S.?

Obvious. Do I need to spend any time here? What? Oh, I see a concern. You just gotta have an employee and most of the people that are willing to work for you are of questionable legality.

This falls back to the concept we drill many times over. It is your choice to be 100 percent legal and worry free or attempt to bend the rules and take the chance. When you take the chance, you *will* get caught and when you do get caught, it will not be worth it.

If you get a questionable response to this question, it may indicate a possible problem. Now is a good time to let them know your company policy is to do a background check to verify information to find out if will this be a problem.

Congratulations… you just filtered out another possible problem.

5. How do you plan to get to work?

This will let you know their dependability in getting to work. If they are using the bus system, you know there may be a case where you get the excuse, "Sorry I'm late. I missed the bus". I'm not saying this is a bad thing. It's just something that you need to decide if it will be OK for the position you need to fill. Example, if the person will be given a key and open your store for you, you may want to warrant a guaranteed arrival time which is best suited by reliable transportation.

Things that you may hear that may not be desirable, "Um, I don't know. I can hitch a ride with my friend or ride my bicycle."

Anyway, I think you get the idea. It will give you a feeling for reliable transportation and possible problems.
On to the next one.

6. What hours are you looking to work?

This is where you match up what you have to offer compared to what they are willing to work.

Example. If you have a part time job and the person is looking for full time but willing to work part time to start. Good chance as soon as they DO find a full time job somewhere else, they are gone and you are left finding someone else. OR if you need a full time person, but they are in school and can only work part time, you may have a problem there too.

Same as before. Just another thing that can be cleared up in advance so neither you nor the applicant do not waste time.

7. What pay are you looking to make?

This is just to make sure the wage you pay matches the applicants' expectations.

If you hear they want to make $15 an hour and your top pay is only $12, then you are done. If you are willing to start at $10 but they ask for $8, then it could be a good thing *or* an indication the person does not place too much value on them self.

Many times, the person will not tell you what they want to make, but instead ask you how much the position pays.

Remember… you are asking the questions. Just say, "That's why we ask that question, to get a feel of what you would like to make. So, what pay are you looking to make?" and send it back on them. They are playing a game to see if you are willing to pay more than they are willing to work for and visa versa.

Again… you will be surprised at some of the answers you get and from those answers, you will get a better feel for the applicant.

8. What are your skills as it relates to (your business)?

This is where you can check out their actual knowledge of your business. Example, if they say they have extensive experience in being a short order cook, you can further screen with specific questions. Example: What type of omelet pan do you prefer? If they know the brand name, they probably know their stuff. If not, then they are snowballing ya.

It's always nice to have a few back up clarifying questions that relate to the position to see if they really have experience or are just trying to get higher pay.

9. Are you looking for a temporary position or long term employment?

This is where you get a feel for their overall feeling about working for you. Example: they may have a degree in computer networking, but can't get a job because of no openings so they are just looking for something to fill in time until they can get a job in computer networking. They may say they are currently in school and just looking for a job until they can earn enough to go back to school. They are *not* looking for a career in your field.

This may be great if you are looking for temporary help. That is entirely up to you and your business. Obviously, the training issue makes it such that the best employee is one who will be there for years to come, but, we are in the people business and people change their minds. So it is *not* a bad thing to find someone who has great work ethics to hire on temporary. Who knows, they may just like it well enough to keep working for you for years to come.

10. & 11. Are you currently working for someone else? And, if we were to hire you, how soon would you be willing to start?

These are great questions. It ties into other questions we have already asked. Example: If they have said they are currently working for someone and they tell you they can start any time. That tells you they plan to give no notice to their existing employer. They will do the same to you when it comes time to quitting. Not a good thing.

Make sure you feel their answer shows respect for their current employer if applicable.

If they are not working... then you have no problem. Sometimes they will say they have an event that is coming up in a couple of weeks and may need time off early. That is respectable that they mention that up front and not surprise you with it after they get the job and it gives you opportunity to plan for it... etc.

As you can see, all of these questions are designed to give you a good feel for the applicant before they even come down to fill out the application.

Here's a cool thing. The above 10 questions are the main course. Here's the desert.

You are not done with the phone interview with just those questions. The other half is to let them know about your company and give an initial impression.

Reason: If a person calls, gets and address, fills out an application... etc. You are just another job, just like any other job. They will be an employee, just like any other employee.

Our mission: To attract and find and keep the good employees.

This is done by letting them know right from the very first contact, you are *not* just another job. People who work for you compete for the job. We have a tough screening process and the people who work here get good pay and have benefits, just like the big companies.

We still have them on the phone, so let's give them that message in a real cool way and see what happens next.

Preface the finale by telling them about your company. It may sound something like this:

"Our company is not like most other companies. We have a specific wage program that allows our employees to get regular raises based on actual performance and work ethics. We offer full benefits to include vacation pay, holiday pay, sick leave, medical plan and cash bonuses. That makes this position highly desirable. We are looking for someone who meets our standards which we realize may not apply to everyone."

"A few things you should know before you come down to fill out an application. We are a drug free company. You will be required to take a drug test before you are hired and we do random drug testing at least twice a year. The information you provide on the application will be sent to legal agencies for verification. If there are any problems in these areas, you do not need to use your time in coming here to fill out the application. With these items in mind, do you want to schedule an appointment to come in and fill out the application?"

Assuming everything is favorable and they set the interview appointment, here are some great things that will help you demonstrate your sincerity and drive the point home getting rid of many potential undesirable employee applicants. It goes like this:

"Great! We accept applications on Thursday at 2:30PM. There are three things you need to do to prepare for this appointment.

    1. Come dressed as you feel an employee should appear to our customers.
    2. Bring (tools of the trade, pencil, calculator... etc as it applies to your business).

3. Arrive 15 minutes early so you can fill out the paper work prior to the application interview.

Do you have any questions?"

Many times, they will ask, "What type of clothes do you want me to wear?" To which you just repeat item number 1 above.

DO NOT TELL them what to wear. Let them know, "That is the first part of the interview. I can not tell you specifics, just come dressed as you feel would be appropriate for our customers."

Same thing if they ask you what specific tools they need to bring. Let them know it is the first part of the interview. Leave it up to them to bring what they feel is needed.

Notice the time issue. *You* are the manager of your business. You set the time that fits in your schedule to meet with applicants. If they really want the job, they will make arrangements to meet you on your schedule. It is a hint if you can set a schedule that they will follow when / if they are hired.

The end of telephone interview:

This is where you take their name only and put them on a list of people who want to apply. Note. It is easy for you to set one day a week at a specific time to orchestrate your application process. Don't let the employee who "sounds" good rope you into a special application time that fits their schedule. It indicates they expect you to bend to them instead of them working for you. That will be your judgment call because only you know what the telephone interview revealed.

Now. I wanna go just a little off track here because I can read some minds out there.

You are thinking, "but Lynn. I just gotta have someone start work as soon as possible and it's hard to find anyone who wants to do the kind of work we do."

OK. First, I would just give a friendly reminder to read the first three chapters of this book. This is where the preface is making your company a desirable company to work for so you *can* attract more people to work for you.

Second, when you hire them just because they seem to want to work for you, you *will* learn all the bad things later and at a potentially huge expense.

We had a drywall contractor hire a person because the person was "well spoken, demonstrated knowledge of drywall and was foreman quality". They had a total of a ten minute talk on the phone, filled out the application, got the job after about five minutes of talking in the office. The new employee was assigned a van full of equipment and tools.

At the end of the day, the employee did not report in. The customer said the employee never showed up. You guessed it. The new "foreman quality" employee took the van, and all the equipment and drove off to another state. The van was found two states away, empty.

How's that for an educational experience?

When you take the time to telephone screen and personal screen, you will get a much better feel and filter out many things that could and will be costly mistakes on your part.

Oh. One more thing before we shift into the application interview.

Go ahead and schedule as many people as you can for the same time. This is important because you want all applicants to see a bunch of other people applying for the same job. It brings in an element of competition. You have set the stage where they applicant realizes they will have to compete for this job. It will not be handed to them just because they showed up.

OK. Let's take a quick breather here. Stretch, blink a bunch of times, shake your head back and forth a few times, un-kink your neck…. OK, let's continue with the interviewing process.

Now that the telephone interview is done, and you have a few people that show up on Thursday at 2:10 to 2:15 (remember… they were supposed to get there 15 minutes early), what happens next?

As they come in, greet each one individually. Remember, you had three things that you ask of them.

> 1. Come dressed appropriately.

If they came in wearing blue jeans with holes in them and a t-shirt with the print of a marijuana leaf, they blew it big time. You would say, "Thank you for showing interesting working for our company, however you have failed the first part of the application interview. We asked you to come in dressed in a way that will be acceptable to our customers. Let me explain. Had you come to work dressed like that, you would have been sent home without pay and be put on probation for a week. Would you like to try again next week?"

What really happened here? You demonstrated beyond a shadow of a doubt that you are a professional company with expectations that are required. When you do not follow our rules, there will be consequences. It let's the employee know the best job is earned when you are the best employee. All of these are messages that we want to get across to the applicant. Are they a fit? That will be proven to both you and them.

> 2. Bring (whatever you requested).

This will be different from servicers and retailers. Retailers may only require they bring pencil, calculator and a list of references… etc. Check to see what they brought.

If they did not bring what you requested… same thing as above. You say, "Thank you for showing interesting working for our company, however you have failed the first part of the application interview. We asked you to bring (whatever) and you have failed to do so. Please let me explain. When we ask you to do something and you fail to follow directions, we send you home without pay and put you on probation for a week. Would you like to try again next week".

For the servicers… the difference is you may have asked them to bring in all the "tools of the trade". Example: For our painting company above, you asked them to bring in all the painting tools needed for a job site. They may say, "You mean I have to buy a whole bunch of brushes, rollers and other stuff just to get a job here?" This is a typical response to which you would say, "No. You are required to have tools of the trade just to apply for a position here. Just because you may have the tools does not mean you automatically get the job. This is industry standard for a professional company like ours. Would you like to try again next week?"

Getting the drift? I am sure you are. Let's check out the last condition:

3. Come 15 minutes early:

Well? Did they?

If they show up ten minutes early, you greet them at the door with... Wanna guess?

Right! "Thank you for showing interesting working for our company, however you have failed the first part of the application interview. We asked you to arrive 15 minutes early. Please let me explain. We require all of our employees to get here 15 minutes early so they can get properly groomed, wash hands, check the schedule, and basically get ready for work so when the start time comes (they punch in), they go directly to work and are not getting ready to work on your time. If a person is 10 minutes early, that is the same as being late and they will be sent home without pay, and be put on probation for a week. Would you like to try again next week?"

Notice in all three situations. They were met at the door and informed of their failure (if applicable) and were invited to come back next week. They were *not* offered an application. If they ask for one, let them know it will be provided for them next week.

Why waste the paper and the time if all they want is the recorded application and they really don't want the job?

For the rest of the group who did show up with the perfect appearance, brought what was asked of them and showed up at least 15 minutes early... Here we go.

You pass out the application to everyone along with a written test.

(Did he say "written test"? Whadda ya mean, "written test?").

Yes. I said written test. Here is the cool thing about a written test. The purpose is to test their existing knowledge of your business or the work they will be performing for you.

Preface hint. The applicant is playing what I call the employer dating game. Just like the real life dating game where boy meets girl, they like what they see, they get the first date. What is really going on at the first date? He will say anything he thinks she wants to hear and visa versa. Why? They want the other person to like them.

Come on now. We all know it happens. I did it. You probably did it. When you get married, that's when the real person comes out and you discover all kinds of unique things. Heck, I learned my wife really doesn't like my homemade hamburger soup! Go figure.

Same game is going on with your applicants.

They are thinking, "I'll tell the owner that I know everything about the business, I have lots of experience. I am worth getting paid a high wage. If I really need $12 an hour, I'll tell them $15 and maybe they will offer me $13...".

Sound about right? Darn tootin it is.

The written test will put things in true perspective. Here's an example of things you may want to have on your written test.

Servicers can apply it directly to their trade. Examples are for a:
  Accounting service: "How do you bring up the check book register in Quickbooks?"
  Landscape service: "What is the oil / fuel ratio for a typical leaf blower?"
  Painting service: "What size tip would you use for spraying block filler?"
  Etc.
For retailers examples may be:
Restaurant: "What does the term 'set up' refer to?"
Candy Store: "What does 'stock rotation' refer to?"
Shoe sales: "What does 'instep' refer to?"
Etc.

You should prepare a written test of about 20 to 25 questions that relate to your business or general business ethics.

Oh. Here are some generic questions good for any business:

"You arrive at work at 8:03 AM and leave at 11:58 AM How many hours do you record on your time card?"

Correct answer 3 ½ or 3 ¾ hours depending on your view. Most people round up to four hours thinking it's ok to be a little late and leave early daily. Warning!

Another question to ask: "When is it OK to use illegal, non-prescription drugs?"

Obvious answer is 'never' since you are a drug free company. You will be surprised how often this is left blank or they write "only during off hours". Warning!

These kinds of questions will help you see their work ethics and moral standards.

Here's am important point on the written test.

Your objective is to let them know beyond a shadow of a doubt where they fall in to your pay scale. When they score low on the written test and don't have much experience, they *cannot* tell you they are the best. The test scores prove otherwise and let's you give them the pay they deserve.

Now, I don't wanna go off on the pay scale system yet. I have a whole chapter on that coming up next.

OK… Back to our interview process:

They have been given the application and the written test. Tell them, "when you are finished with both, please just come and tap on my door (or notify me at the table over there… etc.)." Let them know you will review each one individually so if you are already with another applicant, just line up over "there", wherever "there" may be.

Once they have completed the paper work, sit down with them. Here's a good sequence I like to follow:

  1. Look at the application and compare it to what they told you on the phone

2. Ask questions that relate to the application. You will be surprised how often a person will write down a lie and when asked the same question only a few minutes later, they will give you a different answer.

3. Ask them to expound on their past employment and reasons for leaving. Compare this to what they told you on the phone.

4. Go over the written test question by question letting them know where they got the answers wrong. This will humble them out of the dating game and into the reality game.

5. Give them a skill test if applicable to your business.

What? You're thinking "Can you run that last one by me again?"

Here's an example of a skill test for servicers:

Resume Preparation company: Have them load and use MS Word to type something.

Business Evaluation firm: Have them load MS Excel and build a cell formula.

Plumbing: Have them remove and replace a toilet.

Etc.

Retailers:

Fast Food place: Have them cook a couple of easy over eggs (for you, not a customer).

Book store: Have them bring up an ISBN number on the computer for a specific book.

Beauty salon: Have them work on a wig doing a color highlight technique.

Etc.

The point is to see the applicant in action. The worst thing you can do is trust them to do an Excellent job based on their word. When you observe them at work, that's when you get the real story.

Story? Ok.

When I was screening for a person to do office work for my business, I had a person tell me they were Excellent in Quickbooks and MS Excel. When they came in, they looked nice, arrived early, brought everything requested, and seemed to have a very professional attitude. I was tickled. I had them sit at my computer. I ask them to "load Quickbooks from the desktop". They did. I punched in the password and brought it up to the main screen. I told them to "Bring up the checkbook register". This person started clicking on anything and everything just looking for it. I ended up having to show them.

Expert at Quickbooks? Don't think so.

Next I had them "Load MS Excel from the START menu" to which they did just fine.

I then told them to build a simple budget and bring up the total at the bottom of the column.

I gave them a printed example of the format. They said, "OK" and took over 20 minutes setting up and punching in a ten item list. Most "experts" can do this in less than ten.

By the way, they had to ask, "Where is the button that does the total thing?"

Expert at MS Excel? NOT!

Had it not been for this test, I would have spent countless hours training someone who was overpaid based on my first impression.

See. Told ya so. It *is* important to get a good feel for the *real* skills and knowledge of the applicant before you hire them.

Why? You're asking why? Ok. Fair enough.

When you hire someone and discover they lied about their actual skill, you *cannot* reduce their pay or fire them without potential huge problems with the labor board.

Another story… We had a client that hired a person based on a telephone interview and initial personal interview based on the applicant's word. They worked them for a little over a month.

When it was blatantly obvious this person was *way* under qualified, required constant baby sitting, made huge mistakes that cost way too much time to correct their work, they let the person know they misrepresented what was on their application and would have to let them go.

This person went to the department of labor and industries and said she was laid off and wanted to collect un-employment (which we all know the owner pays).

When the owner explained their side of the story, the department of labor reminded them of the law which basically says it is the responsibility of an employer to properly screen and make sure the person is capable of doing the job *before* they hire them.

Once an employee is hired, it indicates they are capable and they cannot be terminated due to the owner's lack of interest to provide training.

The owner lost and ended up paying six months of unemployment.

Ouch! Costly lesson that we can all benefit from.

OK? Anyway, back to our interviewing point.

When you give them a skill test, you get to actually watch them in action. You will get a definite feeling for their exact skill level. You *always* time and measure the work being done. Example: If a good chef can prepare a salad in 30 seconds or less, but your applicant just took two minutes. You know something is not right. If a painter takes 15 minutes to paint 10 ft of trim, you have a problem.

Oh, it's kinda fun to hear them say, "I'm just nervous. I'm really faster at this…" which translated into English means, "I lied about how good I am."

Again… you *both* know their real skill which makes it easier to establish their wage based on the facts. Or better yet, if you want them working for you in the first place or not.

So… are we done with the interview process yet?

Nope.
One last thing I like to do is to determine the proactive / leader type person from the reactive / follower type person.

The proactive person needs far less supervision. They will take the ball and run with it. They will find things to do when it gets slow.

The reactive person will wait for your instructions before doing anything. They will do only what they are told. When it gets slow, they will zone out and do nothing… etc.

How to test for this?

Great question.

When you are done with their skill test, let them know how they did over all and wrap it up.

It may sound something like, "You did really great. As you can see, we have a lot of interest from people wanting to work here. We will be reviewing all the results and will hire who we feel is the best applicant when a position becomes open. Do you have any questions?"

Answer questions and let them leave. Even if you are *dying* to hire them right now because they are one of the best applicants you have seen in a long time.

Now, think of it this way. If it was you, and you really wanted the job, what would you do?

Right! You would call back the next day or within two days of the interview. You would ask the owner if they had made a decision yet.

Bingo! That is your pro-active leader type person. They are hired.

Now, don't go off on me here. I'm not saying only the good employees call back. We need both leaders and followers. This is just the final test on filtering out their inner attributes.

If you had a great interview and want to hire someone, even if they don't call back, you can always call them and congratulate them on their new job.

I like using something like, "This is Lynn, the manager of Evergreen Technology. I would like to know if you are still interested in the position we have available for you. Are you still interested?"

When they say yes, you then let them know you had over X number of applicants and you feel they were the best candidate (pump 'em up). That will make them rejoice and give them a feeling of pride. All good stuff.

So, there you have it. I know I could write a whole other book on just the interviewing process, but I think you have the basic idea.

Really now? May I humbly suggest you go back and read this chapter again and again.

Here's some things you will need to work on to get your interviewing process down pat.

1. List of questions to ask for your telephone answer. This should be a form that allows you to write down their name and a space after each question to write down what they said during your phone interview. Remember, you do not need their address and telephone since it will be up to them to come in for the application interview. If they are a no show, they are done.

Note: At the bottom of the telephone interview questions, make sure to put down the three qualifications we mentioned earlier. You know... the show up 15 minutes early, dress appropriately and bring stuff. This note at the bottom of this form will remind you to tell them how to prepare for the application interview.

2. Application form. You can get these at any office supply place.

3. Prepare your written test. That's the one you give them with the application.

4. Prepare an application interview checklist. This will have things on it such as, "skill test - MS Excel portion... etc." The purpose it to make sure you don't forget to follow all the steps of the application interview sequence as noted above.

5. Prepare a location for building a file for everyone who comes in to apply for a job. You may wish to have a file folder of blank application forms, blank written test, filled out application, application approved for hire... etc. Trust me. It shouldn't take long to have the "Applicants Approved for Hire" file starting to fill up. The idea is to have a bunch of people waiting to come to work for you. Thus, you won't have to have an on-going interviewing process. When your "approved for hire" folder starts to get low, then advertise and fill-er-up again. It will help you avoid "crisis hiring" or, hiring the first breathing body that walks in the door.

You now have enough to get you going on finding and how to screen out the undesirables.

Whadda ya say we move on to the pay scale thing I mentioned earlier.

Notes:

Where The Good Employees Are: Chapter Five
The Pay That Fits

We start this chapter with the question, "Why do your employees work for you anyway?"
The answer: _____

Right! To make money. The same reason you are in business. Amazing huh? One of the biggest mistakes people make in business is… they think employees are their little money makers. I hire them, hope they are willing to work for as little as possible so I can keep my payroll down and the more they work, the more money I make.

That, my friends, is normal, typical thinking for business owners. So, where does this type of thinking go wrong?

Employees are *not* your little money makers. They are people. They have the same basic desires and needs that you do. They do not wanted to be treated like a machine. They do not like to feel that they are just another insignificant part of your business. They *do* like to feel they are treated fairly or even better than most employees with other jobs. When they feel important and valuable, they will want to hang around more. In the business world, they call this employee loyalty.

But let's not forget the main reason they are working for you. It *is* mostly about money. They could have a warm, toasty feeling but if they feel they are under paid, it will install a negative feeling and perhaps overwhelm the positive warm and fuzzy feelings they have. They leave looking for the better buck.

Makes sense doesn't it? So, this entire chapter is dedicated to helping the employee learn what is a fair wage *and* more importantly, how the employee can learn how to increase their wage the good 'ol fashion way. "They earn it (said with a kinda gruff voice like the commercial)."

Before we jump into the specifics of how to determine a fair wage and how to establish a specific system to give raises (or demote someone). Let's start with the internal thinking of the typical modern employee.

Key word… Modern. In the past, well, at least when I got my first job as a painter, the idea was to give the boss an honest eight hours a day work. Most workers would get there early, take only what was needed for breaks, work right up to the cut off time and even a little extra (which was usually the case) such that the owner always got at least eight hours of labor and more each day. When I did something wrong (spill paint or paint something the wrong color), I would fix my error on my own time by either deducting it from my time card or working late to make up for it.

Is that how employees think today? NoooOOOOoooo!

Someone stepped in there and started teaching employees about this thing called, "their rights".

Now, don't get me wrong. I am all for employee rights when you have a situation where the employer is abusing their labor. Goodness knows, we need to have someplace to go to protect ourselves from wrongful doing. The only thing is, like all things, you can go to far with it.

What this is getting at is this. The modern employee has learned he has rights. Minimum wage (a good thing). Break time rights (another good thing). If an employer requires you to drive from your house to your office and then to a job site, they have to pay you from the time you leave the office (another good thing).

Ready to flip the coin?

If an employee makes a blatant mistake that cost the company a bunch of money, the owner must pay you for every minute you work weather the time is spent cleaning up the employee mistake or not (borderline).

If the employee is done with an assigned task, they can sit there and do nothing and still get paid (not a good thing).

If the employee stops work to smoke, you still have to pay them (not good).

If the employee is authorized to purchase goods, and they buy stuff for their personal needs, you can't deduct it from their paycheck without their express permission (not good).

You cannot fire someone because they were not as good as they told you (not good).

You cannot decrease an employees pay for poor performance without it being documented in a specific company operations manual or company policy (not so good)… and the list goes on.

So, when it comes to a legal issue, who will the law usually favor?

Employees or employers?

Did you guess Employees? Correct-a-mundo.

With that as a background… let's take a look at what you *can* do both legally and motivationally for you and your employees.

The idea is we *want* to give the employee as much money as they are worth. The business world calls this the "merit" system.

To keep things legal, an owner is required to have a specific written wage program in order to justify and verify an employee's current pay or any pay changes.

Here's the basic idea:

Start by thinking of the lowest paid person in your company. A person who is completely un-trained and starting from scratch. When thinking of this person, think in two different areas. 1. The area of knowledge and 2. the area of skill.

Under the knowledge area, start to list everything you feel this person should know in order to qualify for the starting wage.

Next, do the same for the skill area by making a list of any specific skill they should have to qualify for the starting wage.

Once your starting point is finished… move up to the next pay increase level.

Just in case this is a little fuzzy, let me give you a few examples. It may look like this:

(This line is just filler so the example will start at the top of the next page)

(So is this line)

My Welding Company Wage Program

Entry Level Helper   Wage $8.00 Per Hour

Knowledge:
      Basic knowledge of metals (ferrous vs. non-ferrous… etc.)
      Basic knowledge of fire safety (working around fuel tanks… etc.)
      Etc.

Skills:
      Good work ethics… willing to work hard and lift heavy metal items
      Safety conscious… willing to follow all safety requirements
      Etc.

Then… for the next level up, it may look like this:

Apprentice Level 1   Wage $10.00 Per hour

Knowledge:

	1	2	3	4	5
Understand Oxy-acetylene technique	1	2	3	4	5
Understand MSDS Safety sheets	1	2	3	4	5
Understand proper rod selection for arc welding	1	2	3	4	5
Understand basics of MIG welding	1	2	3	4	5
Etc.					

Skill:

	1	2	3	4	5
Ability to do simple welds with Oxy-acetylene	1	2	3	4	5
Clamp and spot weld for arc welding	1	2	3	4	5
Set up equipment properly for MIG welding.	1	2	3	4	5
Etc.					

I think you get the main idea.

I really wish I could give you examples for each company out there, but it would end up being an encyclopedia. If you need help for your specific business, you can always give us a call. Just look us up on our website *www.evergreentech.net*. We are happy to take your phone call and give you some pointers absolutely free. We also have a template as an optional item. It too can be found on the website under the downloadable forms section. Remember, your personal security code is on the table of contents.

For those who like to do it yourself, go ahead and get going.

Really now. It won't take you that long if you just sit down, put it in your pro-active business plan (book 1 of this series) and just bang it out on the 'ol keyboard. You will be surprised how quickly it can be done.

Now don't go running out there and passing this out to your employees yet. Let's go over a few ground rules for this system.

First rule is… the employees must understand this is a guide and is always open for what we call "owner discretionary judgment". That means, you can use your judgment to vary from the list based on other "value" elements of an employee. I like to call this the "non-productive" value.

The non-productive value of an employee applies to those good 'ol fashioned work ethics. Stuff like, do they show up for work early? Do they pitch in a few extra minutes once in a while? Do they always so up looking neat, clean shaven, smell good… etc.? If they are running late, do they call in advance to let you know? Stuff like that.

Once you have your knowledge and skill list down pat, then you can build your non-productive list.

It works like this:

You explain to the employees their value to the company is measured in two different ways. The first is non-productive ways (ethics) and the other is in production (knowledge and skill).

Your mission as the owner is to build a team of the best employees any owner could ever hope for. When you have good employees, they make good money and benefits (benefits coming later in this book).

The "Wage Program" is a program where you evaluate an employees value to the company and assign a wage that meets their current value. When the employee is interviewed (like we suggested in previous chapters), the interviewing process included an application, a written test and a skill test. These test were given to provide documented verification of the employees pay justification.

Every six months or sooner, based on employee merit, each employee will be given an evaluation. That is where you the owner, sits down with the employee and give them a written evaluation. It may look like this:

My Antique Shop Employee Evaluation:

Employee Name: _____ Date: _____

1. Employee always shows up early for work: 1   2   3   4   5
       Reason:_____
       Suggestion: _____

2. Employee follows company uniform policy: 1   2   3   4   5
       Reason:_____
       Suggestion: _____

Etc.

BONUS TIME:

That's right. As an extra free bonus, we have created this section template for you absolutely free for you to download. Here's how:

Go to our website www.evergreentech.net. Just below the picture of "The Guaranteed Profit System" book, you will see a button that reads, "Free Downloadable Forms – Click Here". Click on this button.

The next page will ask you for the personal security code which is found on the table of contents at the beginning of this book.

You then will be taken to a page that allows you to click on the free downloadable forms you want.

This one is called, "Employee Evaluation Ethics Section". Go ahead and download it.

You will notice it comes to you in MS Word format which allows you to change and edit it to your hearts content. My! What value!

Back to the technique of evaluations.

There are two ways to conduct this evaluation. You choose. I see value in both:

Option 1: Have the employees evaluate themselves the day before the actual evaluation. They do this at home so it does not take your valuable time to wait for them to fill it out.

Then you meet and you look at their evaluation while making comment on your observations. Example: The employee may give themselves five points for always showing up for work early. You do not look at what they wrote. You start by saying, "well Tim, Last month you came to work late only once and that was only five minutes late. Most of the time you get here about five minutes early and end up scrambling to get yourself ready. Sometimes still combing your hair. With that in mind, how many points do you think we should put down…" You discuss it and come to a mutual agreement.

On to the next item on the evaluation:

This can work if you have employees you feel confident are open to being fair and honest. If not, you may want to just go to option two:

Option 2: The owner does the evaluation the day before sitting down with the employee. When the owner meets with the employee, they go over the evaluation explaining why the point values were given and ask the employee if they have any comments.

Both options give the employee an opportunity to voice their opinion and sometimes, believe it or not, they bring to light something that is valid that may alter their score.

Whichever option you feel comfortable with is fine. The objective is to have them end up with a specific score for non-productive value. Then you can move on to the production value.

This is where you go to your wage scale knowledge and skill description. You can assign the same point value for each knowledge and skill item. You will then go over the production score with the employee.

Bingo! You have a total score when you combine non-productive with production points.

You start with their current wage and evaluate each item to see if they qualify for their existing wage.

If they have slowed down or shown a lack of skill that is on their current wage page *or* if their overall point value has dropped, then you can say, "I hate to cut anyone's pay, so I'm going to give you two week notice. Your overall score for non-productive and production points has gone down to the next pay level. If you can't get it back up to where it should be in the next two weeks, we will have to reduce your pay to represent your new score."

The way cool thing about this is, it's completely legal and it is completely fair. You have documentation as to why their pay is being cut.

Now. Most of the time, (well, at least we hope so) the employee score goes up.

Oh… I almost forgot. Don't forget to assign a total point value for a specific pay. Example: 200 points to 230 points = $8.00 , 231 points to 260 points = $9.00 etc.

Are you ready for even more great stuff about this program?

Ok, then!

Let's call this the "special rules" section. Here are some special rules that will help keep everything fair.

Rule 1. Evaluations will be done every six months (or how ever often you want to hold them).

This lets the employee know they can expect it in the event they are shy about talking about money. Nothing makes an employee feel better when the boss is pro-active in giving them a raise they deserve. It makes them feel appreciated.

Rule 2. Evaluations can be done anytime the owner feels it is warranted.

This applies to the situation where you just gave someone a raise because they really put forth the effort. As soon as they got the raise, they slipped back into the older, let productive or less desirable attributes.

You can call an immediate evaluation. Even if it is two weeks after their regular evaluation. The score can be re-evaluated and wage adjusted accordingly.

It also works in reverse. If you have a super person that was just evaluated two months ago and you feel they deserve another raise earlier than the 6 month schedule, then you can give an immediate evaluation and give 'em the raise.

Good call. Talk about pumping someone up to give them a raise ahead of schedule.

Rule 3. Employees do not get paid to attend an evaluation.

It is done off hours and they volunteer their time. The evaluation is NOT required, thus if they fail to show up for their evaluation appointment, they will forfeit any wage increase intended until the next evaluation period.

Note: If you "require" them to attend any meeting, you must pay them for that time. I hate the idea of paying them to explain why they are getting a raise. They should be more than willing to come in on their own time.

Rule 4. All employees must sign their review signifying they have heard and understand the evaluation process.

Signature is absolutely required for a pay decrease. If they refuse to sign a pay decrease, then they will not be eligible for discretionary benefits (bonus… etc. as explained later in this book).

Yes. This is legal because discretionary benefits are not required by law. Discretionary means it is fully up to the owner when, if, how and who is to receive optional benefits.

Yup. We got them all in there (when, if, how, who and what).

I can hear it already.

There are a bunch of you out there pounding your fist on the coffee table screaming, "this guy is nuts! Why would I want to pay more than I have to? If the employees are happy with their wage, let it be. Higher wages only mean less money for me…". And on and on we go.

All I can say is, "I hear you. I've been there. I have the T-shirt. Got the degree from the college of hard knocks".

Before we get all upset, think about this:

I have come to realize my price is based on what a typical employee can produce. When they can produce more, I am still making my estimated profit plus. If I lose this employee and have to start over, I now lose money in training time and time waiting for them to become skilled to the point that matches my price structure. The better choice, well, at least for me, is to pay the great producer more money.

After all, as you may remember from the first book, your price structure is based on actual wages, cost of sale expenses and overhead expenses carefully calculated to determine the right price to your customers. As wages change and production increases, it really will *not* affect your price that much. If any, the price goes down due to more work is getting done in less time. And, we all know "time is _____".

So. There you have it. A fantastic wage program that is fair, firm and consistent. Just for grins and giggles, mention the concept of this program to your employees and see if they like it. Don't be surprised if they tell you they love it. That is usually what we discover.

As a wrap up for this chapter, let me summarize some steps to get your wage program up and running:

1. Write your production evaluation wage scale (knowledge and skill definitions as shown earlier).
2. Write your non-production evaluation sheet (ethics as shown earlier).
3. Write your special rules for your company operations manual.
4. Hold a training meeting with your employees to introduce and start the program.
5. Call Evergreen Technology if you need help or have questions. We can help you get this done in no time at all. We've done it literally hundreds of times. One more time is just another drop in the bucket.

For the last step, you can get our current information from the internet. Go to any search engine and type in, "Lynn Fife, Evergreen Technology" and we should come up within the top 10 items. With that as a short checklist, it's time to move on to the next chapter where we can discuss some more cool stuff about employees.

Where The Good Employees Are: Chapter Six
Who Needs A Handbook

Here's something interesting.

Every time I put on a seminar or give a presentation on employees, I ask the audience, "by raise of hands, how many of you have a written company policy or employee hand book?"

Guess how many hands go up?

Right about 25 to 30 percent of the group.

The next question I ask is where it gets kind of funny. I ask, "How many of you wrote your company policy or employee handbook in anger?"

Guess how many hands go up that time.

Right again. Almost everyone who had their hand up the first time.

It's true. The business owner gets to a point where one of their employees does something that just hacks them off to the boiling point. They think, "dang it, it happened again! OK! That's it! I'm writing a company policy! I'll put my foot down and let them know, if they don't follow the rules, they're fired! That will fix 'em!"

Sound familiar? Too often, that's the case. Employers think the employee handbook (same as the company policy) is a book of rules given to the employees to make them stop doing stuff the owner does not like.

I would like to change your thinking a bit here.

Let's go back to the point where we mentioned employees are people. They have emotions, needs, wants, desires… blah, blah, blah. Here's what reeeeeeeely happens with employees handbooks.

Employees are handed a book, told to read it, sign it and they are expected to follow it.

Do they really read it?
Well, maybe once.

That goes back to our first book where we mentioned the average person, with brain turned on and totally focused will only remember 30 percent of what they hear (or read) the first time around. That means, when they read an employee handbook once, they know they have read it but do not realize they only caught 30 percent of it.

Can you see how this still leaves the door open to them breaking the rules? That's why they still *do* break the rules even after reading the handbook. It's normal. It's typical.

When they *do* continue to break a rule (knowingly or not) and nothing is done about it, well, they just learned the rule was not that important because the boss let it slide. They keep doing it. Boss finally catches them. Boss gets mad. Tells the employee they broke a rule in the handbook. Employee says they didn't know it was in there. The saga goes on.

If it goes on far enough... the employee gets flustered from being "yelled" at all the time and quits. You get to hire someone else, train them, and again repeat the same thing.

Sound familiar? I can sense all the heads bobbing up and down. It's true.

So, what can we do about it?

Do we really need a handbook if it isn't really going to fix the problem?

What *can* we do to get them to follow the rules without being a great, big, fat negative all the time?

All these questions and more will be answered after a quick announcement from our sponsor...

Just kidding.

The question of what we can do about it all starts with implementing all the cool stuff we have talked about so far which is:

1. Decide what you want to offer your employees in the way of higher wages and benefits (I know... how we pay for the benefits is still yet to come. Hang in there). When you have a great package you will get their attention and sincere interest in getting and keeping a job working for you.

2. Build your interviewing process complete with written and skill tests as mentioned in earlier chapters in this book.

3. Build your wage program and employee evaluation program.

With these items as a foundation, the handbook all starts at the screening/interviewing process.

When you give the screening and interviewing process as outlined in this book, the applicant is *wowed* by the extreme professionalism. They get a very strong message, "This company is not like most companies. This company has great pay and benefits. I have to compete for this job. I have to earn higher pay and benefits... etc."

Can you see how this system gets them mentally in tune to working for a more professional company? Working with your company is going to be different for them. A whole new experience. Something they actually want! When they have this attitude, that is, when they are wide open to the employee handbook. At the point of being a new hire, the will do whatever you ask, whenever you ask them to do it and they will do it with enthusiasm.

Now, you don't just toss the handbook at them and tell them to read it. We do what I like to call a "pre-employment orientation".

This is *way* important so please stay focused to the max here.

The Pre-employment Orientation works like this:

225

After your interviewing is over and you have made the decision to hire the person, you can call them and say, "We would like to congratulate you on getting the position... (etc. as mentioned earlier in this book). As you can see, we are not like most companies. We have very strict rules and procedures that are expected of all our employees. Before you are officially hired, there are a few things we need to take care of. Do you have a pencil ready?"

Wait for them to get it.

Continue with, "First thing, we need you to get a drug test at (give location) today. You will need to pay for this drug test however, if you test negative for drugs, we will reimburse you the expense and welcome aboard. If you don't pass this test, then we wish you well."

Note... Make sure they get the test the same day you call them. Many people know how to hide or pass test if they are given several days to clean out their system.

Don't be surprised if you don't hear from them again. This is a good thing. They are telling you they have a problem with drugs and you may not want that in your business.

Continue the phone conversation with, "The next thing to write down is... we will be holding a pre-employment orientation meeting at our business location on Thursday at 3:00 PM. You must bring the drug test results and plan on spending about one and a half to two hours at this meeting. We want to make it clear, you are not officially hired until after the meeting is over. The purpose of this orientation is to advise you of what your position includes, our company policy and other expectations we have for our employees. The main purpose is to make sure we both feel comfortable that your employment with this company is a good match. After the meeting, if you feel you are not comfortable with working the way we work, you are free to decline our offer of employment. If we come to an agreement, then welcome aboard. We also want to make it clear that you do not get paid to come in for the orientation. You will be officially hired after you sign the handbook agreement form and will start to get paid on your first shift after this meeting. Do you have any questions?"

Set the appointment to have them come in for the orientation.

Let's talk about this a little more, shall we? The very important thing with this type of introducing a new employee to your company is to continue to prove your company is not like any other they have worked for. When you say something, you mean it.

Skipping ahead to the point where the employee gets the drug test, passes it and is now sitting in front of you waiting for the world's best orientation. Here's how it goes.

Obviously, welcome them to the company.

Use your company handbook as a guide. (We will go over all the neat stuff that needs to be in there later in this chapter).

You go over each and every item. Read it with them and in the right hand column, you have them initial that they understand each item.

This is where you have to be a little bit careful. You can say, "Our policy is to have your company uniform clean at the beginning of each shift. Do you understand?" They will always say, "uh-huh?" or something real exciting like that. What may have gone through their mind was, "Ok... my shirt looks clean even though I have worn it for three days now. They didn't say anything about smell... etc.".

A good teaching technique is to tell them the rule, then ask them a question that will force them to repeat the rule so you can make sure they understood it correctly.

It would sound something like, "Our policy is to have your company uniform clean at the beginning of each shift. What does 'clean uniform mean to you'?"

You listen to their response and correct if needed. This way, you can be sure the term "clean" means freshly washed, no spots, not showing signs of being worn out... etc.

Same concept is true for each item in your employee handbook.

Once you have gone over each item of the handbook, the last page in the handbook will be a summary sheet (sample provided later in this book). This will be a list of all the important company policies as noted in the handbook. The purpose is for you to quickly go over each item in a reverse manner. This means... you get to ask the employee to tell you what they understand the policy is on (whatever). As they tell you the correct policy, you check it off, they initial it and you move on to the next policy.

When complete, you ask them to sign it, witnessed by you and they now have a good understanding of what is expected of them.

OK... You have a great idea of the orientation system.

What? Some of you are thinking... this takes a ton of time. Well, just think of it this way. If you don't give them the two hour orientation and they *do* break the rules, what will it cost you. Here comes another one of those stereotypical clichés... "an ounce of _____ is worth a pound of _____."

Just in case some of our readers didn't have a grandma that pounded them with that cliché, use the words caution or prevention and cure. Translated to this subject. A couple of hours of training is worth months of frustration trying to fix your employees.

What? More questions?

"This is great for new employees. What about your existing employees?"

Great question.

Existing employees must be handled a little different. I will give you a warning here.

Statistics show that 25 percent of the work force simply do *not* want to take responsibility for their actions. When confronted with rules and consequences, they would rather quit and work for someone else who will let them just be themselves and not be "ridden" by a bunch of rules.

They are *not* broken. They just have not grown up enough yet to realize happiness and success comes from serving others instead of themselves. These types of people do not work well with this program. You may have a great "worker" but they may have a terrible attitude.

I have had it happen where the world's best worker did nothing but talk down the benefits program". It always means a better company overall.

So, with new employees, they need to have the same mental shift in their thinking. They need to first realize that you are going through some company changes.

First change is so they (the employees) can make higher wages and get better benefits. This is a good thing and will get them mentally excited. Well, *maybe* anyway.

You let them know in order to pay better wages and provide better benefits, the company must go through changes and it is important all employees learn those changes. One of the changes is to develop an employee handbook that will be used to introduce new employees into the company. You want the existing employees to have a voice in the handbook so all employees are on the same page.

Explain to the employees, "We will be having a benefits meeting next (whenever). At this meeting we will be discussing the new benefits for the employees. This is a voluntary meeting. That means you do not get paid to attend. You must understand benefits are *not* required by law and they will be given at the owners discretion. This means we can choose who receives benefits and who does not. If you choose to miss this meeting, then you will forfeit your benefits and get nothing."

Note: This will let you know who cares enough about their job to donate their time to learn about the benefits program. When they come to this meeting, *that* is where you get to explain how it all comes together.

I know we are not ready to discuss this yet because we still have a few more chapters to go through before we understand how it all comes together.

Anyway… This meeting is the time and place to go over the employee handbook and get them on the same page as new employees.

Same technique is used. Explain it. Have the employees initial the right margin. Have them explain the summary page at the end. They sign it and it goes in their file.

Shift gears now… Let's talk about what goes in the employee handbook. Most of this will apply to both retailers and servicers. When different, I'll let you know.

Oh! One *very* important thing before we get into the technical stuff in the handbook.

That is: Every rule must have a consequence.
We learn this from our kids. Here's a great story that makes it crystal clear.

There was this eight year old child who loved video games. As soon as the kid came home from school, guess where they went. Right. Straight to the video game. They would kick off their shoes and leave them right in the middle of the walkway.

Well, dad looked at the shoes and said, "Honey, please pick up your shoes". Guess what the kid did? Right. They just said, "OK" then went right back to playing the game.

About 5 minutes later, dad came back and said, "Hey! I thought I told you to pick up your shoes?" The kid said (without even breaking eye contact with the game), "OK, OK. I heard you." And went right back to playing the game.

This cycle went on about five times when dad finally got furious and at full volume, demanded the kid picked up their shoes right now while standing in front of the game. It worked! Kid finally moved. Dad went to mom and said, "I just can't get that kid to do anything without getting furious. It ruins my whole evening not to mention the mood that hangs around the whole house".

Mom suggested she handle it the next day. Dad Agreed.

Next day, same thing. Shoes flew in the air and landed wherever. Game came on. Kid sucked in. Mom goes over and calmly says, "Honey, would you please pick up your shoes?"

Guess what? Right.

Same thing. The kid said, "OK" but went back to playing the game.

Mom lets it go for about 5 minutes, then returns. She sees the kid still playing the game, shoes untouched. She walks over calmly, grabs the kid by the ear and pulls them to their feet. Still pulling the ear she leads them over to the shoes, bends them down, they pick up the shoes, still holding the ear escorts them to their room.

The entire time, the kid is screaming, "Ouch, ouch, ouch! You're hurting my ear…" to which mom just ignores until the shoes are done. The kid said, "That was mean"!

Mom says, "You're right. It *is* mean that make us tell you several times to pick up your shoes. I just want you to understand one thing. From now on, this is how I tell you the second time. Understand?"

Next day, the kid comes home. Shoes fly in the air and land wherever. Game comes on. The kid hears a voice that says, "Honey, pick up your shoes."

A very funny thing happened. The kid looks to see who's talking. If it was dad, it was ignored. If it was Mom, instantly, they jumped to their feet picking up the shoes.

What do we learn from this little story?

Easy… To every rule there must be a consequence *that counts*.

In the above story, with dad, it didn't count until dad got furious. Everyone in the whole house suffered from the mood of anger. With Mom, only the kid suffered if and only if they broke the rule. If the rule was not broken, everyone was happy.

Can you see the power in that?

Not only does this work for employees but you also got some great parenting tips.

My! What value for your book dollar!

Now I am not saying you should cause excessive pain to your kids or employees. That is *not* the message.

The message is this:

With each rule you set, make sure there is a consequence that is strong enough to count and make sure you follow through with it.

Let's face it. If you keep saying, "I'm really going to give you a beating if you don't move right now!" Doesn't work. You most likely will never give them a beating. The rule keeps getting broken. You keep getting frustrated.

Now let's apply this to your employee handbook.

Our first step of actually making this important document is to make a list of everything you would like to address. I will give you some areas to choose from just in case you don't know where to start or what to include.

After you make your generic list, then you start to write out a clear, easy to understand description of the rule you desire.

Stop and think for a minute. What would be a fair, firm and consistent consequence for each rule?

Remember, *all* rules have to have a consequence. If there is no consequence, it tells the employee the item is not important and they can break it all they want without concern.

For many rules, the consequences I like to use is what I call the, "standard consequences". It works like this:

For minor infractions:

First offence: A verbal warning is documented and signed.

Second offence: An official written warning and possible probation (day(s) off).

Third offence: Disqualifies them from any monthly benefits (described later).

Fourth offence: Grounds for termination.

This will apply for many of the employee handbook items. Which leads us to, well, the handbook items.

Here are a bunch of things you may want to address in your employee handbook:

Appearance / dress code / uniform policy
Time card policy
How your scheduling works
Arriving to work early policy
Working all the way to the end of your shift (no leaving early without permission)
Overtime policy (not allowed without express permission)
Tools of the trade / tools you must have at all times (service industry)
Safety policy
Requesting time off
Requesting vacation time off

Calling in if you are going to be late for your shift policy (before shift start time… etc)

Smoking policy

Drug testing / random and frequency

Alcohol or influence of alcohol on the job (hang over from previous night)

Customer conduct (being polite, customer is always right… etc.)

Fellow employee relations (no fighting, arguing, being loud, party, horseplay… etc.)

Foul language (hopefully, you don't allow this unless you're a biker bar)

Disrespect for authority (not following orders from management… etc.)

Personal Hygiene (before starting work and /or during work)

Paperwork (neatness and completeness)

Compliance to job description as defined in your Company Operations Manual

Harassment awareness and compliance

Work location cleanliness (Retail sales area cleaning or service job site cleaning)

That should get you started with your list of items you feel would be appropriate for your employee handbook.

Wait! I hear some of you saying, "That's going to take me a ton of time. Do I really have to do all that work?"

Well, there is a short cut. We do have templates that are optional items listed on our website. This is where we already have a complete employee handbook in one of two forms. One is the Company Policy more specific to employee rules and consequences, and another we call the Company Operations Manual which is far more detailed and is best described as a "Job Description" book.

These templates come to you in MS Word format so you can edit what is there to fit your company. This will save tons of time since we have already done the ground work for you. Check it out and see if you think it will help you with your situation.

For those who want to write the employee handbook themselves, let me give you an example of a good employee handbook.

It starts with the understanding the handbook is for *the employees* reading and comprehension. Do not write it such that it reads like a college textbook. Write it in short, sweet, easy to understand sentences. You can put the generic stuff first so it can be referenced throughout the document. Here's an example:

(Intro paragraph… welcome… blah, blah, blah)

Throughout this handbook, you will see paragraphs indicating consequences for breaking the rules in this handbook. Typically, we will note the consequences as "Standard Consequences" which are as follows:

Standard Consequences

First offence is a verbal warning, which is documented as such.

Second offence is a official written warning and possible probation (day(s) off)

Third offence disqualifies them from any monthly benefits.

Fourth offence is grounds for termination.

Some violations may result in a more severe consequence, which will be noted as needed.

Company Uniform Policy:

The company uniform is the company logo shirt, black Levi pants, black socks and black leather top / rubber sole shoes. Hats are not permitted at any time.

Each employee will be given six shirts when they are hired. It is the employee responsibility to make sure they are laundered properly.

Each employee will be responsible to furnish their own pants, socks and shoes.

All uniform items are to be free of holes and must be in good condition.

If a uniform shirt starts to wear out, ask the management for a replacement.

If an employee does not follow all of these rules, the standard consequences will apply.

End of this section…

That should give you a good format to follow. Just keep it simple. Easy to understand. Nothing to question.

So. Did I answer the question of who needs a handbook?

Hopefully, you agree all business owners should have a handbook. It is an Excellent tutorial for your new employees and an Excellent fall back for your existing employees.

It really does not take that much time to write your handbook. If you are having a hard time with it, be sure to give us a call. As mentioned earlier, we have a few templates already done that can save you a ton of time.

OK. Now, on to the really cool chapter we have all been waiting for. The chapter on those seemingly expensive benefits.

Just wait and see…

Where The Good Employees Are: Chapter Seven
Benefits: Are you Kidding?

Drum roll…. Now… Finally… The chapter we have all been waiting for. The chapter on benefits and bonus and how you can have them with little or no expense!

Let's do this a different way. Take a look at the benefit items listed below and circle your choice as to what you think is mostly true. The first column explains the item and the area of choices is the relation to expense. Give it a go.

Medical Benefits:	Cost a lot	Somewhat expensive	inexpensive	Free
Paid vacation:	Cost a lot	Somewhat expensive	inexpensive	Free
Paid Holidays:	Cost a lot	Somewhat expensive	inexpensive	Free
Paid Sick Leave:	Cost a lot	Somewhat expensive	inexpensive	Free
Monthly cash bonus:	Cost a lot	Somewhat expensive	inexpensive	Free

Got 'er done? Great.

If you are like most people who have a grasp on the world of reality, most of the above were either circled "Cost a lot" or "Somewhat expensive".

That is why almost all business owners offer none of the above.

When they do pay for these things, it only drives the price up and they are not as competitive. Nobody else offers these things (except for the big corporations who deal in big dollars). So why do it? That is the *old* way of thinking.

We are here today, reading this book to learn how to think different. To stop thinking like "most" businesses of which 95 percent will be out of business in the next 10 years. We need to start thinking like the companies who are still in business.

What if I were to tell you that *all* of the above items are *free*. You would think I am nuts. After all, there isn't an insurance company alive who will give me medical benefits for free. Paying for benefits and bonus means paying more money which is spending more money so how can it be free?

This is the point where we leave that kind of thinking behind. This is the place where I will show you a completely astounding system that will change your thinking altogether.

Are ya ready?

The thought process is this:

Yes. These things technically cost money. I raise another question.

Where does all money come from?

Write in your best answer: The_____.

The correct answer: The customer. After all, that *is* the source of all money that comes into your company.

How *much* money your customers give you is 100 percent dependent on your price. They only give you as much as you ask for. When (not if) you apply *all* the principles that are taught in all four books in "*The Guaranteed Profit System*", you learned how to budget all your expenses and how to establish a price that will guarantee your success. In book one and two, you learned how to understand cash flow, financial reports and how to use this information to adjust your prices monthly to guarantee your profit target is reached.

Here's the bonus! This "guaranteed profit structure" is the foundation to your benefits program. If you do *not* have this profit structure, then you are absolutely correct. Paying for benefits can put you right out of business.

So where *does* the money come from for the benefits (besides the customer)?

Another great question.

Follow the logic here:

Benefits are *not* required by law. You do not have to give them. They do not have to be a firm part of your company policy. The smart business person sets up benefits such that they can come and go at the owners discretion.

Here's a clear example:

If the owner of a company tells his employees they *will* get paid vacation guaranteed. The owner *must* pay for it. It becomes an overhead expense item.

If on the other hand, the owner tells the employees, "Paid vacation cost money. The money comes from "extra profit" the company can or *may* make. *When* we have extra profit, we may have extra money to pay for paid vacation. *If* we don't have extra profit, we *won't* have money to pay for vacation, and you will not get it.

Here are some key words that will keep things in harmony with the law. They are:

"ALL BENEFITS ARE SOLELY AT THE DISCRETIONARY JUDGMENT OF THE OWNER AND MAY COME AND GO AT WILL OF THE OWNER. THEY ARE NOT A RIGHT OR A PRIVILEDGE OF THE EMPLOYEE."

Double read, triple read that. It is very important your employees understand that.

Now for you, the business owner, the key word is "extra profit". We do *not* call this program a "profit sharing" program because that would make it such that you are sharing *all* of your profit and not the "extra" profit.

Example: If a business owner has a "net profit structure" (explained in book one) of say, 10 percent, and they do $10,000 in sales in a month, their net profit for the company would be 10 percent of $10,000 or $1,000. The owner keeps this amount for wealth building.

If the same business does $12,000 in sales, and end up with $1,800.00 net profit, the target profit of 10% is $1,200. This would leave an extra $600 in profit (the amount over the target net profit or $1,800 actual profit minus $1,200 target profit for the $600 extra profit.

I know it went past you kind of quick. Go back and read 'er again and it should be clear.

Thus, the "extra profit" is money we can use to pay for extra benefits. Key word there is "extra".

So, where or how do we get extra profit? Great question.

This is where we have a split between our retailers and servicers. For the service industry it is a no brainer. For the retailers, it's going to take some extra deep thinking.

Let's start with the retailers this time. Ok?

By the way, if your mind is not fresh and fully focused, now is a great time to put the book down 'cause, mister, you're going to need all the brain power you have for this next section.

Ready? OK. Here we go.

There was this interesting thing on the Internet that was circulated. It was a video clip of a person who had a mission to go to McDonalds and order everything on the menu. I mean everything. The object was to see if McDonalds employees would still try to "up sell" the customer. You know... Up selling is where they always suggest something else. "Would you like some fries with that order?" Etc.

It was hilarious. They ordered small, medium, large drinks of every flavor. Small, medium, large size of all the side order items... etc. When the person got done, the last thing on the list was a double cheeseburger. Guess what the person behind the counter said?

Bingo! They said, "would you like to get the 'meal deal' with that double cheese burger?" BAM! Still up selling.

Now McDonalds has it as part of their policy to "up sell" every customer because they know it brings in extra sales which yields extra profit. Do they share it with the employee? Nope. It's part of the employees' job.

McDonalds is a big company. You are a small business. You can "tell" your employees to up sell, but do they do it or will they do it in your absence? Probably not.

Take that same employee in a retail business and say, "our benefits program is based on extra profit. Extra profit comes from getting our customers to spend more money than they planned on spending. We have feature items that are really cool that most of our customers do not see. When you take a few seconds extra to show it to them, wait for their response, there is a good chance we just got an extra sale. That adds to our extra profit. You just earned more benefits."

Re-read that whole paragraph again. See if you can pick out the most important word or concept that will be the foundation to your benefits program.

Did you find it? Good!

For those who didn't, the key word was "earn".
The entire concept is to get the employees to understand benefits are *not* free.

Here's another way that works as an explanation to your employees: "You get paid an hourly wage. For this wage you are expected to follow all the items in the employee handbook and work diligently as we ask. Your paycheck is payment in full for your work. Benefits are a gift from the management. The only way we can afford to pay for benefits is from the up-sales. Up selling brings in more money, which brings in extra profit, which pays for benefits. Extra benefits are earned by putting in extra efforts."

I know. Long sentence there. The concept is the important thing. Use your own words.

Let's get a little bit more specific. There are other things an employee can do to bring in more sales. Here's a more detailed list of some of the things I can think of:

1. Suggestive selling or up selling (already discussed).

2. Employees talking to family, friends… etc. outside of work to have them come in.

3. Store appearance. A clean store makes customers feel welcome. A dirty store will turn your customers away and you will lose sales (hurts extra profit goal).

4. Personal appearance. Same thing as the store appearance.

5. Employee attitude. A friendly and happy employee gives a fun and welcome feeling to your customers. A boring or even worse attitude drives customers away effecting profits.

6. Inventory control. When items are stolen from the store, profit is lost. Benefits are lost. Employees should be always looking for possible shoplifting and worse yet, they themselves do not steal from the owner in any way, shape or form. When shoplifting or theft happens, it only takes money away from their benefits.

7. Time card accuracy. When someone records time they didn't actually work, it is a form of theft (taking money they are not entitled to), which will affect their benefits as mentioned in item 6.

8. Motivation: An employee working quickly can get a lot more work done and can spend more time with customers… etc. Moving quickly without wasted moves and not walking slowly… etc. will all mean higher production. All this means the owner does not spend as much money on labor and has more extra profit… etc.

As you can see, all the things in your employee handbook become important to the benefits program.

Get this. You are building a sincere desire for them to actually follow all the rules because it does affect their benefits. Cool!

Now. Retailers. Take a break for a moment while I address the servicers.

Servicers. Spark up now. Here's the concept for you.

The service industry pricing is based on how long it should take to do the work.

Example: You know it should take X hours to install the item, paint the specified surface, prepare the document… whatever your service is. When you give the price to the customer, they will give you the money for the amount of time it takes.

Where the extra profit kicks in is when the employees do the work in less time. In other words, say your customer gives you 10 hours worth of money. You get the work done in 8 hours. Do you give the two hours of money back? No. You keep that.

The typical business owner thinking is, "I win some, I lose some, overall, I hope to break even or maybe make a little money by the end of the year".

That was normal thinking.

Our new way of thinking (the "guaranteed profit" way of thinking, that is) goes like this: "My objective is to find a way to make money on every single job and to never have a losing job".

Possible? You bet!

How that works is like this:

We keep track of the estimated hours (the hours you used to estimate your labor price) compared to the hours it actually took.

Each time a project comes under the estimated hours (took less time), I take the money I saved on labor and put that into a "benefits" account. If the project takes longer than expected, I take money out of the benefits account and put it back in my company to pay for the loss. This way… as long as there is *any* money in the benefits account, I am guaranteed a profit on every single job."

Now, that last paragraph is so very, very important, I think it would be a great idea to slip back and re-read it until you have it down pat. Even so far as to have the concept memorized.

That, my servicer friends, is how you pay for your benefits program.

Back to both servicers and retailers.

Here are some issues that come up with all benefit programs that apply to all small businesses. You've probably already thought about a few all by yourself.

First, you will have an employee (if not all) that will say, "This all sounds great, but what if the other employees keep goofing off. That will mean I will be the one putting in all the extra profit and they will take it out. It's not worth it."

The answer to *all* concerns brought to you by your employees stem from one thing. It is called reactive thinking instead of proactive thinking. Is the glass half empty or half full?

A reactive thinker is thinking of all the problems so they have an excuse for it (and them) not to put forth the extra work. The proactive thinker always stays focused on *how* to make it work.

Think of it in the terms of climbing Mount Everest.

Every living soul can think of literally thousands of reasons why they can't do it. "I don't have time, money, patience, health, experience... blah, blah, blah".

Know what? They are 100 percent right. They, who think that way, will *never* accomplish climbing Mount Everest. Heck, they won't even try. They are focused on why they can't.

The only people who do accomplish this task are those who say, "I will find a way to make the money, find the time, get in shape, gain the experience I need... etc."

When any of your employees start any comment with the magic words, "what if", they are screaming at you, "it won't work because I found an excuse for it not to work".

How do you handle this or any question like it?

The magic answer: Turn it around. Do *not* play their game of failure. Play your game of success. How you turn it around is by not answering their question. Simply say, "What do you suggest we *can* do to address that problem?"

Notice: I didn't ignore the question. I didn't show any disrespect by insulting their thinking or putting them down in any way. I simply changed the focus from negative ("what if" problem) to positive (what *can* we do) constructive thinking.

Most of the time, they don't have a clue how to answer your question of what can be done. They are asking because they expect you to do all the thinking. As soon as you come up with the answer, guess what is waiting right behind it? Right! Another "what if" problem. And they cycle goes around and around.

Also, this typical cycle happens because, as soon as your employees hear the words, "make extra profit" or "get the work done in less time" they translate these words into their own minds as "This means I have to work my butt off for the promise of benefits I will probably never see, so let's bring out all the concerns that will prove to the owner it won't work. This way, I can go back to being a typical employee and just get my pay check."

These last few paragraphs were a good preface to all concerns we will be discussing. We have thought out all possible questions or concerns employees have come up with and we have some pretty good answers.

Regardless of the answers we provide, make sure the *you* ask the question to the employees, "what do you suggest"? Get their brains thinking positive and help *them* come up with a winning, positive answer.

Back to more specific concerns.

We already started with "the other employees won't contribute as much as me" problem.

For all solutions, remember: Fair, firm and consistent.

Whatever you come up with must be fair for *everyone*, and not just the person with the concern. Everyone includes the customer (first and foremost), the employee and the owner.

With the above problem, the first thing I like to do is always agree with the employee. I give them an opportunity to think about a solution.

If nothing comes out, I pose the solution in the form of a question to keep the employee thinking positive. I would say, "What about a system that will reward the person who contributes but not the person who doesn't? How does that sound?"

They get all excited and say, "Yea, man. That sounds great".

The owner then would explain, "To do this, we will have to come up with specific things that would disqualify an employee from benefits. What are some things you can think of that would disqualify an employee?"

Let them answer. Write them down. Add suggestions.

What typically comes up is, "If a person shows up late and leaves early, that money comes out of our benefits program. We should first warn them verbally once. Then, if it happens again within a month, we write them up. If it happens a third time, they become disqualified from the benefits program."

Great! Notice how this follows our suggested consequences in the employee handbook. Perfect match.

What happens if a person is doing about ½ of the work because they are slower.

I love this one. Here's a situation that was proved in the painting industry:

The question is asked, "If a person starts painting today, how long will it take them to become an "expert" brush person"?

The answer received from most painters is, "about two years". Now, if you take the same person and from day one, stay with them, watch every move, every wipe on the bucket lip, count brush strokes, watch pressure… etc. and correct everything immediately as you see it. In other words, stay with that painter until they become an "expert" brush person, how long does it take?

The answer came back, "two weeks".

What this all proves is this other fact about people. When a person is left alone to discover their own speed and skill level, they will settle into whatever is comfortable for them. Some people may be hyper (faster paces) while others more laid back (slower paced).

When *all* employees understand their benefits are based on speed and efficiency, they get the drift. They learn, "We all need to be moving at a speed that is considered acceptable for whatever task is being performed".

Now you got it!

When a person is not performing up to speed, it is not because they are not capable. They have just not been properly trained or informed properly.

This is where your company may need some work. You would start by defining time lines for specific work tasks.

Watch everyone to determine what is a fair time line. Document it. Put it in your employee evaluation as mentioned earlier in this book.

Now, you have something specific to measure an employees' actual performance.

When they do not meet the company standards, we can tell them, show them, watch them and stay with them until we see them performing up to our expectations.

Once you have witnessed the employee performing work up to your standards, then, when they slip back into their "comfort zone", without discrimination of any form, you can now verbally warn them (first offence), give them written warning (second offence) and then at the third offence, disqualify them from benefits.

The great thing is, disqualification is documented by specific and recordable instances. You are no longer discriminating and it makes it perfectly legal, not to mention fair.

So much for the non-performer.

Next issue an employee may address.

"I work full time and the other guy only works 20 hours a week. Do we both get the same benefits?"

Answer you would give, "I agree. What do you suggest?"

You thought you were going to get an answer didn't you. I will provide an answer. I did that just as a reminder that all concerns have that as the immediate response, then you can have them think out the real answer with you.

Full time employees would be eligible for vacation, holiday and sick leave after they work X number of months / years for the company. Your choice.

Cash bonus will be based on actual hours worked.

Example: You have employee A and employee B. Employee A works full time and Employee B works 20 hours. They are both employees on the same skill level. All employees are entitled to a full share of the cash bonus money as it relates to the hours they contribute. Both employees are entitled to a full share (one share). Since employee B only puts in 20 hours or 50% of the hours required for full time, they would only get 50% of a full share or ½ a share.

Sound's fair and is a piece of cake to track with a simple MS Excel program (part of our workshop training. See our website for info.)

Another possible issue: Your employees may say, "How do we know if there *is* any "extra profit" and how do we know it will be enough to pay for everything so our efforts are not wasted?"

WOW! Is that negative or what.

I hear them screaming, "I don't wanna work extra hard for the promise of money!"

Not a problem. Same answer as before. You ask them what they suggest.

It boils down to common sense overall thinking. If we do nothing, you will get nothing. Or on the positive side, I love the way T.S. Elliot said it:

"Only those who will risk going too far can possibly find out how far one can go."

Simply put (said to an employee): "Do nothing – get nothing. Do something - get something. The choice is yours. What do you want? If you like the first choice of doing nothing and not wanting to take the risk, you may not be a good match for our company. Have a nice life."

As you can see, *how* the employee thinks is more important than *what* the employee thinks.

OK, those are the biggie concerns. Let's move on to how you can pay for all these benefits.

We have already presented the concept of "the money comes from extra profit" so this time around we will talk about how to allocate the extra profit to pay for benefits.

First… Servicers:

From book one in this series, we learned: For each hour you estimate, you charge a labor rate. Your labor rate includes average wage, labor burden, overhead and profit.

Each hour saved means extra profit.

Why?

When you save time, you don't just sit at home and do nothing. You keep your employees busy on the next job.

When you think of the math, each hour saved saves *all* of the labor rate you charge. Meaning, you collected money to pay for labor wages, burden and overhead that is not needed for those items.

I know it gets a little fuzzy because you are thinking you still have to pay your overhead.

Yes, but the hours they continue to work will also bring in the overhead money. *All* of your overhead is paid by the hours they actually worked, thus the hours they save, none of the saved overhead money is actually needed for overhead.

Still confused… You won't be when you read those last two paragraphs. Keep reading them. It should be clear after a while.

Here's how we like to suggest you distribute that extra money from hours saved.

Let's say your labor rate is $50 per hour.

Broken down: Your average wage is $20 per hour. Your labor burden is $8.00 per hour. Your overhead is $17.00 per hour and that leaves $5.00 for profit (10% target).

Each hour you save:

$5.00 profit you get to keep as part of your target net profit.
$20.00 per hour for average wage is used to pay cash bonus.
$ 8.00 per hour is still paid out in labor burden (gotta pay taxes on bonus too)
$17.00 per hour is split 50 / 50
   50% of this stays in the company profit picture boosting profit above target
   50% of this goes to pay for benefits (medical, vacation, holiday, sick)

Note: If the employees do not save enough hours, you may not have enough to pay for all the benefits so we put that on a sliding scale.

HEY RETAILERS: PAY ATTENTION HERE BECAUSE THIS APPLIES TO BOTH SERVICERS AND REATAILERS:

The benefits will kick in *after* you have saved enough money to get them started. Thus, when you start, your employees must understand they are coming *when* they are earned. You need a six month period to see how much money you can contribute to their benefits. Based on the money you have in extra profits, that will determine which benefits you can kick in for the next six months.

Did you catch that?

It means, when you do well and contribute to extra profits, benefits kick in. If you slow down and go back to no extra profits, the benefits can go away. Yes, they can come and go based on the fact of how much money we have from extra profit to pay for them.

Let me give you an example to help make this clear:

The Fifester Company has six employees. Each month, their employees managed to increase production by 20 % because they are really excited to get these benefits.

Six employees working 160 hours a month is 960 hours of which 20 % was saved which calculates out to 192 hours saved. Using the above breakdown:

Cash bonus pool has 192 hours X $20 = $3,840
Labor burden is a wash since it will be used to pay burden on bonus money.
Extra profit (above target profit) 192 hours at $5 per hour = $960 went to the owner.
Extra profit from unused overhead 192 hours at $17 = $3,264
   Owner keeps half = $ 1,632 goes in the owners pocket (increased profit)
   Money for benefits = $ 1,632

So, the benefits program has an average of $1,632 bucks per month to pay for the extra benefits.

Break down the expense:

	Item	Bal.
Medical: Only 4 employees want it and it cost $300 per mo. Each for	$ 1,200	$1,200
Vacation: Only 1 employee qualifies for 1 week vacation cost per mo	$ 68	$1,268
Holiday: Only 3 employees qualify for holiday pay, cost per mo. Is:	$ 240	$1,508
Sick leave: Only 3 employees qualify for sick leave, cost per mo. Is:	$ 80	$1,588

As you can see from the balance column, the owner needs $1,588 bucks to pay for all the benefits. The extra profit just from ½ of the overhead money saved is $1,632. The owner has enough to pay for ALL the benefits for the next six months. Employees are told and congratulated on their efforts.

Next six months comes through. The employees only increase production by 16 percent. Numbers change to only saving 154 hours. Just the extra benefits (not counting cash bonus) works out to 154 hours X $17 = $2,618 which when split 50% leaves only $1,309 for the benefits.

Looking at the above chart only three paragraphs ago… you can see the owner still has money to pay for *just* the medical and vacation. There is not enough money to pay for the others, so the employees hear, "Well, this six months, we earned enough to keep your medical and vacation in place, but we lost, holiday and sick leave for the next six month period."

Tears swell in the employees' eyes. They know they can do it because they did it before. Time to get back on track.

Servicers. You will notice this example may be pretty close to your situation.

Retailers. You have a different story since your extra profit is based on pure increase in sales. You don't estimate hours and your labor is more an overhead expense.

Thus, retailers, this is your section of this chapter.

Retailers would calculate their available benefits money by taking their P & L statement and making adjustments to the reserve accounts as explained in detail in book two of this series. It is critical you not only pay your current bills and the bills yet to come before you calculate your actual profit.

Once you have adjusted for your reserve accounts, then you can see what is left over for "actual profit".

Probably the best way for me to explain this is in the form of an example:

We have the Fifester Retail company who has six employees. We used to do sales of about $20,000 per month with total budget expenses of $18,000 leaving the company a $2,000 net profit.

Over the next six months (after implementing *all* the components of the guaranteed profit system) their employees really got serious with the up selling, friendliness… etc.

Sales went up to $25,000 per month average. Cost of sales is about 40% (so you subtract 40% of the $5,000 extra sales which is $2,000). This leaves $3,000 in extra profit. The company takes out their target 10% ($300) leaving $2,700. The owner splits this 50% with the employee benefit program leaving $1,350 for the owner to put in their pocket (per month) and the other half of $1,350 going to the benefits program.

Assuming the qualifications are the same for this retailer as they were for the servicer above, this company qualified for both the medical and the vacation pay benefits but do not have enough for the holiday or sick leave.

I realize this is a bunch of math stuff and many people just get lost with that type of stuff. Here again, it will help you to reread the above paragraphs over and over again until it becomes more clear.

You can develop a wonderful Excel spreadsheet to help you calculate exactly when certain benefits kick in and when they drop off. This can be given to the employees so they can have specific targets to hit giving them motivation to hit those targets in order to enjoy all the benefits.

Here again, we have an Excel template available on our website as an optional item that will help you with the qualification calculations. This template may save you time and confusion on the mathy part. (Yes, I used mathy. It's not a real word, but kinda fun to use).

Before we leave these benefits that are paid for out of the extra profit, excluding the cash bonus, which we will discuss later, let's talk about ways we can make some of them more affordable.

First is the medical insurance thing. Your options for medical benefits are:

1. Regular medical insurance, which is very expensive (Avg. $400 to $600 per mo)
    a. All employees must be offered this medical coverage
    b. Owners and employees split the expense (Avg. $200 to $300 each)
    c. A majority of employees must participate (Most companies require 80%)
    d. Employees co-pay as a deduction out of their paycheck

This option is hard to sell because many employees may have spouses that work who have insurance, or they don't want to contribute a couple of hundred dollars each month towards insurance. They would rather have spending money to blow.

2. Catastrophic insurance which *only* covers life threatening items (avg. $100 per mo)
    a. All employees must be offered this medical coverage
    b. Owners can pay all or employees can co pay half (Avg. $50 to $75 ea)
    c. Any number of employees can choose to participate (usually not restricted)
    d. Employees co-pay as a deduction out of their paycheck

This option will greatly reduce your medical insurance expense, but does not cover broken bones, medication... etc. It only covers life threatening items like cancer, M.S., Diabetes... etc.

Wait. Each and every year, someone comes out with a different program. Example: One insurance company offers to pay a set amount per incident. You get the check. You chose where to spend it. Very affordable.

If you would like current information and our opinion based on what we have found to be current, please feel free to call. We can let you know what we have found that will be more current than what may be in this book (remember, this book is dated and is not updated each month).

Note: The math above shows option 1, thus if option 2 is selected, it would make it easier for the employees to qualify for additional benefits.

Option 3: Medical Discount Plan (Avg. $50 per mo per employee)
    a. Any employee can choose to participate or not.
    b. It is *not* insurance. It is a discount plan giving a discount on:
        1. Medical expenses (up to x%)
        2. Dental (up to X% - which most insurance plans do no cover at all)
        3. Chiropractic (up to X% - which most insurance plans don't cover)
        4. Prescriptions (avg. X%)

      5. Vet care for your pets (avg. X%)
c. No age limits, pre-existing conditions OK, no one denied
d. Employees pay for it directly, owner reimburses the employee
e. Employer can set them up as a distributor and make commissions from it
f. When employee leaves, they keep the program if they choose

As you can see, this option is the least expensive to the employee as it cost them nothing because you reimburse them all the expense. If they don't want it, they don't have to have it. If they do want it, it cost them nothing when they keep production up and get reimbursed from the employer. A no brainer if you ask me.

Anyway. Option 3 is the one that will cost the least and usually only requires about 3 to 5% increase in sales / production to pay for it. It makes all the other benefits kick in at an easier to achieve level.

Warning: Not all discount plans are what they claim to be. It is your responsibility to look at the fine print.

Example: Many will tell you they have free Identity Theft program that other companies charge for. I have found that most of the time, if your identity is stolen, all they do is tell you what to do. You still have tons of work and time to do all the work. No actual benefit is it?

I would love to tell you my favorite company, but alas, things change and I'm not comfortable promoting someone in a book, only to find out they changed their policy to something that is really not a good deal.

Yup. It happens.

Anyway, if you would like to find out whom we currently like, just give us a call. Our phone number is on our website. We're more than happy to get you going with the best there is for your specific needs.

Your goal is to make a list of all of your employees along with who qualifies for each benefit. Figure out how much each benefit will cost based on the actual benefit you want to offer.

When you have the total annual expense for each item, divide by 12 to come up with your monthly amount, then you can chart out your benefits program similar to the one we had above for the Fifester Company.

I know this is thinking *way* outside the box and we appreciate the fact that you may not have got it 100 percent the first time around.

Keep reading it. If you still have difficulties, please give us a call. Lines are always open to you, my family of readers.

Now, let's shift to the cash bonus part of the extra profit. After all, that is the one the employees are interested the most. Yes. We saved the best for last.

Cash bonus for the retailers is based on the money left over from the extra profit after paying for all benefits.

Example: When you have say $5,000 in extra profit *after* you took out your cost of sales and net profit as explained above, you split that to $2,500 for you and $2,500 for the benefits program.

Let's say you go with the Medical Discount plan (option 3) and the total for all benefits comes out to $800 per month. You subtract the $800 from the available $2,500 leaving you $1,700.00 to pay out in cash bonus.

SERVICERS: Quickly review your section a few pages back. Your cash bonus comes from the hours saved multiplied by the average wage you pay them. Ok?

BOTH servicers and retailers. Distributing cash bonus is the same.

Some preface thinking here. Typical business owners say, "Why give those buggers my extra profit. Next month or period, when I go backwards, I end up losing money over all, so forget the whole thing". Or, "I've tried it. Employees don't really change. They expect it and don't get what they expect and start complaining, so forget the whole thing." And on we go.

New thinking for you successful thinkers. The only way your employees will ever see a bonus is if there is extra money to give them. I need a system that will make it so I never have a bad month and end up losing money, wishing I had not paid out bonuses in the earlier months.

Here's how we do just that.

Fact is, employees do *not* appreciate annual bonus. Once a year? Big deal! They only get $X for all years efforts. So what?

Employees *do* keep motivated and *do* keep up production and up selling when they are rewarded frequently *and* with understanding.

Thus, we like to suggest a monthly cash bonus pay out system that works like this:

You track your extra profits as explained earlier in this book and come up with monthly totals. You determine how much money was applied for the cash bonus for each month (not that hard with Excel. Again, part of our Extreme Business Makeover workshop training).

You do *not* pay out cash bonus at the end of each month. You hold it for three months, and then pay it out.

That means: January, you have say $2,000 to pass out in cash bonus. You count three months out meaning (Jan, Feb, Mar...) such that the first of April is when the bonus money is paid out that was earned in January.

February happens. You have added say $1,800 to your cash bonus pool. Your pool now has $3,800 because you have not yet paid out January. March comes around and you lost money that month. Say you lost $500. That $500 comes out of the bonus pool and back to your company to pay for the loss. Literally, you still hit your guaranteed profit target because the loss was paid for out of the bonus pool. This negative $500 now makes your account sitting at $3,300 ($3,800 minus the $500).

April first comes along. Back in January, you earned $2,000 for your bonus pool. Do you have enough in the pool to pay it?   Yes   No

Answer: Sure thing. So you pay out the $2,000 leaving $1,300 in the pool. By the end of April (April results), you put another $1,400 in the bonus pool making the new bonus pool sitting at $2,700.

May first comes along. Here's a test to see if you are following this. How much to you pay out? $_____

Hint: to get the answer, go back to what was earned in February. Ask yourself, "Self, does the bonus pool have enough to pay out what was earned in February?"

If the answer is yes… then you pay it. In this case our February earnings was $1,800. Our pool had $2,700. Plenty of money. So you pay out the $1,800 on the first of May.

One last test because this next one has some tricky stuff to it.

Let's move ahead to June first. How much money would you pay out for the June first bonus? $_____

Hum…. We are supposed to pay out March bonus in June. March contributed how much? $_____ Right! A negative number.

This is where you remember you have already taken out the money in advance.

Anytime your month goes negative profit, you end up with zero bonus money. Employees sob. We identify why we lost money that month. Make suggestions for corrections. Fix it and on we go with our bonus program.

I think you see how this works now. The summary is this. Your bonus pool should *always* have money in it such that you will never have a losing month where you have no money to pay for it. If you do have a losing month, or losing project, the bonus pool pays the loss. You have "guaranteed profit" (hence the name of this book series).

Any questions? Great! I think you have it.

Wait. I see a question that has not been addressed, "How much does each employee get?"

Great question. You are such a good audience!

This is where you identify each person in your company by a "title". You, as the owner obviously have the title of "Owner". You may have a manger, assistant manager, crew lead, project manager, estimator, foreman, employee, apprentice, helper… etc. Just make your list of titles that apply to your company.

To each title, assign a share value. Here's an example of how that works:

Owner gets 2 shares
Assistant manager gets 1.5 shares
Crew leader gets 1.25 shares
Employee gets 1 share.

Now assign the number of employees you have under each title. One owner. One assistant manager. One crew leader and 4 employees.

Hey! We have a great form for you to use. You can download it right off the Internet website www.evergreentech.net. You can find this form from our home page by clicking the button that reads,

247

"Free Downloadable Forms – Click here", then enter your code (table of contents page) and click on the forms you want.

This one is called, "Bonus Program Share Worksheet". Go ahead and download / print it now.

Calculate out the total shares your company will pass out. It may look like this:

Position	Share Value	No. of People	Total Shares
Owner	2	1	2
Assist. Manager	1.5	1	1.5
Crew Leader	1.25	1	1.25
Employee	1	4	4
Total shares:			8.75

Finally, you take the total cash bonus amount and divide it by the number of shares.

Example: You have $2,000 for January bonus. Divide by 8.75 shares = $228.57 Each.

Your new chart looks like this:

Position	Share Value	No. of People	Total Shares	Bonus
Owner	2	1	2	$457.14
Assist. Manager	1.5	1	1.5	$342.85
Crew Leader	1.25	1	1.25	$285.71
Employee	1	4	4	$228.50

Will there be modifications? You bet. Check it out.

If an employee breaks the rules and gets his verbal, written and disqualification notice, you now only have three employees that qualify dropping the total shares to 7.75 instead of 8.75 which means bigger bonus for those who still qualified.

Also, remember our part timer that only works 20 hours a week. They only get a half a share dropping the share value to 7.25. Now $2,000 divide by 7.25 = $275.85 for a full share.

Think about this deeply now. Do the employees care about others not performing? If an employee does not perform and gets disqualified, they are out bumping the bonus amount up per person. You just eliminated that concern.

Excel? Did someone say MS Excel?

Yes, we have an Excel template as an optional item on our website that has all of these fancy calculations all spelled out. Just another option to save you lots of hours trying to re-create the wheel in accounting all this stuff. It really is easy. My users tell me it takes them about ½ hour per month to do all the accounting for the incentive program using our Excel template. It's called "Excel Bonus Tracking". Cool thing.

Well, that's all I can think to tell you about all the basics of the bonus and benefits program.

Oh yea. I must warn you. Setting it up will get you nothing. *Using* it to its full potential will increase your profit and wealth building program off the charts. That's the good news. The bad news: Be prepared to lose 25 percent of your employees (those who just don't like responsibility or bad attitude employees) and be prepared for about three to six months of pure living hell!

There is a lot of planning (budgets, estimating, pricing, employee handbook, wage program, bonus program pay out tracking system, training meetings with the employees to explain it to them, production tracking and reporting… etc.) Plus the biggie: Your constant supervision to make sure you follow up on all the rules, consequences, production observation and meetings to make it all happen.

There is a ton of stuff that will put you way out of your comfort zone, so get ready for some really uncomfortable times. When you feel the new problems arise, that means it's working. Just like fishing. When you have a huge fight on the line, you have a big fish! You eat a long time! The rewards are huge! It's worth it!

If it all seems to overwhelming, please feel free to surf our website taking a look at our special employee workshop. We can save you literally months of time and set you up with everything you need to get this going the right way in record time.

Also remember. Phone lines are always open. Give us a call if you have specific questions for clarification or other questions that may not have been addressed in this book. We look forward to hearing from you.

Your success is our success and you will be surprised at our response when you call. Information is free.

Now that you have had that commercial interruption… let's move on to the next chapter, shall we?

Notes:

Where The Good Employees Are: Chapter Eight
Greatly Improved Production!

Now that your owner administration stuff is done, you now have a great idea of how the benefits program is set up, designed and paid for. The only problem remains. Seeing it on paper and understanding the theory is only the starting point.

You introduce this to your existing employees and they all seem to be excited about it, but are they really.

Let's get back to human nature. Employees hear the good things you are telling them. Yes, they would love a cash bonus. They would love all the other benefits of vacation pay, holiday pay... etc.

That part sounds good.

As soon as you leave them alone to think about it, what starts going through their mind is, "Yea right. Heard it before. Got the T-shirt. I'll believe it when I see it. I am already working hard and now the boss is just trying to get me to break a sweat, get out of my comfort zone for the promise of benefits and money of which I probably will never see..." And on it goes.

They do not reeeeeeely buy into it. All they see is "working harder". So, how to we overcome this obstacle?

Yet another great question. You are good.

The root of the answer stems from something everybody already knows. I'm sure you can fill it in:

It's not about working harder, it's about working _____.

Right! We have all been taught to come to work, get instructions from the boss, and do what they ask. When we are finished with the task, what do we do? Right! Wait around for more instructions.

Example: We have our service industry boss in the pipe fitting industry. He sees a worker using a wrench that is too small. The boss says, "Hey Charley, Get a bigger wrench for that". The employee says ok, goes to his truck and gets the bigger wrench. By the way, how fast do they walk to and from the truck? Why is the tool in the truck and not in a toolbox next to them or at least closer to the work area? Did they take time to light up a cigarette or go to the bathroom as long as they were on this approved mini break?

I can feel the tension already building up in you owner. You're probably thinking, "That happens with my employees too".

Don't get upset. This is normal. As far as the employee is concerned, he is doing what the boss told him to do. He is working. Are they thinking about "production"? Nope. Doesn't even enter their mind because, well, there's nothing in it for them if they do walk faster, or think to have all the tools near at hand... etc.

Back to our situation: The very next day, the owner goes out to the job site and there is Charlie. Guess which tool he is using for the same work he was doing yesterday? Right again. The same wrench that was too small. So what does the boss say? "Hey Charley... go get the bigger wrench!" Charley says OK and off he goes for another mini break all the way to his truck again. Note: I left out the profanity that typically occurs. Gotta keep it clean ya know.

Sound familiar. Just out of curiosity, how many of you readers out there have said to yourself, "Self, I keep telling these employees the same thing over and over again. They just don't seem to get it. It's driving me crazy!! Grrrrrr!"

Now I don't want you to get mad at me. After all, it's not like you can smack the book or anything, but… It's not the employees who are at fault. It is the owner doing what most owners do. They tell employees *what* to do. There is a huge difference between *telling* someone what to do and *teaching* them what to do.

Like we said in the first book. You can give a person a fish and feed them for a day or you can teach them how to fish and feed them for a lifetime. The real problem is, the owner is not aware of a better teaching process.

Here we go.

This is really powerful stuff that will give you far more production from your employees and warrant your benefits program will jump into full swing. It's more of the "my what value for your book dollar" part.

The sequence of teaching through training is:

1. Remember the employee is doing what they are doing for a reason that makes sense to the employee. Find out why they are doing what they are doing so you can fix what is wrong and not just toss out useless or meaningless information.

2. Identify if the employee learns by (discussed in detail in book three), a. verbal explanation (thinker) b. adjustment of their technique (doer), c. visual observation (seer) or d. reminders / forgetfulness due to possible mood (feeler). You identify their learning style by what they say. If they say, explain it… they need explanation (thinker). If they keep the tool, and follow what they hear and ask you to confirm what they are doing, they do NOT want you to take the tool away from them and demonstrate. They want to do it themselves and have you affirm correct procedures (doers). If they ask you to show them, they need a demonstration (seer). If they seem peeved or have a negative attitude, forget the training for now and focus on what is bothering them. When neutralized then find the secondary learning style as mentioned above… they are receptive and ready to learn.

3. Take time to give full training and not just surface training. Example. Don't just tell them what to do, but add why, how, when… etc. as it applies to what is being learned.

The best way to illustrate this point is going back to our pipe fitter company. The owner would observe Charlie using wrong size wrench. Go up to Charlie and say, "I noticed you are using a size X wrench. I'm just curious… why do you like that wrench for this task?"

Charlie comes back and says, "It's much lighter than those bigger wrenches, easier to use and lighter to carry. Besides, it will just fit in the widest position".

The wise owner must remember, that is the reason Charlie gave and he thinks it makes sense. Matter of fact… it does based on the way they are thinking.

The owner in all his wisdom does not insult the employee. He makes it a learning experience by saying, "You know, I never thought about it that way. That makes sense. There is one thing about this situation that may be a problem. Let me explain it and see if you think it has any merit..." (Note: ask the employee for their opinion shows you respect what they think. They don't even realize it is a learning experience. Cool).

The boss continues, "When I got my training, my boss told me about torque. You know what this is? It's the amount of pressure applied to a coupling that will guarantee a tight seal. If I don't apply enough torque, the joint may sometime down the line, spring a leak, which creates havoc after these pipes are buried. We now have contamination... etc. Not good for environment. Torque is easy with a bigger wrench because you have a much longer pivot point that allows a lot more pressure to provide the required torque for a tight seal. What do you think of this theory?"

Charlie says, "Oh yea. I never thought of it this way. But, I think I can get the required torque with this smaller wrench."

Boss comes back and says, "No doubt you can. You are some strong dude. I have always liked the saying, it's not about working harder, but about working smarter. It seems to me that in order to get the smaller wrench to give the necessary torque, it takes a lot of strength, where the larger wrench takes hardly any at all. With a larger wrench, wouldn't it guarantee we have enough torque with less effort? This idea may out shine the lighter weight wrench and easier to carry theory. What do you think?"

Charlie finally sees the point and agrees.

The boss can now address the tools being kept near the work area and the avoidance of unnecessary mini breaks walking to and from the truck.

Here's how: "Charlie, You know our company cash bonus and benefits is 100 percent dependent on increasing production in the field. Can you think of anything we can do to pick up production without actually working harder? Just little things?"

Charlie can't think of anything because he never has been asked to think before. He has always just been following directions. Could be a new experience for him, so he says his mind is a blank.

The boss offers, "what about keeping all the tools you need near you instead of keeping all your tools in the truck?"

Charlie starts to get peeved because he thinks he's being chewed out so he says, "Come on boss, it's only a few minutes! It's no big deal!"

Boss calmly comes back and agrees by saying, "You are absolutely right. We never wanted this thing to turn into a micro management butt chewing session. It IS a small thing. Heck, it's a tiny thing, really no big deal.

Just for grins... let's expand it to see how small a deal it really is. This morning I noticed you, Bob and Ted all went to your truck an average of 5 times each. That's 15 times total and each time it only took three minute each trip. That is 45 minutes. That is just the morning so keep going for the afternoon and that gives us 1½ hours a day. Take 21 workdays a month and that gives us almost 31 hours all month. Our benefits program contributes $25 an hour for each hour that is saved plus about $7 from the saved overhead. That is $32 per hour times the 31 hours we lost means we lost $992 or almost $1,000 was lost out of our benefits and cash bonus because of this little item. WOW! I didn't realize it added up to that much. What do you think Charlie?"

Charlie's face changes because he didn't realize it either.

The boss then affirms… "Charlie, what if we just focus on putting all the tools we typically need in a tool box and keep it near the work area. That will greatly reduce this time. Oh, yea, it will still happen but maybe only ¼ as much meaning we can all enjoy the $750 in our cash bonus pool and benefits program."

Now Charlie understands. *Now* Charlie *wants* to use a bigger wrench and *wants* to keep his tools close at hand because *He* will benefit from it personally. There is something in it for *him*. (Lots of emphasis in there, huh).

OK… I hear ya. You're thinking, "This sounds like a good plan, but dude, It takes so darn long. It's just easier to tell them about tork and tell them you expect them to keep their tools close by. I don't have that much time in my day…"

Am I right?

My response:

Well, actually, you don't have enough time *not* to do it. Ok, I said that a little bit strange. What I mean is… If you don't take the time to train them, they will keep doing the same thing over and over again without correction. How much time do you lose in production by not taking time to properly motivate them?

Yes, you will spend 15 minutes explaining something. When the employee understands and wants to comply, you just saved countless hours in lost production for the future. You have taught your employee how to fish.

Still think it's not worth the time? Hope not.

I hear the retailers out there saying, "is this the same thing for us?"

You bet!

Same concept, just a different situation.

When your customers come in, do your employees suggestive sell each and every time?

Are they showing your new feature product to each customer?

When there is no one at the cash register, do they just stand there and do nothing, or do they find another customer and help them or suggestive sell other items or do they clean… stay busy?

Do they understand why all these things help their bonus and benefits program?

I think the most important concept we are getting across is this.

Do not just tell your employees what to do. Take the time to understand their current thinking. Take the time to help them understand the what, why, who, when, where, and how as much as possible. Then, finally, follow up with how it applies to their bonus and benefit program.

Will they get it first time around? Absolutely not! Don't even expect it and for laughing in quiet (no wait… that's crying out loud), don't get mad because they don't seem to get it the first time around.

Here's some facts about human nature. Remember from the first book and even in this book, we mentioned the average person with their brain focused, will only remember 30 percent of what they hear the first time. It takes about 3 or 4 times before the mind registers it.

Even worse, lets learn from a ski instructor. Anyone out there who has ever learned to snow ski will relate to this.

A new student is taught how to put on skis, how to fall and how to stop. The first moving position they learn is the snowplow. You know, make the wedge with your ski tips together and the ski tail far apart. They teach you about pressure on one ski will make you turn the opposite direction and visa versa.

The ski instructor in their training have been taught, the average person must apply correct pressure and balance at least 25 times before it starts to become automatic.

The student becomes comfortable and proud of their snowplow control then BAM! The instructor messes up their entire day. They show them the parallel skiing system.

Now the weight and pressure are exactly reversed. Weight goes on both skis and pressure is adjusted to both edges in the direction you want to turn. Knees bend in unison, body twists exactly opposite of what they learned before.

Ski instructors are taught, it takes the average skilled person not 25 times but now 50 times to do it correctly before it starts to become automatic (mind doesn't have to be forced to think about it).

What we learn about human nature is this. Your employees have been working for you and other people and have learned their work ethics and habits that are "normal" to them.

This whole concept of teaching them to think of things they can do to be more productive is new to them. They will have to do it 50 times before it starts to become automatic. That means you may have to work with them twice a day for a full month before you will have the fine tuned, well balanced and in control employee you desire.

Patience??? You bet!

So much for physical production.

We now can address the non-productive items that can have a huge effect on your bonus and benefits program.

Non productive stuff is stuff like… Do they:
- Show up exactly on time and spend time getting ready to work? Example: They arrive at 8:00 AM. What time does the work actually start? How much time is lost?
- Lose time talking on their cell phone or on the company phone for personal calls?

- Lose time talking to customers about topics that have nothing to do with business?
- Lose time talking to other employees about last nights date?
- Smoke, and with your no smoking policy have to go outside when its not break time?
- Take longer on their breaks than they are supposed to (to go a local fast food joint and get back 10 minutes late… etc.)?
- Leave work a few minutes early because no one will notice or care?
- Stop work ½ hour before quitting time to "clean up" when clean up should only take 10 minutes… soon as they are done cleaning up, they sit around waiting for quit time… etc.?

Go back and put a check mark in front of each one of those that applies to your employees.

Funny thing. When I go to a company on a consulting assignment where the goal is to train the employees and set up the benefits program, I always have the employees in a two day meeting (or more depending on the type of business). In that meeting, I bring up these exact same things and I ask the employees how much time they think is spent doing these types of things.

I always take the smallest amount of time from them and usually almost always come up with anywhere between ½ hour per day up to two hours per day. The ½ hour per day works out to 10 hours per month where the two hours a day works out to 40 hours a month.

The name of the game is, "If this stuff is happening and always has been happening, it is because it has always been considered part of the job".

Our choice is this: We can either ignore it (reactive thinking), and lose the money which could be used for the benefits program, or we can do something about it (pro-active thinking) and put money in our benefits program.

Each time I ask the employees in a group, which choice do they want, guess which one they always pick?

Right. The proactive choice.

Why? Because they know it's the right choice.

That is where it becomes very important that you have this type of meeting, get them thinking proactive, *then* introduce the employee handbook concept.

You would say, "I agree. So, let's discuss what we *can* do about each of these…". Then you can discuss each one and come up with a rule everyone agrees to follow along with the related consequence (see standard consequences in earlier chapters).

The fixes are:

Company policy to arrive to work 15 minutes early so you can get ready to work. The work starts at your start time.

Talk as much as you want while you are working. Just don't stop the tool or task.

Cell phones must be in the OFF position during work. When management asks to see your cell phone, if it is even on, you will be in violation and will lose benefits.

Work up to the stop time. Clean up is to be done after hours (discretionary judgment on this one, depending on the type of company you have.

Smoking is not permitted except during breaks in designated smoking areas. Period.

The rules go on. Can you see a really slick system here?

Let's assume for a minute that you just dropped the above rules on the employees. They would all groan and think you are being mean.

With this system, they understand these are things that, when stopped, will put more money in their cash bonus pool and give them full benefits. They *want* these rules so everyone will stop losing non-productive time. Everyone wins. Complete mind change. They are thinking like company people instead of individual money hounds with rights.

That, my friends, is the true power of this program. It can only happen when you have a good training meeting to explain this entire system to your employees. All the cards on the table, face up.

Again, if you need help, feel free to call us. Telephone consulting of this type is free.

Now, on to the final chapter of this book.

Where The Good Employees Are: Chapter Nine
OK! You're Done! (Termination)

This is a chapter where we've got to be very, very careful.

This is when you have an employee that just doesn't want to seem to get with the program. They have just got to go. They're Fired!

The important thing is this. You are a professional business. Termination is not a good thing or a bad thing. It is just a part of being in business and having employees. The most important thing about termination is being fair, firm and legal.

You probably already know, our government has set up this thing called unemployment.

The intent is to help a person who was working for a company and is no longer working because of a lay off. They are capable of work, are looking for work, but just have not found work. When a person meets these qualifications, they are entitled to unemployment pay.

So, who pays for their unemployment? Right! You do. In effect, you will be sending money to an employee and get no work out of them in return.

If your business is known to have slow periods where lay off is part of your regular annual routine, you need to plan for this unemployment expense in your budget and pay it gladly. You *do* want these good employees to be taken care of for a while until they get back on their feet or you get busy again and can re-hire them.

You do not want to pay unemployment for an employee who gets fired because, well, they were a terrible employee and don't deserve it.

The government agrees. If you fire an employee because they broke specific company policies repeatedly, steals from you, gets in a fist fight with your customer... etc. they don't deserve unemployment pay.

So, let's get started with how to properly terminate someone so you never have to worry about getting stuck paying unemployment to someone who does not deserve it.

In the earlier chapters, we came up with a wonderful system called the "standard consequences". Quick refresher here:
First offence, they get a verbal warning, which is documented on a warning slip as the first warning.

The second offence on the same issue becomes an official written warning where all the details are written out.

Third offence is also a written warning with all the details and the employee waives their cash bonus and benefits for that month.

Your employee handbook clearly states that the fourth offence for the same issue is grounds for termination.

IMPORTANT: They must sign each warning. Note: This gives you three instances where you will have their signature agreeing that the offence did occur. Proof positive that they are breaking company policy. That is the thing that will cover your back side from any problem with an employee attempting to collect unemployment. All you do is show the written warning slips of which all three have the employee signature. No problem.

So… What if the employee doesn't sign it? Another great question.

At the bottom of the warning slip, you have a paragraph that says something like:

"The employee signature signifies the employee has been issued this warning and they understand the reason for the warning. In the event the employee fails to sign this warning, a signature of a witness will be submitted as verification of the authenticity of the infraction being made and the employee will agree to lose any or all discretionary benefits or cash bonus offered by the company…"

As you can see, it simply states, if the employee does not sign, you will get someone else to sign as a witness that the employee did in fact get the warning *and* the employee will not get *any* benefits or cash bonus offered by the company.

If this situation occurs when the employee says, "I'm not signing that…". You would say back to them, "That is your option. I must let you know that your signature only acknowledges you received it. If you want to make comment, you can do so, right on the notice. You must also realize that if you do not sign it, you will not get any benefits, vacation pay, sick leave, medical, holiday pay or cash bonus. When you don't sign, it shows an attitude of not caring. Warnings are there to protect our benefits program and if you don't care about the benefits program, you do not have to receive the benefits intended for you. Are you sure you don't want to sign?"

Usually, they will sign. If not, make sure you have a witness. Call over another employee and let the other employee know what is going on.

It may sound like this: "Hey Tony, can I get you to come over here for a minute? Thanks. Tony, we have a situation here where Jason arrived 10 minutes late without prior notification. We have prepared a warning slip but Jason, here, doesn't want to sign. We just need your signature as a witness. Your signature *only* means you were present and have personally witnessed the warning slip being written up and presented. Now, Jason, did you want to change your mind and sign it or do you still refuse?"

If he still refuses, then you have Tony sign as a witness. This *must* be done in front of Jason (the employee who made the infraction).

So, Jason blows up and says, "This is all a bunch of crap. I quit!"

Great. He has just told you he has been doing it for a long time and plans to do it over and over again, which means he plans to steal money from you in time card inaccuracy.

He got caught. He does not care. Maybe you don't want this type of person working for you in the first place.

Question comes up. "Can Jason collect unemployment"?

Absolutely not. He was not laid off. You did not fire him. You still offered him a place to work. He, on his own decision chose not to work.

The government says, if you have a job and you voluntarily leave on your own knowing the owner still wanted you to work, then you do not qualify for unemployment.

The same employee warning slip comes out and you have one of the other employees witness it. If Tony is standing there, you already have your witness and you will eliminate all possible problems.

Another form of termination is where you may have an employee with a short fuse. You never know. They may be 99 percent sweetheart and 1 percent jerk.

A customer comes up to this employee. They start talking business. The customer doesn't like or believe what they are hearing, so they start disagreeing and asking more questions for which the employee does not know the answer. The employee starts to make something up. The customer comes right out and says, "I don't think you know what your talking about...". The one percent button was pushed and the employee hauls off and punches the customer right in the kisser.

Do you warn them or fire them on the spot? Dah!

I would hope you fire them.

Same thing as if you go to an area where your employees are getting ready for work, you see one of your employees snorting a line of cocaine. Do you warn them? I hope not! Immediate termination!

With either of these cases, are the employees eligible for unemployment?

Nope. However, it is amazing how they will try.

They go to the department of labor and tell them they were laid off. Or, they tell them the boss was having a bad day and just pointed fingers to a couple of people and said they didn't have any more work. They *know* what they should say to collect unemployment, and they will lie. After all, it is free money.

The sad thing is, it's your burden of proof to prove otherwise.

This is where paperwork is so very important.

When you fire someone on the spot for a major infraction, it is important that you have done all the ground work, current work and aftermath work to cover yourself.

The ground work is your employee handbook, which identifies all the reasons an employee can be fired immediately. You list any form of fist fighting, loud shouting matches with employees or customers, disrespect for management, drug use... etc. This way, you have documented the employee has been forewarned.

Current work is the warning slip being prepare immediately at the point of termination.

If, for example, you are standing back and you see your employee put their hand in the cash drawer, slip out a $20 bill and slide it in their pocket. You *first* go get the warning slip and fill it out. Then you pull the cash register and count it out to verify the money is missing, then you approach the employee and ask

259

him to show you the $20 in their left front pocket. They turn red because they got caught. You show them the warning slip. They sign it (maybe thinking it's a warning, duh). You let them know this is grounds for termination. They can come back tomorrow to pick up their final paycheck.

OH. Here's a very important item.

Before they go, as they are leaving, tell them, "We will have your final paycheck ready tomorrow. In order to get this paycheck, I need you to write down a quick sentence on why you think you were let go. It will save time so you won't have to write it down on your employment severance sheet when you come to pick up your check".

If the employee says, "Just mail the check to me." Let them know, "I'm sorry, legally, we have to hand this check to you in person and document the conditions of your termination. I know it is very uncomfortable for both of us, believe me, I am as upset about this probably more than you are. It will just save us time. If you don't feel comfortable writing it down beforehand, then you can save your comments for when you come to pick up your check and write them down then".

Just a note: Most states require that you pay an employee within 24 hours of immediate termination.

It's a good thing so you don't have to drag out the negative feelings from it all for the entire week waiting for the payday show down. You are in full compliance because the check is ready and available to the terminated employee within 24 hours of termination.

It's up to the employee as to how long they want to take to actually pick it up. *Do not mail it to them.* Remind them you *must* give them the check personally so you can fill out the legally required documents for termination.

Next important thing is the last part. The aftermath documentation.

This is where you fill out a completely different form that you have called "Employment Severance Sheet".

On this sheet, you write out name, date and a detailed description as to why they were terminated. Most of the time the employee will follow your directions to write a comment on why they think they were terminated. It will usually be short and sweet. "I got caught borrowing $20 out of the cash register without permission".

Amazing how they avoid the words like stealing, fist fighting, using illegal drugs… etc.

On this sheet, your detailed description is made concrete with their statement. If their statement is way off and they did not identify the real reason, you need to let them know, "I can not accept this statement. It must have not been clear. You were terminated because you (whatever they did). I would like you to re-write what you now understand is my reason for letting you go."

Get a more accurate statement.

OK. You have your three strikes. Strike one - Written handbook. Strike two - written employee warning signed and/or witnessed (if needed). Strike three – employee severance sheet. THEY'RE OUT!

If an employee still files for unemployment knowing they really should not, you can call the employee and let them know that you do not take unemployment fraud lightly. Let them know you have documentation as to why they are not eligible and if they choose to pursue unemployment they are not entitled to, then your option as an employer is to press charges for intentional fraud. Jail time.

Here again, we can refer you to a great legal service that cost next to nothing for these types of situations. As an employer, you should never be without legal council or representation. Please call me on this if you don't have access to the best legal firm in your area for dirt cheap! Contact information is on the website.

Once you have had this discussion with the employee attempting to get unjustified unemployment, your problems should be over.

It rarely goes this far. Typically if they still attempt to collect unemployment, all you have to do is show the unemployment company all of your documentation showing and proving (three strikes) that they are not eligible.

They will usually drop it *if* and *when* you have documentation. This is where many companies get in trouble and end up paying unemployment they should not have to pay. It all boils down the company firing an employee without written documentation. They lose.

Well. I hope that didn't scare you. It really is not big deal when you remember you are a professional company. This is just professional company stuff and is not an emotional thing.

Well, OK, it really is because we can't avoid it, but the more you emphasize business professionalism the less problems, emotional stress and worries you will have when the time comes to let go an undesirable employee.

Let's see. We've talked about how to find the good employees, how to phone interview them, live interview them, put together benefit packages, how to pay cash bonus on only the extra profit in your company, how to get better production through specific training of production and non production items and how to terminate them if needed. I think that covers it all.

I realize you may have a specific and special thing that is eating at your brain. Please remember the offer is valid and real. Give us a call. We are happy to help with things that may not be covered in this book.

Oh, One clarification to be fair to you and me. If I get a call where someone wants me to explain how to deal with a specific problem with an in-law who is bending the rules but not quite breaking them... what do I do" type question. No problem. No charge. If on the other hand, I get a call with someone wanting me to read the book to them or explain a part of the book just using different words, well, then I would consider this a reading service and may want to charge for my time. Don't worry. I will always let you know in advance if there is a charge. Most of the time. No problem.

Anyway... Deep breath. There you have it. I hope to hear from you in the future weather it be during one of our fantastic live seminars or workshops or via the phone.

In any case, I truly have a desire that your business success is greatly improved from applying some or all of the things you have learned in this book and all the other books in this series.

Your success is my success, so go get 'em.

www.ingramcontent.com/pod-product-compliance
Lightning Source LLC
Chambersburg PA
CBHW061357210326

41598CB00035B/6017